Anonymous

Seed-Truths

Or, Bible views of mind, morals, and religion

Anonymous

Seed-Truths
Or, Bible views of mind, morals, and religion

ISBN/EAN: 9783337097899

Printed in Europe, USA, Canada, Australia, Japan

Cover: Foto ©Lupo / pixelio.de

More available books at **www.hansebooks.com**

SEED-TRUTHS;

OR,

BIBLE VIEWS OF MIND, MORALS, AND RELIGION.

BY

PHARCELLUS CHURCH, D.D.,

AUTHOR OF 'PHILOSOPHY OF BENEVOLENCE;' 'RELIGIOUS DISSENSIONS: THEIR CAUSE AND CURE, A PRIZE ESSAY;' 'ANTIOCH; OR, THE INCREASE OF MORAL POWER IN THE CHURCH,' ETC. ETC.

Search the Scriptures.—JOHN V. 39.
Comparing spiritual things with spiritual.—1 COR. II. 13.

NEW YORK:
SHELDON & CO., No. 677 BROADWAY
AND 214 & 216 MERCER STREET,
UNDER GRAND CENTRAL HOTEL.
1871.

PREFACE.

READING the Bible in course, or by verse and chapter, fails in many cases to bring to light the truths which underlie all its documents, and which are the same to us as to any previous generation. Human nature and its relations, in their essential principles, are a unit in all ages. But we are prone to think of what we read as pertaining to another sphere, or quite remote from the order of our present experiences. A more interior view of the subject dissipates this illusion, and makes the Bible, more than any other book, a painting of what we now see and experience.

There may be unfitness of mind for this interior view, just as there may be for enjoying the poets; and we may turn away from Scripture, as having nothing to interest us, as many readers do from Shakspeare and Milton. But this is not all. The reading is too fragmentary to reach foundation-truths. Can we know what a tree is as a whole, by seeing its leaves and its chips? Commentaries are too ponderous, sermons too excursive, and creeds too summary, great as their value is, to meet this exact demand. Questions are ever recurring to inquisitive readers, which they find it difficult to answer. Why a revelation in such form?

Why such a record of the first man, and his trifling aberration? Why doom his posterity for a sin in which they had no participation? Why such a life as that of Abraham, and such a law as that of Moses? Why such a murderous raid on the Canaanites? Why such lists of unmeaning names? On account of such questionings, the Catholics deem the Bible an unsafe book in the hands of the people, unless a priest is present to indoctrinate them in the dogmas of the church.

That the writer has met all these questions he does not claim, but only that he has developed certain principles in which all those anomalies and our present experiences alike cohere; just as in nature there are forces binding into one both its explained and unexplained phenomena. His plan is, first, to sketch the Bible man in his mental, moral, and religious characteristics; and then to trace him out in the states, transitions, and histories recorded of him in Scripture; and showing, at the same time, their agreement with what we are, what our forefathers have been, and what our posterity is to be to the end of time.

It is usual, in our systems of education, to detach the science of mind, morals, and natural theology from revelation, and treat them on the basis of consciousness, our relations, or the evidences of design which we see around us. What is thus acquired, on merely human grounds of evidence, is preparatory to the study of the Bible. The divinity student, after being drilled in the study of man as conducted by the schools, is put to interpreting the word of God, as a Chinese lady is put to walking after her feet have been crippled in iron shoes. His mental muscles are indurated into a form, in judging of the man of the Bible, to compel him to be thus and not otherwise; or to be a puppet of the schools, rather than a piece of God's handiwork. The young preacher must have a strong decoction of philosophy, just a little tinctured with revelation, and then be sent abroad to give the mixture to the sheep and lambs of Christ's flock.

But can the philosophical man act the part of the Bible man? Is there anything in a metaphysical Adam, or a metaphysical new man in Christ, to meet the descriptions of Moses or the apostles? Suppose the professor, after shaping human nature by his science of mind, morals, and theology, were to say to his pupils, 'Now you see that a being so constituted might eat an apple and damn a world,' would not the class laugh him in the face? There is no fitness in the man elaborated out of his material to act any such part. The idea of being born again would be foreign to his nature. 'If MORALS are not taken up distinctively on the principles of revelation, they had better, as subjects of prelection for young men, be let alone altogether. Not only can there be no true morality without religion; but the teaching of moral virtues to sinful creatures, on grounds independent of the mercy revealed by the gospel, is an inlet to antiscriptural and soul-destroying delusions.'[1] This remark is as true of the science of mind as of morals. No honest pupil can compare the science of man, as studied on merely natural grounds, with what he reads of the race in the Bible, without feeling that there are grave and inexplicable discrepancies.

There must be something in human nature that philosophy has not reached, or the Bible must be given up as a revelation from God. Many of those who

[1] *Christian Ethics*, by Dr. Ralph Wardlaw, p. 378.

strongly adhere to the view of the schools become infidels; and others adhere to revelation on the principle of withdrawing it from the category of humanity, and assigning it to quite another order of things. While speculative philosophy is a very unsettled science, with as many theories of it as there are powerful minds to treat the subject, it should be considered that the writers of the Bible, in all their varied ages and circumstances, are perfectly agreed in their views of man's nature, relations, history, and necessities. They keep to those practical views which ensure uniformity among themselves, and which must have a like effect upon others so far as they are studied.

The Bible man stands between two distinct worlds—that of nature, and that of spirits; taking impressions and ideas from both, though unlike each other as spirit is to matter, and heaven or hell is to earth. He trims his sails to breezes from the seen and unseen, from the temporal and the eternal. These opposite influences act upon him through distinct modes of apprehension; and it is for him to determine whether the one or the other shall rule him. This is a prerogative that allies him to God. It is the basis of his law and of his principle of duty. So totally distinct and unlike is what comes to him from God from what comes to him from nature, that his whole character, his moral status, and that of those born of him or trained under his influence, are necessarily determined, according as he continues under the rule of spirit from God, or as he recedes to the ruling of flesh, as acted upon by the world. The two necessarily bar each other as ruling powers.[1] Can we wonder that man, as so constituted and so situated, should by one act detach himself, and

---

[1] 1 Cor. ii. 14; Matt. xvi. 23; Rom. viii. 6-8.

those born of him, from innocence, or at the extraordinary means necessary to his recovery? How much does it cost to civilise a savage, or to make an innocent man of a voluptuary, drunkard, and murderer?

Plato, a heathen philosopher, came nearer the Bible idea of man than most others who have considered him merely from a natural point of view. He supposed the soul had a pre-existent life, and that ideas from another world were born with him. He therefore, like the inspired writers, united two worlds in man, though he mistook the manner of it. Kant has a sublime passage on the subject, though he stops short of the Bible idea of a spiritual and natural universe: 'Two things there are which, the oftener and the more stedfastly we consider, fill the mind with an ever-new, an ever-rising admiration and reverence—*the* STARRY HEAVENS *above, the* MORAL LAW *within.* Of neither am I compelled to seek out the reality, as veiled in darkness, or only to conjecture the possibility, as beyond the hemisphere of my knowledge. Both I contemplate lying clear before me, and connect both with my consciousness of existence. The one departs from the place I occupy in the outward world of sense; expands, beyond the bounds of imagination, this connection of my body with worlds, and systems blending into systems; and protends it also into the illimitable times of their periodic movement—to its commencement and perpetuity. The other departs from my invisible self, from my personality; and represents me in a world truly infinite indeed, but whose infinity can be tracked out only by the intellect, with which also my connection, unlike the fortuitous relation I stand in to all worlds of sense, I am compelled to recognise as universal and necessary. In the former, the first view of a countless multitude of worlds annihilates, as it were, my importance as an *animal product*, which, after a brief, and that incomprehensible, endowment with the powers of life, is compelled to refund its constituent matter to the planet—itself an atom in the universe—on which I grow. The other, on the contrary, elevates my worth as an *intelligence* even without limit; and this through my personality, in which the moral law reveals a faculty of life independent of my animal nature, nay, of the whole material world;—at least, if it be permitted to infer as much from the regulation of my being, which conformity with that law exacts; proposing, as it does, my moral worth for the absolute end of my activity, conceding no compromise of its imperative to a necessitation of nature, and spurning in its infinity the conditions and boundaries of my transitory life.'[1]

Thus the Bible view of man, as acted upon by two worlds, is not without a certain kind of response from philosophy. The sense of amenableness to God pervading ordinary minds, however, is a much stronger proof of the fact. Every one who honestly consults his own heart will find responses from the spirit-realm as unmistakeable as those which he receives from nature through the senses.

After revolving this subject for some time, it occurred to the author to collate what is said in the Bible of the nature of man; and when he had done so, he saw clearly that its histories, its ceremonials, its morals, its doctrines, its views of sin and redemption, were all adjusted to certain attributes and relations of human nature. The principles ruling in the case are few and simple, and they are a complete index to the

[1] As quoted by Sir W. Hamilton, *Metaphysics*, pp. 28, 29.

whole subject-matter of revealed religion. These are treated in the first eleven chapters of his work.

The writer gave to the public some years ago a volume issued as a Prize Essay on Christian Union, in preparing which he became convinced that our sectarian divisions begin with interpreting Scripture by something out of Scripture; and that, if we would be united, we must 'search' for its true sense and spirit by 'comparing spiritual things only with spiritual;' interpreting the word by the word, or doctrine by ceremony, law by gospel, the historical by the devotional, the obscure by the plain, and the Old Testament by the New, and *vice versa*. This might not restore Papal uniformity in the dark ages,—a state of things far worse than our divisions,—but it would tend to abate the rancour of schism, by showing each sect the wisdom of moderating its extreme positions by those of its equally zealous and conscientious neighbours. The writer did not expect to attempt a work on this principle of comparing spiritual things with spiritual; but, Providence favouring, he has devoted about five years to the studies which have resulted in this unpretending work.

The chief part of his labour has consisted in an endeavour to draw his materials from original sources, ignoring what others had made out of those materials. The reading of the original Scriptures throughout, and the re-reading of parts of them over and over again, have been his chief resource. He desired to look beyond translations as far as possible, to the human or material 'form of sound words,' or to the derivation of 'the words which the Holy Ghost teacheth.'[1] He does not claim to be a critic in language, but only to

[1] 1 Cor. ii. 13; 2 Tim. i. 13.

look beneath the derived word, which translations do little more than give, if they do that, to the germinal idea which its root was used to express.

The writer has found much instruction in collating all the passages in which important words occur, to eliminate the stem-thought in each of them. *Ruach*, spirit; *nephesh*, soul; *torah*, law; *kapporeth*, atonement, and many others, thus collated and compared, have proved a rich placer of the purest gold. He finds, in the use of these words, a discrimination of meaning not to be detected by any other process. The 'spirit, and soul, and body,' as used by the apostle in 1 Thess. v. 23, is a Hebraistic mode of speaking as old as language.

The writer has also collated much of the Bible reflected in the articles of our most renowned creeds. This has enabled him the better to judge of the standpoint of our old interpreters. Their work is of great service as a breakwater to lawless innovations, but not as reflecting an unbiassed comparison of spiritual things with spiritual. They were too much affected by the controversies of their several periods to admit of this. And their definitions have extensively modified commentaries, sermons, interpretation, and the whole range of religious thinking and reasoning. Even the latitudinarian sects have taken form, as the water-line of an iron-bound coast by its jagged rocks and granite bluffs, through the mighty resisting force of these old Athanasian, Augustinian, and Calvinistic creed-makers.

The writer has not the vanity to attempt to improve upon such men, but only to hint, as the result of fifty years' reflection on the subject, that orthodoxy, to retain its hold on the restless thought of the age that is and is to come, must look to a more interior and untrammelled examination of the word. There is a fear of relaxing our hold upon the old standards, even for the Bible itself; the cry of heresy may perhaps assail him that attempts it; but still the work must go on, and the writer trusts that his feeble efforts may prompt others to do better. To indicate a few points of difference between an exterior and interior examination of the sacred text, let a few examples suffice.

The exterior view makes the primeval man holy in his creation; the interior finds him innocent and upright, and the candidate for a virtue and holiness to be acquired by trial.

The exterior ascribes his fall to an outward tempter; the interior finds in his doubt, appetite, æsthetical nature, and various specific impulses, a basis for temptation, apart from extraneous malign influence.

The exterior makes depravity total; the interior makes it the extinction of spiritual life, or life in God, but not of natural conscience and conservative qualities.

The exterior confines its ideas of sin chiefly to vices and crimes; the interior makes it a nature ruled by the flesh and the world. Everything is sin under that ruling.

The exterior makes law a series of specific enactments; the interior makes it a principle of duty, of which specific enactments are an emanation.

The exterior makes penalty an overt infliction of death upon men and animals in this world, and hell-torments in the next; the interior makes it that extinction of spiritual life which began on the day of the first sin, to continue till that life is restored by divine grace.

The exterior view regards a decree of election, consigning a portion of mankind to eternal life, as the first act in redemption; the interior view refers specific manifestations of grace, as with believers in Rome and Ephesus, to God's gracious working from the beginning of time, as recorded in the Old Testament. As Dr. Wardlaw says, the way is, 'not to begin with the purpose, and reason forward to the event, but to begin with the event, and reason backward to the purpose.'[1] This is the order in which the apostles uniformly state the case.

To the exterior, the sacrifice of Christ upon the cross is a price paid to law and justice; to the interior, it is power to reproduce itself in every believer.

To the one, the atonement is an abstraction of government; to the other, it is bruising the serpent's head, or killing the nature which is the head of his power over man, in order to resurrection to a new and heavenly life.

To the one, the crucifixion was a spectacular scene like a public execution, to exhibit to the universe the vengeance of law; to the other, it is God on the mercy-seat restoring union between Himself and His mourning people at the door of the sanctuary, or 'that repentance and remission of sins should be preached in His name among all nations.'[2]

To the one, regeneration is a change of affections and conduct; to the other, it is God's restored dominion in the soul, of which the changed affections and conduct are a consequence. It is 'seeing' and 'entering the kingdom of God.'[3]

To the one, the blood of Christ is a wrath-appeaser; to the other, it is spiritual life purifying the heart through faith, and pervading man's whole outward life. 'He that eateth me shall *live* by me;' and all things are purified by blood.

[1] *Christian Ethics*, p. 158.   [2] Luke xxiv. 47.   [3] John iii. 3–6.

To the one, the church is an outward organization; to the other, it is a company of believers, who 'by one spirit are baptized into one body.'[1]

The author states these as a few of the many points on which the views of thousands will undergo essential modifications as they advance towards a more interior and untrammelled view of the word of God.

He gives his authorities at the bottom of each page, which the reader can refer to or not as he pleases. The body of the work is complete without them. The same passages and the same sentiments are repeated under different aspects, or to ensure clearness. This seemed to the writer unavoidable.

He desires to record his grateful acknowledgments to the curators of the University Library of Bonn, Prussia, where the work was written, for the free access allowed him to their valuable collection of books.

[1] 1 Cor. xii. 13.

CONTENTS.

		PAGE
I.	HOW TRUTHS BECOME THE SEEDING OF IDEAS,	1
II.	TWO MINDS OR MODES OF CONCEIVING TRUTH,	7
III.	ARCHETYPE OF MAN IN GOD,	14
IV.	TERMS OF MIND IN FLESH,	24
V.	INHALING LIFE FROM THE EXPANSE,	34
VI.	THE SOUL AS THE CONSCIOUS SELFHOOD,	44
VII.	THE REALM OF SPIRITS,	50
VIII.	SPIRIT IN INSTITUTIONS,	69
IX.	SPIRIT IN MORALS,	81
X.	SPIRIT IN CONSCIENCE,	94
XI.	HISTORY AN OUTGROWTH OF SEED-TRUTHS,	107
XII.	HAPPINESS OF BEING RULED BY SPIRIT,	116
XIII.	HOW HEAVEN IS LOST,	128
XIV.	THE SPIRITS IN PRISON,	144
XV.	DOCTRINE IN HISTORY,	161
XVI.	DOCTRINE IN WORDS AND SYMBOLS,	176
XVII.	WORDS AND SYMBOLS IN POWER,	189
XVIII.	LAW THE BASIS OF GOD'S RULE IN THE SOUL,	203
XIX.	THE NATURE AND USE OF THE LAW IN STONE,	216
XX.	THE DIVINE INDWELLING IN OUR SOCIAL RELATIONS,	235

		PAGE
XXI. THE THEOCRATIC AS A TYPE OF THE SPIRITUAL MAN,	.	253
XXII. GOD BORN OF MAN, THAT MAN MAY BE BORN OF GOD,	,	264
XXIII. DYING TO LIVE, ...	.	281
XXIV. THE KINGDOM OF GOD WITH POWER, . . .	.	294
XXV. SUFFERING AS THE INITIATIVE OF POWER, . .	.	308

SEED-TRUTHS;

OR,

BIBLE VIEWS OF MIND, MORALS, AND RELIGION.

CHAPTER I.

HOW TRUTHS BECOME THE SEEDING OF IDEAS.

A TRUTH can take no root in our minds until it is embodied in words and symbols. Like a wheat-corn, it must die and incorporate its life with elements gross and unlike itself, before it can reappear in enlarged knowledge or improved character. As the identity of the seed is lost in the process, and cannot be known to one who has only seen the plant, so of truths, especially those farthest removed from the senses: they cannot be known without careful searching, and are often sadly perverted by those who stop with their symbols. SEARCH THE SCRIPTURES has a peculiar force of meaning in the lips of our Lord.

The honour bestowed upon a plant has reference to the value of its seed. A mean shrub that enriches us by its products is highly esteemed. So God has magnified His word above all His name,[1] by making that part of the infinite truth in Himself, which He

[1] Ps. cxxxviii. 2.

has deposited in language, fruitful in knowledge, virtue, and salvation to a lost race. This is the word on which He has caused us to hope, and for the fulfilment of which He has taught us to pray.[1] It was incarnated, or made flesh, that we might behold its glory, and be changed into its image.[2]

How much of truth in thought and feeling fails of the embodiment necessary to make it the seeding of ideas to other minds! How many a poem, great, perhaps, as Homer's or Milton's, has been felt or sung in hearts that had not the tongue to give it expression! How many inventions in art, that might have blessed the world, passed away like a forgotten dream, because they were not put into wood, iron, or brass! More are the seeds that perish without germination, than those which yield our harvests.

Every well-thought-out book has a few leading truths, of which the rest is the husk, into which they are expanded for transmission to other minds. Cowper's idea of the ridiculous spectacle of plain people seeking pleasure in unwonted ways, by shaping itself into his John Gilpin, has yielded amusement to thousands. The analogies of natural and revealed religion, by taking on the reasoning of Butler's *Analogy*, have given instruction to succeeding ages. Though the truths in such cases were the same, those results could no more follow, than a harvest from parched corn or burned wheat, if the words were not added. A book with a few good and great thoughts will live and bear fruit in spite of defects of style. Some of our most prolific truths appeared at first in a clumsy form, just as our greatest machines began with unartistic models. But, having an idea in them, it worked itself out, as the

[1] Ps. cxix. 49.   [2] John i. 14; 2 Cor. iii. 18.

crab-apple is said to have produced by culture all the delicious varieties of the apple kind. What a poor thing must have been the first plough! But, having in it a great idea, it has gone on increasing, till it now breaks up millions of square miles of soil, and triplicates the inhabitants of the globe by giving them bread.

Seed-truths are the only things in the whole harvest which are unchanged. They are the same in all ages. The oaks that shade the valleys, and are reflected from the placid surface of lake or river, tall, expanding, majestic, come from a like chit with their scrubby, gnarled, tempest-beaten, lightning-riven brethren of the mountain-tops. From the first planting by the Creator's hand, this chit truth has remained the same,—nothing having changed but the external form, as affected by soil or climate. The vegetable kingdom, however, furnishes no greater examples of identity, in all ages and circumstances, than the word on which God has caused us to hope. In the vast product of ideas from the seeding of revealed truth, which has appeared from Adam to this day, there are a few underlying principles which have never changed. The process has not been one of mutation, so far as they are concerned, but of development. The gospel preached to us was before preached to Abraham.[1] 'Before Abraham was, I am,'[2] are words asserting a oneness of thought in redemption from the beginning of time. One mind, one idea, one class of truths. These are the truths of our inquiry in this work.

That the Bible has yielded a great harvest of ideas, none will deny. And why is it? Why is it to-day more read and circulated than any other book? Why

[1] Gal. iii. 8. [2] John viii. 58.

is it so impressed upon the fabric of our common law ? Why is it so wrought into our civilisation ? Why is it so generally quoted, and preached, and reverently listened to ? Why have the most gifted minds, in many cases, ascribed to it their best culture ? Not certainly because its wars are a model for ours. Not because its ritual of bleeding beasts could edify us. Not because we hope to grow its inspired men in our schools. Not because its details of legislation, under the old theocracy, are adapted to our age; nor because the present descendants of the subjects of that theocracy, in their shrewd practices on 'Change, are at all fitted to recommend it to our adoption. Not because the Papal and Mohammedan hierarchies, fashioned after this ancient model of a divine civil government among men, afford the least encouragement for us to attempt anything of the kind. If a theocracy was a blessing under David, it is a curse under popes and sultans. And those who look for its restoration in the Holy Land, to rule all the nations by means of converted Jewish satraps, 'do err, not knowing the Scriptures nor the power of God.'

Seed-truths live in all ages and climes, because they adjust themselves to the intelligence and wants of a people. Abraham's career, Moses' miracles, David's reign, Solomon's golden and gorgeous throne, was each suited to its age; though, if attempted in our times, it would prove as dead a failure as a crop of polar mosses under equatorial suns. And yet is this any evidence that the same great spiritual truths did not underlie all these histories ? Liberty has allied itself to many a bloody scene in the last three centuries; but is it therefore to be repudiated by those who shall live in the quieter days of the future ? Its glory is that it has survived so many a hard-fought field. And the glory of revealed truths is that they have prosecuted their great work of man's redemption with such tools, and in the midst of such scenes. They owe their perpetuity to their inherent vitality, and also to taking on forms of thought adapted to the several ages,—just as the plough-idea has survived, both by its necessity to human use and by allying itself to the clumsy models, which have repeated themselves from the crotched stick of savages to the shining shares with wheels which now upturn the soil. Realities at bottom, great, momentous, infinite realities, that man was born to feel, put into a form to be comprehended by all,—this is the law.

As every one of these truths is from a human standpoint, like all seeing from the eye, our first inquiry is as to what the seers saw in man. What sort of being is that to whom truths of God, truths of nature, truths of providence, truths of redeeming love, truths of heaven, hell, and judgment, are addressed? What fits him for receiving them? Pictures are not for the blind, nor music for the deaf. Revelation is not for brutes, but for men; and what in men makes a divine revelation apropos to their case? The answer of these questions we take from prophets themselves, not from analysing the facts of consciousness after the manner of our speculative philosophers. The prophets saw what was in man by intuition and not by reasoning, and what they saw they describe. Our business, therefore, is with their language and their symbols.

If what the seers saw in man is not to be trusted, nor made a basis of science, what is? Will the metaphysics ever emerge from the quagmire of inconclusive reasoning in which they have been for ages floundering? They may be an excellent discipline to the intellect, as rope-dancing is to the muscles; but their basis is always unsettled,—always veering to and fro between realism and idealism, or between points too subtle to admit of a fixed basis, and which are no nearer settlement to-day than they were two thousand years ago. However excellent as intellectual gymnastics, they are not likely to enter largely into the concerns of practical life.

But there is this to be said of the inspired writers,—they give us fixed ideas of man and his relations. They present the same ideas from Genesis to Revelation, and describe them by like words and images. The external and internal organs of the body—the adytum and exterior of their temple; respiration as an inhalation from two worlds; and like symbols, are the form which their thoughts on the subject assume. Their whole system of doctrinal truth, their record of the race from beginning to end, and, we may add, their anticipations of its final destiny, are to their minds types of the nature and relations of man. The salient points of their teaching on the subject will be considered in the following chapters.

CHAPTER II.

TWO MINDS OR MODES OF CONCEIVING TRUTH.

THE writers of the Bible looked upon human nature as centring in itself currents of thought and influence from the headlands of two worlds, and yet so blended that the thinking agent himself does not always suspect the source of the impulses that direct his conduct. He thinks them wholly of this world if his tendencies are materialistic, or he thinks them from heaven if he is a fanatic, — both views being alike false. What is thought to be from earth may be from the spirit-land, and what is ascribed to heaven may be from hell, like the piety of Simon Magus. Human life, in the Bible view, is the blended result of what acts upon us from this outward scene of things, and what acts upon us from heaven and from hell. We have two distinct modes of conception,—one through our bodily senses, of which we have no doubt; the other through our spiritual susceptibilities, of which perhaps we are not conscious, but which is none the less potent in making up the sum-total of what we are as moral and intellectual beings.

The inspired writers claim for our spiritual susceptibilities, as ruled by the Spirit of God, the right to control us in all things. These are for dominion, the flesh or natural life for subordination; and when they coexist in that relation, they constitute the kingdom of heaven upon earth. 'We are double,' says an able writer,—'one part of earth, another of heaven; one part gross body, the other life of the soul. Which of these is the better it is not hard to determine.'

The apostle speaks of the ruling of the one or the other of these opposite powers in the man as τὸ φρόνημα τῆς σαρκός, the mind of the flesh, and τὸ φρόνημα τοῦ πνεύματος, the mind of the spirit.[1] The one is thought and feeling cast in an earthly mould, and the other is thought and feeling cast in a heavenly mould. In the mind of the flesh natural ideas predominate; in the mind of the spirit heavenly ideas predominate. The one is carnally-minded, the other is spiritually-minded. The one relates to an earthly, the other to a heavenly life. The one outward, the other inward,—not merely as pertaining to body and mind, but according as the ruling influence with the man is from God or the world. 'For ye are dead,' that is, to an earthly life; 'and your life is hid with Christ in God,'[2] or is kindred to that of Christ, and an emanation from Him. Your sources of hope and joy, your principles of activity, your desires and aversions, the scope and end of your lives, are from spiritual impulses coming to you from God through Christ, and are hid, or of a character not to be detected by one who is ruled by earthly ideas. This distinction of two opposite forces acting upon man, and to be dealt with by him voluntarily and in freedom, crops out in the history of his creation; of his first life in God, or under the ruling of spirit; of his subsequent relapse under the ruling of the flesh, and consequent apostasy from God; and is reflected in the inner and outer apartments of the tabernacle and the whole ritual worship for fifteen hundred years.

---

[1] Rom. viii. 6.   [2] 2 Cor. iv. 16; Col. iii. 3.

Man's conscious self is indeed a unit, but with two distinct forms of thought, as also with two directly opposite tendencies of interest and desire,—the one natural, the other spiritual. And what can be wider apart than flesh and spirit? No skill can bridge the chasm between them. Yet they are united in man. Powers animal and angelic meet in his conscious selfhood, and both may be legitimately exercised by him, provided he assigns to the one subordination and to the other dominion. This seed-truth enters into all the Bible representations of human nature. If an earthly palace for Jehovah is to be sketched from Horeb, it must have its adytum, with its surroundings of exterior cloisters and courts. If a Jewish doctor is to be taught the requisites to entering the kingdom of heaven, he must be made to understand the difference between flesh and spirit, or of being born of the one and the other, as the initial lesson on the subject. And if the Christian life is to be unfolded, it must be as a 'walking not after the flesh, but after the spirit.'[1] If there are fundamental ideas in revealed religion, this provision for uniting two worlds in man must be reckoned among the number. It is not a distinction superinduced by regeneration, as some suppose, but original to the race. Regeneration does not create new faculties, but merely puts in order those that already exist. It restores the ruling of spirit to one who had been under the dominion of the flesh.

These two powers of flesh and spirit must coexist under the ruling of the latter, in order to a normal and happy condition of manhood. Yet they tend to bar or exclude each other. To 'the natural man the things of spirit are foolishness, and he cannot receive them,

[1] John iii 1-12; Rom. viii. 1.

because they are spiritually discerned.'[1] When natural ideas and feelings rule us, they exclude from our minds spiritual apprehensions. They are not in harmony with influx from God. But when spiritual truth and love rule us, they enable us to understand not only what is of God, but to appreciate the true value of earthly interests. 'In God's light we see light' in reference to both worlds, and are able to 'judge all things.' Wrongly directed, spiritualism bars true ideas of our outward relations; and we are charged 'not to be righteous over-much; neither make thyself over-wise: why shouldst thou destroy thyself?'[2] Those whose absorption in spiritual things, to the neglect of earthly duties and enjoyments, is made a necessity of the religious life, as in the recluse and the anchorite, are guilty of this sort of perversion; 'which things have indeed a show of wisdom in will-worship and bodily austerity, not in what is honourable to the fulness or perfection of the flesh.'[3] They deny the body to improve the spirit, by a process alike corrupting to both. Thus a spiritualism which is not duly balanced by our earthly relations and duties, is scarcely better than the dominion of the flesh. Jesus, who had the Spirit without measure, never lost sight of what belonged to Him as a citizen of this world. His life is a rebuke to all mystical and impracticable piety. It is true that a soul absorbed in spiritual things may momentarily feel an unsettling of earthly ideas; as when Paul knew not whether he was in the body or out of the body, and Peter was scarcely conscious of what he said.[4] This sort of exclusion of natural thought is an exceptional case, and does not affect the

---

[1] 1 Cor. ii. 14, 15.
[2] Eccles. vii. 16.
[3] Co.. ii. 23.
[4] 2 Cor. xii. 2; Luke ix. 33.

general tone of a holy life. The two powers must coalesce into one in order to perfection of character.

In speaking of these two powers in man, we must not confound them with appetite and reason or conscience, in common parlance. Seneca, the heathen philosopher, makes a distinction between flesh and spirit in the latter sense. Perhaps he borrowed the idea from Paul, of whom he was a contemporary. He no doubt refers to the pleading of lust against philosophical reason, both of which alike pertain to the natural man. How many merely worldly men practise great self-denial! How many a fakir of India, dervish of Turkey, and monk of the Papacy, though totally ignorant of a spiritual mind in the scriptural sense, performs extraordinary feats of bodily discipline! Our seed-thought of flesh and spirit is quite another thing. This thought contemplates the same mind taking in and properly using the ideas and influences of this world, accepting 'every creature as good, and nothing to be refused,'[1] and at the same time drawing truth and love from the heart of God, as the power ruling over all. However seemingly antagonistic, both must dwell in harmony to make us perfect men in Christ Jesus. One is an open window towards heaven, the other towards earth, and glowing with humanitarian sympathies. One makes man a member of the family in heaven, the other of the family on earth,—two branches of the same household under one head and name.[2] The ruling in both is the same, and is reflected in the natural man when reason governs appetite, and conscience passion.

But why reason on the subject? Our business is simply to set before the reader Bible views of human

[1] 1 Tim. iv. 4. [2] Eph. iii. 15.

nature. In those views is a being made to be God's throne, or a representative of the life of heaven, here below. No other animal nature unites in itself the power to look out upon this material scene through a spiritual medium, and from a heavenly standpoint. As man's inner being is God's throne, so his outer tabernacle is God's footstool. The two worlds in him are reduced to a single sovereignty. All this is reflected in the terms spirit and flesh, as used by inspired men. The inbreathed divinity of the first Adam, which proved a failure from his succumbing to the flesh and representing a fleshly seed, and afterwards in the second Adam, who is the Lord from heaven and a quickening Spirit, to restore life to a dead race by re-establishing a spiritual rule, and hence called the kingdom of heaven, to which all who believe are admitted: that kingdom came in the person of Christ, and is established in every spiritual man as a conquering power, to rule out the carnal life of the first Adam, with all its demon influences.[1]

The efflorescence and fruitage of these germinal truths of man are illimitable. As some one pertinently says: 'Were an inhabitant of some distant world able to look down upon our planet, his eye would be most attracted by the glittering painted pagodas of China, Borneo, and Japan; the rich ornamental temples and splendid rock-shrines of India; the dome-topped mosques and slender minarets of Western Asia; the pyramids and vast temples of Egypt, with their avenues of gigantic statues and sphinxes extending for miles; the graceful shrines of classic Greece; the basilicas of Rome and Byzantium; the semi-oriental domes of Moscow; the Gothic cathedrals of Western

[1] 1 Cor. xv. 46; Matt. xii. 28; Dan. ii. 44; Luke xi. 20.

Europe ; and the grand fire temples of Mexico and Peru, where, in the infancy of reason and humanity, human sacrifices were offered up, as if the All-Father were pleased with the agonies of His creatures.'

In these varied architectural devices for intercommunion of humanity with divinity, there was a secret shrine, a consecrated adytum, in which the parties were supposed to meet. This comes, if not from revelation, from man's inner consciousness, that his state of communion with spirit was abstracted and separate from his state of intercourse with the objects and interests of this world. If sense opened the latter to him, something higher, and purer, and holier must constitute his medium of intercourse with God. Flesh and spirit are dimly reflected by nearly all the forms of worship.

CHAPTER III.

ARCHETYPE OF MAN IN GOD.

THE inspired idea of human nature may be seen from the model after which it was fashioned. That model is neither animal nor angelic, but is found only in God. An animal nature acts and is acted upon only by the outward world, or through the bodily senses and organs, while the angels are purely immaterial and heavenly. But God acts both in nature and in the realm of spirits. He is supreme in both kingdoms, and unites their sovereignty in Himself. So man is in communication with matter through his senses, and also with God and spirits through his interior or spiritual nature. The two kingdoms are united in him.

In Moses' vision of creation God appeared, saying, 'WE will make man in OUR image, after OUR likeness.'[1] There is no other instance, except in these first chapters of Genesis, in which God adopts the plural pronouns in speaking of Himself; and it gives the idea that the being in reference to whose creation He uses it was to have inherent differences of constitution suggesting plurality. How else are we to account for this mode of speaking? To suppose that it was a slip of the pen, and without significance, would make this part of Moses' account different from all the rest. Elsewhere each statement

[1] Gen. i. 26, iii. 22.

represents a vast aggregation of facts, as in saying, 'Let light be;' 'Let the earth bring forth.' Each phrase of the kind is like a dot on the spectrum of a telescope, representing a continent on the sun's disk greater perhaps than our globe.

This mode of speaking represents infinite truths. It indicates a basis in God for the distinction of Father, Son, and Holy Spirit, as He existed before all worlds,— a truth here hinted, but fully developed in subsequent revelations, especially of the New Testament. It shows also that the Godhead concentrates His radiant glories in the Son of God *as* the Son of man, whose delights or affinities are 'with the sons of men.'[1] All that is of the Father, and all that is of the Holy Spirit, shine in 'the Son of man,' who is 'the beginning of the creation of God,' and in whom 'dwells the fulness of the Godhead bodily.'[2] He is 'the image of the invisible God, the first-born of every creature ;' by whom 'all things are created that are in heaven, and that are in earth, visible and invisible, whether they be thrones, dominions, principalities, or powers ; all things were created by Him : and He is before all things, and by Him all things consist.'[3] By Him God 'made the worlds, who, being the brightness of His glory, and the express image of His person (or characterization of His essence), upholds all things by the word of His power.'[4] 'He is the Word,' or divinity expressed or revealed, 'being in the beginning with God,' and at first disembodied, but afterwards embodied or 'made flesh, that we might behold His glory.'[5] It might be convenient to dispose of the WE and OUR of God in speaking of

---

[1] Prov. viii. 31.
[2] Rev. iii. 14 ; Col. ii. 9 ; Dan. vii. 13 ; Rev. i. 13.
[3] Col. i. 15. 17.   [4] Heb. i. 2, 3.   [5] John i. 1–14.

Himself, by regarding them as a slip of the pen, or a trick of emphasis, if it were not for the coincident statements of the New Testament. Or these statements might be set aside as the hyperbole of sanguine men in glorifying their hero, if the whole revelation and all its views of the nature of the man who was made in the image of God were not shaped to like ideas. If the warp must go with the woof, what have we left? Without a basis in the divinity for this plurality of representation, how should it have been kept up by men variously educated, and under such diversified circumstances, in documents covering a period of four thousand years?

It should be noted that this manner of representing God began with the first mention of the creation of man. It was in the image and likeness of God *so* represented, that man was said to be created. The image of a being is the form which he assumes in manifesting himself; and that form in God has its reflection in man. That form is 'the Son of man, who came to the Ancient of days,' 'whose garments were white as snow, and the hair of His head like pure wool: His throne was like the fiery flame, and His wheels as burning fire.' A like description is given of 'the Son of man' in the visions of John in Patmos.[1] The form was that of man, but the accompanying imagery reveals the divine attributes concentrated in it, and shining through it. The word was the expression of what there is in God, according to our human types of thought, or a characterization of His essence or substance in a form of humanity. We see not how any other idea can be derived from a careful collation and comparison of the passages of the inspired text which bear upon the

[1] Dan. vii. 9, 13; Rev. i. 13-18.

subject, and we can pretend to no other source of information.

The Father, thus one with the Son of man and the Holy Spirit as the Divine Proceeding through the Son, or as the emanating energy working in creation, providence, and redemption, is the central sun of the universe, whose energy, whose influence, whose beams, operate in infinitely varied forms of manifestation, according to the natures upon which and through which they act. The brooding Spirit gave life to the chaotic world, understanding to man, instinct to beasts, inspiration to prophets, power to the infant Church, having descended upon her Head at the baptismal waters in the form of a dove, and abode upon Him without measure. 'Thou art God that made heaven, and earth, and the sea, and all that in them is,' is a favourite mode of appeal in prayer on the part of a suffering people, giving the idea that, however weak in themselves, they cannot but be strong under the protection of Him who worketh all things in and around them.[1]

Man is formed after a like model. The outflowing energy of his interior conscious selfhood, all that is possible to his voluntary agency, goes forth in the direction of spirit, or in communication with God and heavenly life, and also in the direction of matter wielding the bodily senses, organs, and muscles, and so much of the world besides as he is able to affect by his efforts. What earth is as compared with what it would have been, if no human mind had acted upon it, is difficult to conceive. Its soil would have yielded no such harvests, its animals would have had no such culture, its minerals and precious stones would have

[1] John x. 30, xiv. 26, xv. 26 ; Gen. i. 2 ; Matt. iii. 16, 17 ; Acts i. 8, ii. 4, et al.

performed no such office of utility and adornment, its wood and stone would have had no such construction into cities and navies, and its sciences no such development. It is a nature in the image of God, and exercising like functions, that has created our histories, and brought earth into communication with heaven. Man has spirit, man has soul, man has body, all united in the one selfhood, as God is Father, and God is Word, and God is the Holy Spirit, all revealed under the one image of the Son of man, in whom this divine fulness dwells bodily.

We attempt no lines of demarcation between Father, Son, and Holy Spirit in God, as we cannot always distinguish between spirit, soul, and animal life in ourselves, though we know that they mysteriously coexist in the same conscious selfhood. I know I feel the pain of a burnt finger as well as agony purely mental, moral, and spiritual. Between these extremes of matter, how wide the field for diversity of manifestation! So in God, between His working in crude matter and in seraphic life, can we wonder that Moses saw what suggested to him the idea of plurality?

A Trinity in Unity as the archetype of man's nature crops out in the history of his creation. 'The Lord God formed man of the dust of the ground, and breathed into him the breath of life; and man became a living soul.'[1] We have here three distinct stages in the progress of the work:—1*st*, The creation of man from the ground. 2*d*, The inbreathing into him the breath of lives from God. 3*d*, The result,—man became a living soul.

We have first the ground-nature, or the earth-man, which must have been fitted for the destiny of the race. It was a tabernacle constructed for a certain

[1] Gen. ii. 7.

tenant; and the constitution, convenience, and activities of the destined occupant must have been provided for. The same adjustment obtained in this case, no doubt, as in all animal natures, whose organs and instincts are suited to the element in which they are to live, and the modes by which they are to subsist. As some one has said, No matter how low and bestial a race may be, if it has a human hand, it is susceptible of civilisation. The gorilla and chimpanzee, though above it in capacity to look out for themselves, for the lack of a hand are infinitely below the lowest race of human-kind in their fitness for culture and elevation.

As the tenant in this ground-structure of the Creator is what the Hebrews call *nephesh*, or soul in a peculiar sense, to which was assigned the possession of the lower animals, and the dominion of the world, his fleshly tabernacle must have been suited to so exalted a destiny. What we should expect in this regard, from the general analogy between the natures and habits of living creatures, we actually meet with in the earthly constitution of man. It is fitted to 'rule over the fish of the sea, and over the fowl of the heavens, and over everything that moves on the earth.'[1] The organic nature of man, though not so fleet nor so strong as that of many animals, is every way better fitted for the use of the soul in exercising dominion.

But how much is included in this first act in the process of man's creation? What were the constituents of his ground-nature? Was it merely a mass of clay, shaped in the human form by the plastic hand of the Creator, as the artist shapes his model? Was it without animal life? Was it without a human soul? This, I think, is not the idea of what Moses saw and

[1] Gen. i. 28.

described. For the beasts, with all their instincts, were formed from the earth. They were complete in this first act, and no divine inbreathing added to their faculties or qualities. They came from the earth living, active, sensational, thinking, and almost reasoning creatures. They are gregarious, as we are social; they are great builders; they have a sort of instinctive justice or conscience among themselves to live in harmony, as thousands of bees in the same hive, and as prairie dogs in mimic cities with a sort of police. Thus their ground-nature verges towards human intelligence; and some animals are above some men in ordering their lives. And yet nothing is said of an inbreathing from God, like that which is the crowning fact of man's creation. God simply said in their creation, 'Let the *earth* bring forth the living creature after his kind, cattle, and creeping thing, and beast of the earth after his kind: and it was so.'[1] And chemistry shows that the bodies of men and animals are of the same constituent properties with the earth itself, and at death their dust is not to be distinguished from vegetable mould.

The part of our race formed from the ground constituted it MAN. And what is a man? Is it clay-mould in human shape? Or, if the clay-mould were converted into dead flesh, would that make a man? Or even if animal life and instinct were added, does that reach our conception of manhood, or meet the requirements of Moses' language in saying that 'God formed MAN from the dust of the ground?' No; such a supposition is an outrage upon common sense, and a confounding of language. What was included in this first stage of man's creation was a being, not only with the clay-mould or animal life of a man, but with those

[1] Gen. i. 24.

faculties of thought, intelligence, and reason which supply in our race the place of brutal instincts, or which fit man to be a successful actor among the elements of this world. Anything short of this would not make the first statement in the case true, that 'God formed man from the dust of the ground.' It was the natural or earthly man which was thus formed with understanding, reason, love of the beautiful, powers of social organization, natural conscience, a sense of civil justice, and all those qualities which are necessary to the race as the mere tenants of earth, having dominion over nature and the brute creation. It was a being fitted, indeed, to receive something higher, holier, and more spiritual, to make the *nephesh* or soul 'living' in the highest sense of that term. But these higher endowments were imparted by another act in the drama of creation. The spiritual or divine must be added to constitute 'life' in the Bible sense; and, in the absence of it, all is regarded as death.[1]

The second act is altogether the most significant, and reveals the secret of man's real importance in the scale of being: 'God breathed into him the breath of lives.' The plural is used to denote amplitude, capacity, variety, as including civil and social life of a higher order,—not only a life directed by intellectual and scientific truths, but by those which are divine and heavenly; not only by knowledges reasoned out on natural grounds of evidence, but by intuitional and heart communion with God and angelic beings, and of open visions of the divine glory. God infused into a being earth-born and earthly a spiritual and heavenly nature, that he might live, not as the ruler of a material and brutal kingdom, but reign as king and priest in the kingdom of heaven.

[1] Gal. ii. 20; John xiv. 19; Eph. ii. 1; 1 Tim. v. 6.

These facts prepare us to understand the sense of the last stage in the process,—'and man became a living soul.' The same is said of beasts, where they are called living creatures, or 'the breath of life' is ascribed to them.[1] But the term life is determined by the being to which it is applied, whether to God, to men, or to animals. Of course it means in this case that man became living in the sense of the life for which the divine inbreathing prepared him. It was a life not consequent upon his ground-nature,—for that is described as dead,—but upon the divine and heavenly infusion of which his soul became the receptacle. This allied him to God as spirit; fitted him to receive God's word, which has no response in animal natures; to take his place among the gods, as those are called to whom the word of the Lord came.[2] It made him immortal, and, bodied or disembodied, a citizen of heaven.

Death, when man was created, had been the law of animal life from immemorial ages, if the testimony of the rocks is at all to be believed. The language of Moses by no means contradicts this testimony. And death no doubt would have been the law of man's being as he came from the ground; and even in any case his material nature must have undergone a change to render it immortal. It is imposing upon scientific men too heavy a tax, to require them to believe that a structure like the human body, made up of solids, fluids, gases, and nervous tissues, could keep up its action for ever, without a change like that of Enoch and Elijah fitting it for such a destiny.[3] A misinterpretation of the apostle's words, 'that death entered the world by sin,' and that 'in Adam all die,' has led to the general belief that both animal and human

---
[1] Gen. i. 26.   [2] John x. 35.   [3] 1 Cor. xv. 50.

bodies are rendered mortal by the fall of man. The error comes from failing to consider that the apostles use the term sin for a state as well as an act, and that this state is sometimes called death, and sometimes sin. As an act, 'sin is a transgression of the law,' and as a state, it is the condition of those who are made sinners, or brought into guilt and condemnation through 'the sin of one man.' This is the death that came by sin:[1] 'Flesh and blood cannot inherit the kingdom of God;' 'Dead in trespasses and in sins;' 'She that liveth in pleasure is dead while she liveth.' This is the only death inflicted on man the day he sinned, and therefore must have been intended by the threatening, 'The day thou eatest thereof, dying thou shalt die.'[2]

The account given by Moses of the creation of man is the key-note in the epic of revealed religion. It is the prologue of sacred history, throughout which the *nephesh*—soul—is eliminated from animal life, from spiritual life, and from all the components and relations of man's being, as in no other language and no other book on earth. It shapes not only the language, but the symbols of divine worship; and its ideas are transferred into Greek by the apostles, using words in a sense that Homer, Xenophon, and Plato never imagined. All this comes to view by carefully 'searching the Scriptures,' and 'comparing spiritual things with spiritual,'—the work which we propose to ourselves in these pages.

[1] Rom. v. 12-21; 1 John iii. 4; 1 Cor. xv. 44-51. etc. etc.
[2] Gen. ii. 17.

CHAPTER IV.

TERMS OF MIND IN FLESH.

WRITERS on speculative science represent the body as inert and powerless, except as acted upon by the mind. The mind sees, hears, walks, and performs all like functions. Our bodily organs are merely the instruments with which the mind works, as a lame man uses his crutch; and they might perish one after another, till all were gone, and yet the man in his conscious selfhood remain intact and unchanged. He loses thus only the implements of his work. Socrates very ingeniously sets this forth by a series of questions, in which he eliminates the man from all his bodily organs and senses.

Now this view, in a far more graphic form, is wrought into Hebrew as the language of common life. The *nephesh*, or soul, as permeated by spirit inbreathed from God, and connecting man with God, is the recognised actor in all our members and movements. It is not mind in our sense, but mind in the image of God—mind open to the spiritual as well as material world, and receiving contributions from both as a medium power to unite the two,—thus making man moral and immortal, a citizen of earth and of the spirit-land, and imparting to his actions a significance unknown to speculative philosophy. Seeing, with inspired men, is knowing, believing, enjoying; hearing is hearkening, obeying; smelling is imbibing the sweet odour of goodness, or disgust of wickedness; baring the arm is power; putting under feet is subordinating to authority; carrying in the bosom is affection and care: and thus all muscular movement has a spiritual and divine significance, as the outworking of exalted and enduring forces. I am aware of no language in which these ideas are so framed into the structure of words and speech as in the Hebrew.

In this language the outer organs of the body give names to things that pertain to the outer life of man, and the inner organs to the interior faculties, or mental states. *Adam* ground, *methim* mortals, *basar* flesh, *golgolcth* skull or head, are of the first class; and *lebab* heart, *kelayoth* kidneys, *kereb* inner parts, *meim* bowels, are of the second or inner class.

The term *adam*, ground, was the name of the first man, and is applied to mankind in general. It is about five hundred times variously used for individuals, nations, and the race. The stem-idea is that of a ground-man, or a being allied to God, angels, and the spirit-world, or immortality, but dwelling in a house of clay, to show forth in this material world the attributes and splendours of heavenly life. The subject of 'a kingdom that cannot be moved,' he is surrounded by things shaken and to be removed, in order to give place to ' a building of God, an house not made with hands, eternal in the heavens.'[1] Though thus endowed, he is still a ground-man. His soul, though opaque and grovelling, being of the earth, earthy, was by the divine inbreathing rendered radiant with heavenly light. Heaven is anchored to earth in his person. Eyes refulgent from communion with God

[1] Heb. xii. 27, 28; 2 Cor. v. 1.

look out upon this earthly scene through him, that 'heaven may not want spectators, God want praise.' The ladder reaching heaven finds foothold in him, on which angelic troops ascend and descend. God's kingdom comes, and His will is done spiritually as in heaven, according to our Lord's prayer. Here the two worlds meet in him, who is formed in the image and after the likeness of God. All this is included in the original conception of the ground-man.

Mĕthim, mortals, points to dissolution, and is used as a term of weakness. Jacob uses it in the words rendered 'few in number,'[1] to indicate the weakness of his tribe; and Isaiah, of 'the men of Israel' as being alike weak with the 'worm Jacob.'[2] There seems to be little doubt that it is made from *mûth*, to die, though it is chiefly applied to men as distinguished from women and children. Whether derived from a change original to the race, answerable to what the death of the body now is, or not, we cannot presume to say. It is certain that death in its present form would not have been known had it not been for sin. 'Dust thou art, and unto dust shalt thou return,'[3] is introduced in a way to give the idea that a bodily immortality was originally provided for, without this return to dust. It may have come, as to Enoch and Elijah, without death, or as to Christ, without seeing corruption. One thing is certain, that a glorified body is not a material one, or not subject to material laws, as our Lord's was not after His resurrection. We call men mortals because they die; and the ancient Hebrews would appear to have called them *mĕthim* for the same cause. Death to holy men, however, was not what it is to us. Abraham at his death

[1] Gen. xxxiv. 30.   [2] Isa. xli. 14.   [3] Gen. iii. 19.

was 'gathered to his people,' and was no doubt more alive the day his remains were deposited in the cave of Machpelah than ever before.[1]

Flesh, as a term for man, denotes his exterior life, as that is the enclosing casement of all that is within him. It is often put in contrast with spirit, which is the window of the soul heavenward, as flesh is earthward.[2] 'All flesh' is a term many times used for the whole human family. It is also used for worldly pre-eminence, intellectual and material, in the passage, 'The Egyptians are great of flesh.'[3] That nation in the time of Ezekiel was the centre of the world's civilisation. Still it was all flesh or exterior show, and not founded in spiritual power. 'All flesh is grass' is an expression for the universal frailty of our earthly life.[4]

The *skull*, or head, is used only in the sense of poll, as 'an omer a head;' 'every male according to their polls.'[5] In this connection *golgoleth* denotes personality.

Another class of words denoting mental or spiritual qualities is derived from the internal organs of the body. The inspired writers had no conception of our understanding, heart, and will, or cognitive, esthetic, and conative faculties, as mapped off and divided from each other by our mental philosophers. Their language is rather shaped to their ever-present idea of man as the common centre of two worlds, spirit and matter, angelic and animal; and they offset the foregoing terms, denoting the animal contributions to his material of thought and action, with the internal organs

---

[1] Gen. xxv. 8 ; Matt. xxii. 32.
[2] 2 Chron. xxxii. 8 ; Ps. lvi. 4 ; Job x. 4.
[3] Ezek. xvi. 26. [4] Isa. xl. 6 ; 1 Pet. i. 24.
[5] Ex. xvi. 16 : Num. i. 2.

of his body, as a reflection of his higher relations. These two influences mingle in all he is and does, either for good or for evil; and if he is a mere beast, he is so with a significance and intensity of application which are impossible to the brute creation. He is more than earthly and sensual,—he is devilish.[1]

The word *lebab*, for instance, which we render heart, but with no exactitude to the original, includes both the intellectual and pathematic, or affectional nature, or these attributes as affected by our relations both to God and the world. *Our* heart is used for the affectional, as distinguished from the intellectual. Not so the *lebab* of the Hebrew. The heart, as the seat of animal life, derives its action from absorbing chyle from the digested food of the stomach, and from certain properties of air inhaled by the lungs. Without these united contributions, it would soon cease to beat. So inspired intuition seems to recognise the mental action as uniting in itself both thought and feeling. Both must supply pabulum to every mental state and exercise. Without thought, feeling has no being; and without feeling, thought no impulse. Conscious mental action is permeated and interpenetrated by affectional influences, as melted iron by heat. And as iron loses its fluidity when the heat is gone, so the mind loses thought when no longer impelled by feeling of some sort. I speak of the subject as it seems to me to stand in the representations of inspired men, and this is the case as it exists in fact and in nature. The *nephesh*, mind or soul, is in their view a unit, with influences acting upon it from flesh and from spirit. Whichever way it went the whole man went, and not a part merely. He could not truly give his thoughts

[1] Jas. iii. 15.

to God and withhold his affections, nor his affections and withhold his thoughts. He cannot serve God and mammon. He cannot divide thought from feeling.

Lebab, however, inclines more to the intellectual than the affectional, and was used as a verb, as we use mind when we speak of minding a thing. Thus in Job it is said, ' Man *hearts* to be wise, or thinks to be, though man be born as a wild ass's colt.'[1] Wisdom here includes spiritual perception, of which man by sin has become as destitute as a wild animal. The word is also used for doing things skilfully, as Tamar in baking cakes for Amnon, and the spouse in her arts of captivation.[2] Skill united to affectional influence is the idea in both these cases. It is adding feeling to ingenuity. It is ' mind, purpose, intention, understanding, knowledge, insight.'[3]

Kĕlayoth, kidneys or reins, are used for a lower order of tendencies than heart, and is made from a word which means to consume, as with grief, sorrow, remorse, lust, voluptuousness, or any strong inward feeling that preys upon a man's nature. It is only twelve times used, being connected in several instances with *lebab*, as : ' Search my heart and my kidneys,'[4] that is, my thoughts and emotions. ' My kidneys instruct me in the night season,'[5] is a passage referring to the guiding influence of right emotions, or the inward movings of the divine Spirit, ' teaching us all things.'[6] This is the law written in the fleshly tables of the heart. The kidneys and heart stand related to each other in

---

[1] Job xi. 12.   [2] Cant. iv. 9.
[3] 1 Kings viii. 17,18 ; 1 Chron. xxii. 7, xxviii. 2 ; Job xii. 3, xxxiv. 10 ; Prov. vii. 9.
[4] Ps. vii. 9 ; Jer. xi. 20, xvii. 10 ; Ps. xxvi. 2.
[5] Ps. xvi. 7.   [6] 1 John ii. 27.

Hebrew somewhat like appetite and passion in English, the one tending to a fleshly, the other to an intellectual exercise.

Meim, bowels, is also ten times used, in the sense of a highly emotional state, accompanied by pity or compassion. ' My bowels boiled ;' ' my bowels sounded as a harp ;' ' my bowels resounded within me.'[1] These are expressions of affectionate yearning towards a suffering object, which the New Testament writers have adopted in the expressions, ' tender [bowel] mercies ;' ' in the bowels of Jesus Christ ;' ' bowels of mercies,' and some others.[2] There are other cases of the like use of similar organs, but these will suffice to show the general scope of the whole.

Not only is mind the recognised actor in the bodily members, but the name of God is the added superlative in setting forth in Hebrew what is extraordinary; and the great rivers are rivers of God, the great trees, trees of God, the great mountains, mountains of God, and a fertile country is 'the land the Lord hath blessed.' The lilies are painted with beauty by His pencil, the fowls fed from His storehouse, and the very hairs of our head are all numbered. ' They also that dwell in the uttermost parts are afraid at Thy tokens: Thou makest the outgoings of the morning and evening to rejoice. Thou visitest the earth, and waterest it. Thou greatly enrichest it with the river of God, which is full of water: Thou preparest them corn, when Thou hast so provided for it.' ' Thou crownest the year with goodness.' ' He rode upon a cherub, and did fly ; and He was seen upon the wings of the wind.' ' Deep

[1] Job xxx. 2 ; Isa. xvi. 11 ; Jer. iv. 19, xxxi. 20 ; Lam. i. 20, ii. 11.
[2] Luke i. 78 ; Phil. i. 8 ; Col. iii. 12.

calleth unto deep at the noise of Thy water-spouts; all Thy waves and Thy billows are gone over me.' 'Day unto day uttereth speech; night unto night showeth knowledge.'[1]

Thus in the inspired intuitions God was as really present in all the objects and forces of nature, and all the events transpiring, as mind is in the organs of man's living body. The spiritual world was a greater reality to them than the natural world, just as the power is greater than the machine through which it operates, the mind than the body wielded by it, the life more than raiment.

This sense of God's present working, everywhere manifesting itself in the Bible, is not to be confounded either with the fancies of childhood, the local divinities of the heathen, nor with the pantheism of poetry or philosophy. Everything to a child has life or personality. Fairies disport themselves in the summer woods, utter their sweet notes in the babbling brooks and rustling pines; and thunder, lightning, and storm are to his fervid fancy giant beings over his head, putting the heavens in commotion. This childish feeling may be an index to our spiritual instincts, showing how inseparable religion is from our nature, but it has little affinity with the inspired view of God in the visible scene around us. Still more remote is this view from the Greek mythology, which peopled the world with gods of the hills and gods of the plains, gods of the groves and gods of the fountains, gods of learning, war, agriculture, and of all the occupations of life.[2] Nor is the Hebrew Jehovah the sum of all material forces,

---

[1] Matt. vi. 26-34; Ps. lxv. 8, 9; 2 Sam. xxii. 11; Ps. xlii. 7, xix. 1, 2.
[2] 1 Kings xx. 28.

according to pantheism, but a personal, conscious, designing, acting Being, who 'worketh all things after the counsel of His own will.'[1]

What a delightful sense of security in danger does this faith of a present God give to those who have it! The besieged prophet in Dothan was surrounded by chariots and horses of fire, to assure him that more were they who were for him than against him.[2] Who does not desire to feel himself nestling in the bosom of infinite Wisdom and Love ?—ourselves infants, but controlled and protected by a Father's care. No flower unfolds to us its beauties, but comes as a gift from His hand. No bird sings its matin song which does not resound His praise. No evils can assail us which He cannot turn to our greatest good. We see Him in the revolving planets; feel Him in the pulsating life-current within; hear Him in the voices of nature; and the whole visible scene around us is radiant with His beauties and His glories. Nothing comes by chance, but as the dictate of a Father's love. As, when we enter a furnace, and observe around us the currents of fire and the action of huge iron hammers, or hear the groaning, wheezing, whistling of pent-up steam as a chained lion struggling for freedom, we stand secure, because we have confidence in the mind regulating these forces according to law, so we feel a greater security amid the vaster forces of nature, because Jehovah has fixed the bounds beyond which they cannot pass. His laws assure us that His earth will not fall from under our feet, His stars will not drop upon our heads, His mountains will not crush us, and His raging deep will not overwhelm us. 'Thou rulest the

---

[1] Eph. i. 11 ; Isa. xxviii. 29 ; Jer. xxxii. 19.
[2] 2 Kings vi. 16, 17.

raging of the sea: when the waves thereof arise, Thou stillest them.'[1] Who is so great a god as our God?

Tholuck, in his exposition of the vine emblem in the fifteenth chapter of John, institutes a beautiful parallel between mind and matter. 'The Author of the realm of spirits, he says, 'is likewise the Author of the realm of nature: both kingdoms develope themselves by the same laws. Wherefore those comparisons which the Redeemer derives from the realm of nature are not mere comparisons, serving to throw light upon the topic in hand; they are inward profound analogies, and nature is witness for the realm of spirits. This truth of correspondence floats dimly in the allegorizing Cabalists, and is also present in Swedenborg, who did not lack in apprehension of the principle, but only in an application of the principle. Their principle was,—everything that is in the kingdom of nature is found also in the kingdom of heaven. Were it not so, those comparisons would not have the power of conviction which they exercise over unperverted minds.'

[1] Ps. lxxxix. 9, 11.

CHAPTER V.

INHALING LIFE FROM THE EXPANSE.

A FAR more significant class of words now offer themselves to our consideration. They are four,—two of the Old Testament, and two of the New. The Greek terms are, however, a mere rendering of the Hebrew, with little added except greater clearness. *Nephesh*, of which *psuche* is the synonym, and *ruach*, of which *pneuma* is the synonym, the first in each case being Hebrew, and the others the expression of their meaning in New Testament Greek. *Nephesh* and *psuche* mean soul or mind, and *ruach* and *pneuma* spirit. The primary or physical idea expressed by the two first is breath, and they are both made from a word which signifies to breathe; and the primary or physical meaning of the two last is wind, and they are made from verbs that mean to blow. As wind inhaled is breath, and breath exhaled is wind, these words have a peculiar affinity in a natural sense, and equally so as applied to the spiritual of man and the universe. They are words which direct our thoughts from man to the aerial, translucent expanse, on which he is as dependent for life as the mussel upon his rock, or the fish upon his watery home. Detached, he is as sure to die.

By what association of ideas were the inspired writers led to adopt such a mode of representation?

Why symbolize soul by breath, and spirit by wind? No doubt it comes from the necessity of breathing and atmospheric influences in order to life. As animals are under a like necessity, they are designated by the same terms. 'Every living creature' is in the original every living soul; and *ruach*, spirit, is applied alike to men and beasts, where it is said, 'The spirit of man goeth upward, and the spirit of the beast goeth downward.'[1] The tenuity and evanescence of air, and the shadows and mists encumbering it, are by some thought to be the point of its resemblance to a ghost or ghosts, as they conceive of a soul in its disembodied state. Spirits or ghosts are spoken of as 'shades of the dead.' So far as simple animal life, common to man and beasts, is concerned, or the life that depends upon breathing air, this may be the chief point of comparison. But the soul of man, as a recipient of the divine inbreathing, and rendered immortal, is anything but evanescent in the view of inspired men, and must therefore have its analogy to breath and breathing, to wind and blowing, in a very different class of facts.

Is a being with capacities for endless existence a puff of empty air? Matter or material worship is in the Bible represented as shadow soon passing away, but heaven and the objects of faith are substance.[2] Breath and breathing, therefore, denote life, not death. The absence of them brings death. So long as breathing lasts, there is life. And it was this that constituted the salient point,—'In God we live, move, and have our being.' If 'to live is Christ, to die is gain,' because it opens to us a higher form of life, where the

---

[1] Gen. ii. 19, i. 21; Eccles. iii. 21; Num. xxxi. 28; Lev. xi. 10 xxiv. 17, 18, etc.
[2] Heb. x. 34, xi. 1.

nephesh or soul, instead of being lost as a breath or waif in the unbounded ether, will plume itself for a higher flight, and be borne aloft by another and more enduring atmosphere.[1] Such are clearly the ideas of inspiration, and such of course must be the design of the symbolism which it employs. The soul lives in God as the body in air, and out of Him it dies as in a vacuum.

Still higher ideas are included in the soul as breath. In the atmosphere from which we inhale life, sun, moon, and stars concentrate their radiance and their influence to supply elements wanting to the air itself, without which we should as certainly die as without breathing. Can we live without sunlight? Can the pulsating tides act without lunar influence? Can the earth be held in its orbit without that mysterious power which we call the attraction of gravitation, keeping it in its place in this great family of worlds? And do all these facts stand for nothing in this divine symbolism? No; our dependence upon the expanse for animal life, or for breath and breathing, is the type of the higher and more significant truths of the dependence of our souls upon God, and the spiritual atmosphere investing Him for the more exalted functions of our moral and immortal being. This, I think, is the point of the comparison of animal and soul life which the inspired writers had in view in using the terms breath and wind in this connection. They had in view an immortal soul drawing all right thoughts and affections from God, by a process like that of inhaling bodily life from air; a soul acted upon by God Himself, as wind upon breathing animals, fanning and invigorating them, as it were, by spiritual breezes, like the currents of air

[1] Acts xvii. 28; Phil. i. 21.

which purify and assist our natural respiration. 'Praying without ceasing,'[1] is an exhortation of the apostle which would be impossible on any other principle than such a spiritual respiration. It supposes us living invested by God's real life-giving presence, so that we can draw upon Him by prayer as easily and continuously as upon the air we breathe. He holds us in His loving arms, as we are held by atmospheric pressure or by gravitation.

Our purpose is not to impose upon the reader ideas of our own, or any fanciful interpretation of the sacred text, but simply the thoughts penned by inspiration, and what is clearly legitimate to them. The inspired writers were indeed ignorant of the natural sciences in our sense of that term. But they had what was better, —a clear insight into the real forces working in mind and matter, forces which our laboratories and chemical processes fail to reach. Their induction included facts of the spiritual as well as of the natural world, and had therefore a much broader basis than ours. And those which they derived from a spiritual source, when rightly understood and interpreted, will be found perfectly accordant with all true science. This breathing process, by which they represent spirit and soul life, stands connected with ideas and statements from their pen which singularly accord with our most advanced discoveries in reference to atmospheric influence. We know that our lives do not depend simply upon inhaling atmospheric air, but upon innumerable chords of influence from sun, moon, and stars, radiating through, and interpenetrating as threads of lace, the whole aerial expanse. Every star in heaven supplies so important an element to this aerial tissue, that if it were gone it

---
[1] 1 Thess. v. 17.

would destroy the equilibrium of forces; the earth would be jostled out of its place, and undistinguished ruin would ensue. We should as surely die without sun and moon light, and without the ministering stars, as without an atmosphere to breathe. A congealed ocean and a polar winter overspreading all the earth, would extinguish the last remains of animal and vegetable life.

Thus in the Bible not only are we represented as 'living in God,' as we live in air, but as ministered to by spiritual beings, executing specific commissions from God for the training and preservation of our race. The idea of angelic intermediation in the affairs of men is as constantly kept before our view as the world we live in, or the beings inhabiting it. 'God maketh His angels spirits, and His ministers a flame of fire.' 'Are they not all ministering spirits, sent forth to minister to them who shall be heirs of salvation?'[1] Both these passages are connected with facts of material nature, such as the 'stretching out the heavens as a curtain,' 'laying the beams of His chambers in the waters,' 'making the clouds His chariot,' 'walking upon the wings of the wind,' 'making the worlds,' 'upholding all things by the word of His power,' as if angelic ministrations were symbolized by the ministering elements and heavenly bodies. How much had angels to do in the patriarchal histories, in the career of Moses and subsequent prophets, and in the New Testament events! No one can look at this record with an impartial eye, without feeling that we breathe a spiritual air, and are ministered to by a spiritual sun, moon, and stars, as well as those which are material.

Nor do inspired men confine their ideas merely to

[1] Ps. civ. 4; Heb. i. 14.

good beings and influences from the spiritual world, but include also those which are bad. The bad they liken to a noxious atmosphere, and speak of it as 'the prince of the power of the air, the spirit that worketh in the children of disobedience: among whom we all had our conversation,' or impulse to life and conduct, 'fulfilling the desires of the flesh and of the mind.'[1] As a malarious atmosphere introduces disease to those who breathe it, and excites an abnormal action of the blood, state of the appetite, and of the whole physical man, so inhaling a spiritual atmosphere ruled by the devil and his angels influences lust and voluptuousness, and leads to all manner of error and wickedness. It is only on the principle of an instituted analogy between natural breathing and spiritual influence that such passages as the foregoing can be legitimately interpreted. The prince of the power of the air acts upon our moral nature or soul-life as malarious air upon those who breathe it. Unclean spirits, of which we have such frequent mention in the Gospels, influence men and beasts on analogous principles, as they left the maniac to madden the swine. We here attempt no explanation of these facts, but simply notice the comparison which the Bible institutes between them and those of breathing and atmospheric influences.

The infinite Spirit acts both upon matter and upon mind, giving a life-producing power to the waters, and understanding to man.[2] The two, *ruach* and *nephesh*, spirit and soul, in man commingle their influence, as wind and blood in the lungs, the result being what we see,—a conscious responsible being, uniting in himself what Tholuck calls 'the realm of spirits and the realm of nature.' These two distinct realms meet in the soul

[1] Eph. ii. 2, 3.   [2] Gen. i. 2; Job xxxii. 8.

of man. Soul is interfused by spirit as melted iron by heat, and at the same time it is interpermeated by material or animal influences. It sees God on the one hand, it sees the world on the other. There is no likeness between the two; for nothing is like God, and no material substance approximates spirit, though, to convey ideas of the former, we are compelled to symbolize it by the latter, as we said in our first chapter. The life of a plant is no more soil than breath is soul, or spirit, wind; but can it live and become seeding without soil? But though breath is not soul, it is a necessity of the soul's life in the body, and therefore a fitting symbol to represent it. So wind is a great power in nature, and therefore a fitting representation of Spirit, who came upon the apostles as 'a rushing mighty wind,' and so was their promised gift of 'power from on high.' And 'the wind or breath of our nostrils is the anointed of the Lord,' 'the unction of the Holy One by which we know all things, and is truth, and is no lie.'[1] It is spirit as a breathing medium, analogous to our atmosphere, which imparts to us faith, divine communion, the capacity for acceptable worship, and all the highest qualities of our nature. The apostle takes occasion to say that this sort of inspiration is 'truth, and no lie,' and Jeremiah calls it 'the anointed of the Lord,' to rebuke the tendency in us to regard everything unreal which is not material. This extraordinary gift of power to the Church would have been the normal condition of human nature had it not been for sin. Man was originally created for the exercise of those powers which we now call miraculous; the divine inbreathing insured them to him. But he lost them by abjuring the dominion of spirit for that of the flesh.

[1] Compare Luke xxiv. 49; Acts i. 5, ii. 2; Lam. iv. 20; 1 John ii. 27.

Thus two kinds of respiration are clearly set before us by the inspired writers,—first, that by which our animal life is preserved; and second, that by which our spiritual life subsists. They had both in view, no doubt, in their references to the material expanse,—soul breathing in the properties of air, and spirit breathing in the higher influences supplied by the heavenly bodies. The boundless empyrean, infinite ethereal spaces, the properties of light shining from innumerable orbs, are subjects of frequent reference in the Bible. 'The heavens declare the glory of God, and the expanse showeth His handiwork.' 'When I consider Thy heavens, the work of Thy fingers, the moon and stars, which Thou hast ordained; what is man that Thou art mindful of him, or the son of man, that Thou visitest him?'[1]

But it may be said the seers had not the light of our science to guide them, and they could not therefore have had our enlarged views of nature. True, they knew nothing of the attraction of gravitation; but do *we* know what it is? They had what was better than our name for this unknown thing,—the clear view of a divine Power holding all the orbs and elements in their places, 'guiding Arcturus with her sons,' and 'binding the sweet influences of Pleiades.'[2] Science sees in gravitation a power conterminous with matter; *they* saw a Power alike conterminous with a universe of matter and of mind. One Jehovah rules in both, and was infinitely more to them than the name of an unknown power. Spiritual Omnipotence pervades the domain of nature and of spirits, and affords to the human soul breathing in both, to make sure that, though the animal organism depending upon the one be dis-

[1] Ps. xix. 1, viii. 4, 5.   [2] Job ix. 9, xxxviii. 28-37.

solved, the soul itself will rise like a phœnix from the ashes of its desolation, and plume itself for everlasting progress in holiness and bliss. The *nephesh* of the Hebrews is represented as standing between two worlds, the uniting link between the two,—a son of earth and a son of God.

These views, though pervading the Old Testament, are not so clearly seen as in the New. There centred in the God-man, the archetype of humanity, not only the faculties, attributes, and breathing necessities of an earthly nature, but 'the fulness of the Godhead bodily.' 'All power in heaven and earth' thus took on the forms and conditions of our common manhood. And through Him a like impartation is made to those to whom ' He gives power to become sons of God.' 'They are born, not of blood, nor of the will of the flesh, nor of the will of man, but of God.' 'They have put on the new man, which is renewed in knowledge after the image of Him that created him.' The idea is, that the true Spirit is Christ, whether manifesting Himself as God or in flesh, in His own person or in that of His renewed people,—' He in us, and we in Him.'[1]

It is only by this twofold view of breathing and living, one of flesh, and the other of spirit, that we can explain many things in the Bible. How else can we 'pray without ceasing,' as I have already said?

How else can the *asking* and the *having* be simultaneous? (1 John v. 15.) Inhaling is having breath; and truly desiring a grace or virtue is to have it.

How else can hungering and thirsting after righteousness insure an instant fulness? (Matt. v. 6.)

If God as a Spirit were not investing a supplicating people as their breathing expanse, or if He were not

[1] John i. 13, 14; Col. iii. 10; John xvii. 21, xv. 5, etc. etc.

present as speech to a hearing ear, how could what God says be true, that 'before they call, I will answer; and while they are speaking, I will hear?' (Isa. lxv. 24.)

How else can the Holy Spirit be surer to them that ask Him, than good things are from parents to their pleading children? (Luke xi. 13.)

How else can a hidden life from God reach a soul through Christ? (Col. iii. 3.) Must there not be spiritual respiration to insure such a result?

How else can man live otherwise than by bread alone? (Deut. viii. 3; Matt. iv. 4.)

Where there is a failure to take in these divine sources of life, the breathing is not in that direction, but towards the world: 'Ye ask, and receive not, because ye ask amiss, that ye may consume it upon your lusts.'[1] Even if desire goes towards a spiritual atmosphere it is to subserve a worldly end, like that of Balaam and Simon Magus; nothing but demon influences will follow, and we shall be more than ever 'in the gall of bitterness, and under the bond of iniquity.'[2]

[1] Jas. iv. 3. [2] Acts viii. 23.

CHAPER VI.

THE SOUL AS THE CONSCIOUS SELFHOOD.

WHAT is the exact position which inspired writers assign to the soul, as distinguished from flesh and spirit ? That there is a difference, not only appears from the relation in which they are placed to each other generally in the Bible, but by their being specifically used by the apostle for three separate ideas in the same sentence : That 'your whole spirit and soul and body be preserved blameless unto the coming of our Lord Jesus Christ.'[1] We easily distinguish between soul and body, and spirit and body ; but what is the difference between soul and spirit ? This is the question.

The synonymous words *nephesh* of the Old Testament, and *psuche* of the New, are used with a discrimination which is not expressed by our word soul, by which they are rendered. Soul with us, as applied to mind in distinction from body, is the same as spirit. A man's soul is his spirit. But *psuche* of the New Testament is never used for *ruach*, or spirit, but always, when applied to men, for *nephesh*, or soul. The tendency of *psuche* is towards the flesh ; and the adjective made from it, *psuchikos*, means animal, or the animal nature, and in our common version it is rendered 'natural' and 'sensual.'[2] But *ruach* and *pneuma*,

---

[1] 1 Thess. v. 23.   [1] 1 Cor. ii. 14 ; Jas. iii. 15.

spirit, have a directly opposite tendency, and, from being applied to man's inner being, it supplies a name for God. Or perhaps the order should be reversed, and we should say that, from being applied to God, it became a name for that in man which responds to God, as it was before man's creation, that 'the *ruach*, or Spirit of God, brooded on the face of the waters.' And in the New Testament it supplies the adjective *pneumatikos*, spiritual, which is the direct opposite of *psuchikos*, natural, sensual, or animal. How then can two words, one of which means divine and spiritual life, and the other animal life, be conceived of as expressing the same ideas when applied to the nature of man? No, soul and spirit are heaven-wide apart in their acceptation by inspired men. True, the inner nature of man is called soul, because connected with animal life ; and spirit, because a recipient of influence from God. So we call a person a cottager because he lives in a cottage, and a scholar because he is a learner ; but does that make cottage and scholar synonymous terms?

The stem-thought of soul, as used by inspired men, is that of a conscious, personal, responsible selfhood. It covers the whole ground of man's free voluntary agency. When the limits of that agency are exceeded in any direction, the things we meet with are not part and parcel of a man's soul. They may pertain to somebody else's soul, or to brute force, but not to that particular individual soul to which one applies the word self when he is speaking of his own. My body may be forced, but not my soul. My outward deeds may be distrained, but not my will. The veriest slave wills to be free. Quite another process is necessary to enslave the soul than that of simple force. It must be done by perverting the will through deception, ignorance, or some modification of the selfhood, whereby the man is made to choose what he would not choose in a right state of his faculties. This is trading in the souls of men, of which Rome is not alone guilty, but every government and organization which obstructs the march of truth.

There is no way of moving the soul but through the will; for the moment the soul were distrained against its consent, whether by God or men, its selfhood would end, and another power come into its place. Suppose the laughing-gas be administered to a man, and he plays various unconscious pranks under its influence, is it himself that acts? If he is out of his head, as we say, do we not set his doings to another account than his responsible selfhood? To say that a man's personality is anything but his conscious willing, is to make him a chemical compound, or a mere secretion of matter. He cannot will against his will. Soul inviolability is the great idea of revealed religion. The whole Bible is constructed with reference to it. It is a great argument, influencing men to the choice of truth and good. And what is redemption, but recovering men to the love, preference, and practice of goodness? How could stronger proof be given of the inviolability of the human will, than God's expedients to induce our choice of Him and His service before all others? Popes and kings may use coercion in matters of conscience, but God never,—for the good reason that virtue is *not* virtue, and holiness is *not* holiness, only so far as the soul's unconstrained will and desire go out after them. Man is in the image of God in this absolute supremacy within his own domain, and without partnership in the throne except as he consents

The Soul as the Conscious Selfhood. 47

to admit one. Such is the *nephesh*, or soul of the Bible.

Bunyan's idea of the soul as a castle is biblical and authentic. It is a castle open to spirit on one side, and flesh on the other, but none can enter except at the option of the reigning lord within. His business is to keep guard at ear-gate and eye-gate, and at all the avenues of sense, on the one hand; and, on the other, to 'try the spirits whether they are of God, because many false prophets [malign spiritual influences] are gone out into the world.'[1] If he admits evil from either of these sources, it is at his peril, because law, conscience, God, hold him responsible as the ruling power within. No matter how multitudinous the army, authority is a unit in its head. No matter how various the powers subordinate to the soul, *that*, in the view of inspired men, is the seat of all moral responsibility. Each soul, within its own measure of duty, has the question of its virtue or its vice, its holiness or its sin, its happiness or its misery to all eternity, to decide. What questions in national diplomacy can equal these? God, in making each one his own diplomat, puts the utmost dignity upon the soul.

The metaphysicians have for ages controverted the question as to whether ideas are derived wholly from the external senses, or partly from intuition; and they are as far now as ever from reaching a satisfactory result. But the inspired writers view the subject from quite another standpoint. They looked upon the soul as the centre of a world of flesh, on the one hand, offering him its contributions; and of spirit, on the other, reaching him through another channel, or by

[1] 1 John iv. 1.

a different mode of apprehension. One is an object of sense, the other of faith. Both unite its experiences in the soul, or selfhood. The Hebrew seers had not reached the point of madness to deny the contributions of either the one or the other. They believed the eye did see light, and not a merely subjective illusion of the fancy. They believed that faith did act, as seeing Him who is invisible. The objective reality of both a spiritual and natural world stood to them on the same basis,—the fact of their being conscious of a nature that took truths, influences, and impressions from both. To them a bird's wing supposed the reality of air, and the fish's fin the reality of water. So the power to receive inflowing truth and love from God made His existence a stupendous fact; just as the power to take impressions from this world through the five senses made that also to them a vast domain of substantial thought and expatiation. All aglow with seraphic fire at viewing the divine glory in both, they cry, 'Alleluia: for the Lord God omnipotent reigneth.'[1]

There is recognised in the Bible *nephesh*, or soul, a retributive provision, that when he lets in an enemy he cannot drive him out. A dominating sin or lust once entrenched in the castle is a strong man armed, that can only be dispossessed by One stronger than he. To will oneself into crime is easy, but to will oneself back again into innocence is impossible. The soul is indeed still free to follow desire; but when that is perverted, it is an *ignis fatuus*, to lead into still more inextricable error. He is then "the servant of sin."[2] But this is a servitude of choice, and therefore morally free, like the slave with his ear pinned to the doorpost of his master, who was so by his own election.[3]

[1] Rev. xix. 6.   [2] John viii. 34.   [3] Ex. xxi. 6.

The controversy between free-will and necessity, therefore, ends in this, that men are free and not necessitated, because they do as they choose; and yet they are slaves to evil, because evil dominates their affections, and deprives them of the will to be free from its power.

Another power accorded to the *nephesh* of the Bible, even in its slavery to evil, is that of being a successful actor among the elements of this world. He can apply himself to science, to art, to agriculture, to architecture, and thus lay the foundation of a beneficent civilisation. The loss of one sense leads to a more careful cultivation of those that remain; the loss of heaven, as a power in the soul, has turned all human energy, in a certain sense, upon making the most of a purely intellectual, animal, and material life. True, it is a soil cursed with briars and thorns; and while it causes much labour and misery, it affords infinitely less happiness than under the ruling of the Holy Spirit.

It is a mistake of certain sanguine reasoners, however, to claim for Christianity the sole civilising agency. Nations totally unchristian, and unspiritual except demon-worship, are far advanced in an intellectual and material civilisation. The Chinese were, a few centuries ago, in advance of all the world in printing and paper-making, in inoculation to mitigate contagious disease, in the use of the magnetic needle, in highly-improved methods of agriculture and of certain arts, and in other means of individual and social progress. The Egyptians, Chaldæans, Greeks, and Romans of the ancient heathen ages are to this day our models in art, civil law, and architectural magnificence. Their lost arts are not yet recovered in our age of boasted progress.

No doubt a true spiritual condition for a people is infinitely better than any other, just as virtue is better than vice, and truth than error; but this is not saying that a man without them may not have much valuable knowledge in worldly matters. Those who violate God's laws in some things, and keep them in others, will experience the disadvantage in the one case, and the benefit in the other. I have seen some earnest Christians on neglected farms, with everything going to waste around them, while their infidel neighbours were surrounding themselves with thrift and plenty. The one, perhaps, were faithful to spiritual, but negligent of natural laws; the other, negligent of spiritual laws, but lived up to the letter of those which concern farming and business. Inspired men never represent the subject in any other light, but insist that if a man will not work, neither shall he eat.[1] What we call talent, natural endowments, education, worldly advancement, they recognise in the frequent mention of Egyptian and Chaldæan opulence and glory; but they never regard them as *wisdom*, for that begins with the fear of the Lord.[2] The *nephesh*, or soul, must, in their view, have the Holy Spirit to sanctify and ennoble all worldly good, all material and intellectual achievements. This is the only wisdom, because it alone unites in itself the two worlds of which man is a tenant.

The *nephesh* of the Old Testament is used about seven hundred times, and *psuche*, its synonym of the New, seventy times. In our common version they are nearly four hundred times rendered soul, twenty-seven times as a personal pronoun, seventy times as life, twenty-five times as person, ten times mind, once will, six times desire, three times pleasure, twelve

---

[1] 2 Thess. iii. 10.   [2] Prov. i. 7; Job xxviii. 28; Prov. ix. 10.

times heart, once beauty, twice ghost, once spirit, three times appetite. Its application to beasts and dead bodies we omit as not pertinent to our subject. The stem-idea, as I before said, is that of the man as distinguished from body and from spirit. Hence its use as a pronoun, person, life, mind, spirit, will, desire, pleasure, heart, ghost, appetite. These are mere expressions of what the soul is, or what is consequent upon its existence.

It can live in the body, and it can live out of the body; it can be in communion with God and angels, or with the world and devils. It is not an ethereal essence, as some foolishly speak of it, to be diffused at death; but it has an identity of its own which it will never lose. 'Thou wilt not leave my soul in Hades, nor suffer Thine Holy One to see corruption,'[1] proves that our Lord's soul retained its conscious selfhood in its state of separation from the body. 'To-day shalt thou be with me in paradise'[2] is a promise which insured to the thief on the cross the conscious integrity of his soul after death, as well as to his Redeemer. Of Rachel it is said, 'Her soul was in departing (for she died),'[3]—that is, departing from its dissolving tabernacle of the body, as a nomad from his falling tent. This is the apostle's view of the relation of the soul to a dying body: it leaves a transient for a permanent house.[4] Thus in many passages the soul is detached from the body as a subsistence by itself, or the sole conscious personality of the man, which is nowise dependent upon the body except as a medium of converse with the material world.

So, on the other hand, the soul is eliminated from

[1] Acts ii. 27.
[2] Luke xxiii. 43.
[3] Gen. xxxv. 18.
[4] 2 Cor. v. 1.

spirit, as the receptacle from the substance which it contains, or, as I said before, as heat from the iron which it holds in solution. Indeed, the spiritual atmosphere has the same relation to the soul as air to animal life. 'Because I live, ye shall live also;' 'He that believes in me hath everlasting life;' 'He that eateth me, even he shall live by me,'[1]—are all passages in which the pronouns 'ye' and 'he' denote the soul, the only part of the man capable of everlasting life; while the life itself which it derives from Christ is spiritual, or divine, and heavenly. It involves the soul's holiness and happiness, the means to which are not in itself, but come from living in Christ as in a spiritual atmosphere, or from believing in Him and living upon Him, as upon our daily food. The apostle also speaks of 'dividing between soul and spirit,'[2] which would be impossible if they were identical. It consists in distinguishing between what the soul derives from its natural life, and its life in spirit or in God. 'The anchor of hope' also supposes that the soul may have a hold upon spirit in God, and so enjoy 'strong consolation;' but it is a hold upon what is as distinct from itself as the ship and the bottom of the sea upon which the flukes of its anchor take hold.[3] The spiritual influence of which a witnessing Church is the organ is distinct from 'the soul converted from the error of his ways' by its means.[4] Indeed, if spirit and soul were always the same, then every man, being actuated only by his soul, would be spiritual, whereas we make a broad distinction between being spiritual and having a soul to save or lose. A man's soul may be carnal, sold under sin, and thus remote as possible from

---

[1] John iii. 36, vi. 57, xiv. 19.   [2] Heb. iv. 12.
[3] Heb. vi. 19.   [4] Jas. v. 20.

spirit. Soul is the man, spirit his life from God. The one is Bunyan's castle, the other the heavenly king to whom its occupant owes fealty.

This elimination of the soul from flesh and spirit is wrought into the structure of the Hebrew language. It gives it terms of personality. On a careful review of some hundreds of cases in which soul is used, it will be found that the personal pronouns, or other designation of personality, would in other languages express the same idea, though not with the same discrimination. 'Every soul [person] must eat;' 'Ye know the soul [selfhood] of a stranger;' 'If a soul [person] touch an unclean thing;' 'Serve Him with all your soul' [undivided self]; 'Three thousand souls' [persons]; 'Hungry soul' [hungry man]; 'Full soul' [full man]; and so throughout.[1] Lexicographers speak of it as a Hebraism; but whether original to the language, or infused by the ideas of those using it, is a question. Ideas shape words, rather than words ideas. Hebrew-speaking men, before and after the time of Abraham, had conceptions of human nature that involved the necessity of such a use of words. They were a shepherd-people, with few arts, small trade, and a limited demand for words in those directions, but of deep spiritual insight, making discrimination in that direction a law of speech. Imagine a people shaping their language to the acutest distinctions of the metaphysics, till in that form it became the speech of common life, and we may have some idea how spirit, soul, and animal life came to be so carefully distinguished from each other in the original Scriptures.

This distinction was a necessity of their faith. It

[1] Ex. xii. 16, xxiii. 6; Lev. v. 2; Deut. xi. 13; Acts ii. 41; Prov. xxvii. 7.

was their religion to regard the world, its impressions and its duties, on the one hand, and God, on the other, influencing them as Spirit, and revealing Himself to their spiritual apprehensions. This is the law in the formation of thought from the natural world, the outward scene producing in the infant various sensations, and these sensations terminating in thought and memory. All sensation is not thought, though its tendency is towards thought; nor is all spiritual influence truth to the understanding, but a predisposing cause of objective truth. Religious reasoners are full of nonsense on this subject, fancying that nothing could have existed to influence their moral character which is not included in thought and memory. Thought and memory may cover their responsibility, though even that is greatly increased or diminished by the previous influences acting upon them. What a savage remembers of himself cannot produce the same responsibility with that of a child in a highly civilised and virtuous family. The unseen forces revealing themselves in our consciousness are greater treasures of character, if possible, than the seen.

As I have said, spirit, soul, and body were so radically distinct in the Hebrew mind, and so essential in its worship, as to give form to its temple, with its holiest place, its holy place, and its exterior courts and cloisters. But in the gospel they are more marked, and its piety and its virtue involve 'citizenship in heaven,' 'Christ dwelling in us by faith,' 'the hidden man of the heart,' and the like, as distinguished from 'doing' outwardly 'things contained in the law' on the part of those who are represented as 'without God in the world,' because their inner sense was not open to God, and they did nothing out of a regard to His holiness and love.[1] The soul of inspired men therefore has an outer court of natural virtues, conservative worldly influence, and of civilisation, even when the adytum of spiritual apprehensions is utterly closed against God and heaven, and is actually open to a hell of malign agencies and doctrines of devils. Is not this view a reflection of real life?

[1] Compare Phil. iii. 20, Eph. iii. 17, 18, 1 Pet. iii. 4, with Rom. ii. 14, 15, Eph. ii. 12.

CHAPTER VII.

THE REALM OF SPIRITS.

IF any one asks what spirit is, or where its realm, we should be compelled to answer, as Newton did in reference to gravitation, that we know it in its effects, but not in its nature. That there is a power of mind, extraneous to matter, working out its results in ways that chemistry cannot reach, nor science explore, comes to us with the same sort of evidence as that there are working all around us physical forces that we cannot explain. Who knows but these unknown forces may be spirit, or bordering on its realm? The more subtle the element, the greater the power; and the gnarled oak and granite ledge are riven by an unseen bolt hurled by an unseen hand. Can we tell how the sunbeams are generated, and how they work out results so all-pervading, so stupendous? Can we divine the principles of cohesion by which the sand-grains of a stone are held in such close affinity, explain the needle's adhesion to the pole, or the earthquake's power to upheave continents? Or can we any better explain how it is that spiritual ideas should work out results in human nature so magnificent?

There is much curiosity at present abroad to explore the realm of spirits. More are taxing their ingenuity in this direction than to find the north pole. Mediums profess to put their gaping audiences into communication with the souls of the dead. That these souls exist as substantive entities, or as knowing, conscious, active beings, and in connection with worlds infinitely more populous than our own, is no doubt true; but that they have modes of physical or electrical communication with us needs proof that has not yet come to our knowledge. Furthermore, necromancy, or attempts to converse with the dead, besides being forbidden in Scripture, are found injurious to those who practise them. The soul is substance, but not matter; and when detached from matter by death, it has another and higher sphere of action, or is in an element or realm suited to its disembodied nature. Whether in future ages souls in the body will come into more tangible connection with the departed, who is able to say from anything within the range of our present experience?

Spirit is not matter, nor can it be believed to be matter even in its subtlest forms. What in matter does thought resemble? With what effervescing fluid can we compare a mental emotion? Spirit is substance, no doubt, and of a nature more enduring than any material element; but what on earth can it act through or with, except the soul of man? How can the disembodied effect material changes through any other channel? To suppose that it reverses the order, and works upon the soul by manipulation or magnetism, is to suppose matter a suppler element in the hand of a spirit than the soul which is in affinity with it. When that future age of enlarged spiritual manifestation comes, we imagine it will be through a generation of souls in more intimate affinity with God and heaven, and not one of enlarged magnetic or electric science. We leave all doubtful hypotheses on this subject, and keep to the letter of those inspired men who lived so many ages in open visions of heaven.

These men are clear on one point, that there is in the soul a capacity to take impressions from the realm of spirits, and in due time to become itself an occupant of that realm. This is the *sanctum sanctorum* of human nature. Here God sets up His throne and writes His laws. Here His shechinah of truth is to shine, and His rod of authority to bud and bloom. Thence are to go forth the decrees regulating all our outward life. Spiritualism must work outward from this interior life, instead of working inward through the nerves. Here divine truth and love are to have their seat as a sort of heavenly intuition, guiding us into all truth.[1] Intellectual reasoning is more exterior. It is in the place of daily ministrations, or of natural and worldly knowledges. Those graces which are the fruit of divine influence are independent of the logical faculties; and hence the ablest reasoners are often deficient of them, but they are revealed unto babes.[2] A child's love to his parents is a surer guide to doing their pleasure than any amount of logic. If all the virtue of this world had to be reasoned out as an intellectual problem, how much should we have?

No; the impulses are deep through which God's Spirit works out its results. The deepest fountains, fed from distant headlands, throw their jets highest into the air. So of those impulses in man which are in communication with the realm of spirits. They gush forth in the most demonstrative deeds. We call them heart, affections, which unconscious children and even animals have as well as we, and sometimes even more decisively; and yet they have nothing spiritual

[1] John xvi. 13.   [2] Matt. xi. 25-27.

about them. A change of heart does not express the full idea of regeneration. No; it is a birth of the Spirit, and is effected upon the spiritual nature, upon the conscience-faculties, or upon those powers which connect man with the realm of spirits as his native land. It opens that land to him which erst had been closed. It cleanses the sanctuary of his inner being, that God may resume His alienated throne. God's entrance into the soul of man, through the hitherto closed gates of a fleshly life, is solemnly heralded: 'Lift up your heads, O ye gates; and be ye lifted up, ye everlasting doors; and the King of glory shall come in. Who is this King of glory? The Lord strong and mighty, the Lord mighty in battle.'[1] What is closed against God, but the soul of man walled in and barricaded by fleshly appetites and worldly ideas? Or what more extraordinary than the Holy Spirit's entrance into the soul in regeneration, heralded as it is by gospel truths awakening the conscience and impressing the heart? It is effected by power, or by the 'Lord strong and mighty, the Lord mighty in battle,' who is stronger than the strong man armed, and spoils his goods, and is thus heralded back to His own throne in human nature. The kingdom then comes, ruling within. Is not this a conquest of something more than of the affections?[2] Are not the affections themselves set right by an anterior influence of Spirit, reopening communication between the soul and the spirit-realm to which it appertains?

Besides, all the facts of a Christian life represent it as a walk with God, or walking in the Spirit, or as maintained to the end by perpetual influx from the spiritual world. 'I will come in and sup with him,

[1] Ps. xxiv. 7-10.   [2] Luke xi. 21, 22, xvii. 21.

and he with me;' 'He shall be loved of my Father, and I will love him, and will manifest myself to him.'[1] This is to be the experience of one whose soul is open to God, and who truly loves God. He shall sup with God, and God with him, and have continual manifestations of Christ given to him; and thus the utmost freedom of intercourse is established between himself and the realm of spirits. He is under the guardianship of angels.[2] He has the feelings of a child, to say 'Abba, Father.' 'The Spirit itself beareth witness with our spirit.' The Spirit intercedes within us, and maketh intercession for us, showing a correspondence between what is passing in the man himself and in heaven, as message responds to message through a hidden track in the sea from Europe to America. 'We have an Advocate with the Father, Jesus Christ the righteous,' 'who ever liveth to make intercession for us.' Nor is this an apologetic advocacy or intercession, like that of a barrister for his unfortunate client, to soften the Father's heart towards our sins, but one that consists in a continued supply of spiritual force, to enable us to overcome our sins. The word advocate in the original is *paraclete*—comforter, reprover, guide, to call us away from a sinful to a spiritual and heavenly life, of which He is our Mediator to keep the way of access ever open.[3] Advocacy or intercession, as an abstraction, apart from restored power from the spirit-realm to enable us to overcome the world, is a thing unknown to inspired men. 'I have overcome the world;' 'Greater is He that is in you, than he that is in the world;' 'This is the victory that overcomes the world, even your faith;' 'Whatsoever is born of God overcometh

---

[1] Rev. iii. 20; John xiv. 21. [2] Heb. i. 14; Ps. xci. 12.
[3] Rom. viii. 15, 16, 26, 27; 1 John ii. 1; Heb. vii. 25.

the world.'[1] These are passages which show the nature of Christ's work as our Advocate and Intercessor. It is through Him that spiritual power flows continually into the hearts of them that believe, enabling them to achieve a victory that otherwise would be impossible.

As regeneration and redemption are returning to the realm of spirit, or the ruling of God in the soul, they are so referred to by the apostle : ' Ye are come unto mount Sion, and unto the city of the living God, the heavenly Jerusalem, and to an innumerable company of angels, to the general assembly and Church of the first-born, which are written in heaven, and to God the Judge of all, and to the spirits of just men made perfect, and to Jesus the Mediator of the new covenant, and to the blood of sprinkling, that speaketh better things than the blood of Abel.'[2] Could anything be more explicit as to what redemption and regeneration amount to ? As heaven was open to man in his first creation, but was closed when he came under the ruling of flesh and the world, so it is opened again, and all its blessed inhabitants become his associates, when he returns to them a new man in Christ. This restored connection with God in spirit is cause, of which the renewed affections and the holy life are effects. Hence the sealing or graces of the Holy Spirit are '*after* ye had believed.'[3]

The realm of spirits is unlike that of nature in itself, and in its modes of thought, activity, and happiness. Still, in the normal condition of manhood, it is as accessible as matter to the body. Sin alone can close it to us, and substitute in its place demon influence.

[1] John xvi. 33 ; 1 John iv. 4, v. 4.   [2] Heb. xii. 22-24.
[3] Eph. i. 13.

Owing to this substitution of hell for heaven in the sensual or natural man, the first step in redemption was ' to destroy the works of the devil.' ' For this purpose was the Son of God manifested.'[1] His first battle was with Satan, among the wild beasts of the wilderness, the vanquishing of whom was the preparatory step to our Lord's public ministry.[2] And He anticipates His final triumph, by saying, ' I beheld Satan as lightning fall from heaven.'[3] This was binding the strong man preparatory to spoiling his goods. It was symbolized in the exode from Egypt, which was effected by means of the ten plagues, and the destruction in the Red Sea of Pharaoh and his host, constituting a redemption of power, and not of purchase, except in a figurative sense. So now the malign spiritual powers dominating man, and rioting among 'the wild beasts' of appetite, and passion, and worldliness, are the first to be subdued, in securing to God a spiritual Israel to do Him service in this world's wilderness. All progress begins by a battle with error and the devil.

Nothing can be conceived more imposing than the imagery by which the realm of spirits is represented to us in the Bible: ' I saw the Lord sitting upon a throne, high and lifted up, and His train filled the temple. Above it stood the seraphim: each one had six wings; with twain he covered his face, and with twain he covered his feet, and with twain he did fly. And one cried unto another, and said, Holy, holy, holy is the Lord God of hosts: the whole earth is full of His glory. And the posts of the door moved at the voice of him that cried, and the house was filled with smoke.' The effect upon the prophet, as also

[1] 1 John iii. 8.   [2] Matt. iv. 1-11; Mark i. 13.   [3] Luke x. 18.

upon Daniel of like visions, was a recoil upon self, withering and blighting,—the latter adding, 'I Daniel fainted, and was sick certain days.' But Isaiah exclaims, 'Woe is me! for I am undone; because I am a man of unclean lips, and I dwell in the midst of a people of unclean lips: for mine eyes have seen the King, the Lord of hosts.'[1] 'They saw the God of Israel: and there was under His feet as it were a paved work of a sapphire-stone, and as it were the body of heaven in clearness.'[2] The visions of Ezekiel and John combine attributes of power and glory above everything to be met with in real life.[3] The transfigured Saviour, with heavenly glory investing Him, outshone the sun, and was clothed in a radiance which no art can imitate.[4] And the words which Paul heard in the third heavens exceeded all the powers of earthly speech.[5] All the mines of earth cannot supply the amount of gold and precious stones brought together in the last chapters of Revelation to represent the New Jerusalem. Nor is the spirit-world of evil represented by images of pain and woe less extraordinary.

Such is the nature of the world of which the human soul is the tenant, and of whose influences, for good or for evil, it is a recipient. In reference to this capacity of spiritual reception, the same term is bestowed upon *it* and the Spirit of God. *Ruach* in the Old Testament, and *pneuma* in the New, are, as we have seen, applied both to man and to God. 'The *pneuma*,' says Neander, ' corresponds to the divine *pneuma* or Holy Spirit, which is destined and adapted

---

[1] Isa. vi. 1-5 ; Dan. viii. 27.   [2] Ex. xxiv. 10.
[3] Ezek. i. 4-28 ; Rev. i. 12-16, iv. 2-4.
[4] Matt. xvii. 2 ; Mark ix. 3 ; Acts xxii. 6, xxvi. 13.
[5] 2 Cor. xii. 2.

to receive His influences, and spread them through the whole of human nature.' This is the Divine Proceeding going forth from the Father through the Son, to operate in the souls of His people, 'to will and to do according to His good pleasure,' to realize heaven in them, and at the same time brooding upon the elements of nature, to reduce the two kingdoms to a unit in the person of our Lord Jesus Christ. He is Lord of all. All power in heaven and earth is His.

Graces and gifts in the Church are the divine *pneumatika*, or the result of an impartation from the spirit-realm, and not an exercise of natural gifts, whether inherent or acquired. They were obtained for us when Christ ascended up on high, and thus reopened communication between heaven and the soul of man. And when the field lacks labourers, He sends us not to the schools for a supply, but to the Lord of the harvest, to pray that He would send forth labourers.[1] Spiritual power is what the world needs; no other can explode its errors or alleviate its woes. And the channel is open for its influx; and we have only to 'come boldly unto the throne of grace, that we may obtain mercy, and find grace to help in time of need.'[2]

Our spiritual apprehensions are subject to much the same laws as those which are natural. Ideas of taste and ideas of sense can only be conceived by those who have the taste or the sense. No matter how intellectual we may be, we cannot see without eyes; no matter how finished as mathematicians, we cannot appreciate art and poetry without a feeling for them. So of truths from the realm of spirit. Without a responsive chord in us, how can we know them? 'The wind bloweth where it listeth, and thou hearest the

---

[1] Eph. iv. 8; Matt. ix. 38. [2] Heb. iv. 16.

sound thereof, but canst not tell whence it cometh, and whither it goeth: so is every one that is born of the Spirit.'[1] It is necessarily occult to one who has not opened his mind to the heavenly breeze. How can he speak of the odours of paradise, when he has never inhaled them?

Impartations from the spirit-realm reveal themselves, like light and sound, not merely by their own force, but by that force as responded to by what is in the man himself, as the breeze is responded to by the vibrating strings of the harp which it sets in motion. Does not the muse of the poet act in the same manner? Images from without kindle the poetic feeling within and the inspiration is partly of the man, and partly of the influences acting upon him. Seeing is partly of the eye, and partly of the light, and not of either by itself. So is it with all spiritual influence. It comes from God, but takes its cast from our minds, whether as penitence for sin, faith in Christ, joy in the Holy Ghost, supplication in the Spirit, a gift for edifying others, quiet and patient endurance under suffering, the practice of domestic virtues and daily duties, or in any other form.

In all cases where moral characteristics are ascribed to the spirit, more is meant than outward virtue. It supposes a divine force acting through the soul, to give a spiritual and heavenly stamp to those virtues, or to make them what they would not be without such force, as sunlight makes a plant what it would not be in the shade. Doing things 'as unto God, and not unto men,'[2] may not materially change the outward form of the act, but its spirit how different! The spirit to do things as unto God remains, in some cases, when the

[1] John iii. 8.   [2] Eph. vi. 5-8.

actions are wholly wanting, or are directly of a contrary character. Peter's crime, in not only neglecting to defend his Master under trial, but in actually denying Him, did not unsettle the spiritual basis of love and devotion to that Master. No; his flowing tears testified to the hold which his Master still had upon his spiritual affections. On the contrary, the virtues of which the Pharisee perhaps truthfully boasted in his prayer, were still worldly and unscriptural, and therefore unacceptable.[1]

The term spirit is added to a virtue or a vice, to denote actions performed from a good or an evil impulse from the spirit-world. Hence the expressions, 'the spirit which is of God,' 'the spirit of the world,' 'spiritually minded,' 'carnally minded,' 'walking in the Spirit,' 'seducing spirits,' 'Spirit of truth,' 'deceiving spirits,' and many others.[2] By such forms of expression, the inspired writers keep constantly before our minds the currents of influence inflowing from the world of spirits, to give a good or an evil direction to our lives. The idea is, that we have a nature constantly acted upon by a spiritual as well as a natural world, and that we are to regulate our conduct in reference to this fact. We are to breathe and pant and long after God, but to resist the devil that he may flee from us.

The spiritual laws of association are like the natural. Like affiliates with like. Good angels cluster round the good, and unclean spirits around the unclean. What we are and what we do is never secret, but under the eye of heavenly spectators. 'There is

---

[1] Luke xviii. 11.
[2] 1 Cor. ii. 12; 1 Tim. iv. 1; 2 Cor. xii. 18; 1 Cor. xii. 10; Rom. viii. 6.

The Realm of Spirits.

nothing hid, which shall not be manifested; neither was anything secret, but that it should come abroad.' 'A great cloud of heavenly witnesses ever encompasses us,'—a cloud more imposing by far than ever looked down from a Roman amphitheatre.[1] Our evils are enacted against an ever-resisting heavenly force, and our hearts are hardened by the process, as Pharaoh's was by opposing himself to God, and as the Jews were by withstanding the spiritual power that wrought with Christ and His apostles. The intenser the influence from above, the more rapid the process of spiritual decay in us, as with a carcase under a torrid sun. Our power to be wicked is proportioned to our means of spiritual influence.[2] Tares derive their baneful luxuriance from the same soil that nourishes the fat of the kidneys of wheat.

With a hint to those who would be restored to communication with heaven, we will conclude this chapter. This is to be done by turning away from fleshly ideas, to act upon the truths of faith. 'Enter into thy closet: and when thou hast shut the door, pray to thy Father who is in secret; and thy Father, which seeth in secret, shall reward thee openly.'[3] Communion with spirit must begin by shutting out worldly influences. Truths of faith, truths of prayer, truths of the divine law, truths of Christ and of following Him, truths of the gracious promises, truths of the inner life, truths of spiritual worship, truths of brotherly love, truths of general charity and benevolence, truths from searching the Scriptures, and comparing spiritual things with spiritual, never open upon us, except in a state of abstraction from the thoughts and feelings which dominate our minds as worldly

[1] Mark iv. 22; Heb. xii. 1.   [2] John xv. 22.   [3] Matt. vi. 6.

men. This is coming out from the world, and locking the door behind you. Such a course, persevered in with honest intent, will cause heaven to open upon thy soul, and Jesus to appear standing on the right hand of God. Try it, reader, try it.

CHAPTER VIII.

SPIRIT IN INSTITUTIONS.

WE will here repeat ourselves, to make sure of being understood. Soul in Hebrew is the man as connected with flesh on the one hand, and spirit on the other. From the one he derives natural ideas, and from the other spiritual: the man is distinct from both. He is not sense, nor is he spirit. If he were without the body and its senses, he would still be a man; and the same would be true if he had no spiritual apprehensions. Dives in hell had neither bodily senses nor true apprehensions of God, and yet his personal power of knowing and suffering remained, and his natural ideas of family relations were still present to his mind.

Not only is the man distinct from sense and spirit, but from the objects with which they render him conversant. He is distinct from what he sees in the natural and in the spiritual world. The one he sees through the body, the other through the spiritual apprehension with which he is endowed. Spirit in himself is his power to receive spiritual truths, as sense is his power to receive natural truths. Such, it seems to the writer, must be the view which one will arrive at who carefully collates and compares the facts, symbols, and statements of the Bible on this subject. The soul as a nature is a unit, of capacity for influx from two worlds, with duality of results to character.

The realm of spirits is more populous than that of nature, as would appear from the oft-repeated designation, 'the Lord of Hosts,' and also from the mention of angels 'innumerable,' and the devils in one man, whose 'name was Legion, because they were many.' Christ in the garden speaks of being able to command more than twelve legions of angels.[1] It is not only more populous, but more powerful than nature, just as soul is than body, and God than the universe. Spirit acts from within, matter from without; spirit is the sap-current, matter the efflorescence. The one works out its results not only through individual souls, but by aggregating them into institutions, bound by an occult force, to make it next to impossible to detach them. They stick together like the filings of magnetized iron. Paganism, Romanism, Judaism, Islamism, and Christianity are the general terms by which they are called. As existing in most nations, they have a politico-religious character, enforcing their decrees by the sword of two worlds, or by social ostracism.

The inspired writers regard them as the outworking of spiritual forces, good or evil, in which they are more logical, as well as more truly inspired, than those who ascribe them to climatic influences. If they owe their existence to differences of climate, why does not the same climate produce in all ages the same religion? Why has not the Druid worship been perpetuated in England? Why are not Bel and Nebo still worshipped on the banks of the Euphrates, and Isis and Osiris on those of the Nile? Why does not Jupiter still thunder from Ida, and rule from the Capitoline Hill?

There is something more enduring than earthly

[1] Heb. xii. 22; Luke viii. 30; Matt. xxvi. 53; Dan. vii. 10; Rev. v. 11.

forces in these religious divisions. So far as man's nature is affected by food or climate, it admits of an easy transition from one condition to another. He can live within the tropics or polar circle, on the diet of Peru or Greenland; but does his religion undergo like change? When a thought, or feeling, or usage takes possession of a people, as sanctioned by God, and binding their conscience, they take it wherever they go. Who can persuade the Hindoo out of his caste, or the Chinese out of his ancestral worship? Who can unsettle the Arab's faith in Allah and His prophet? How are two hundred million Romanists to be dissuaded from picture and saint worship, or reliance on the priesthood for the pardon of sin? ' Has a nation changed its gods, which are no gods?'[1] The gospel assumes that the change may be effected, though not by education, not by new climatic influences, not by any earthly power or appliance, but only by the quickening Spirit. 'The gospel is the power of God unto salvation.'[2] As the resistance to be overcome is spiritual power in high places, it must be assailed by a spiritual force. You may break a rock with gunpowder, but to change the currents of human thought, feeling, and desire, quite another power must be brought into requisition. 'Tarry ye in Jerusalem, till ye be endued with power from on high.'[3]

There is behind the reasoning faculties, and the qualities which education affects, an influence directing and determining the ideas and conduct of a people. In the Indian and the Hottentot are not only peculiarities of complexion and conformation, but also of thought and feeling, of which no training can fully dispossess them. I once inquired of a Jew how it was

[1] Jer. ii. 11. [2] Rom. i. 16. [3] Luke xxiv. 49.

that they gave their children so uniformly their own peculiar cast of religious thought. 'Oh,' he said, 'it is our nature.' Minds thus shaped cast their reasoning in the same mould; and the libraries of Europe groan under Jesuitical tomes, bringing all argument, all logic, all reason, to the defence of the Roman type of Christianity. The Hindoo, Chinese, and Mohammedan are equally ingenious in the defence of their several systems. Not that truth is thus contradictory, nor reason incapable of discovering it, but there is a disguising influence in such cases to darken and pervert the mind. Something besides reason and truth determines its convictions.

How are we to account for disguising influences of the kind taking possession of races and aggregations of men, and perpetuating themselves from age to age? Can any better reason for it be given, than those spiritual agencies to which the inspired writers refer them? They represent a spiritual being, under the form of a serpent, as having a hand in bringing our race into its present guilty and suffering state. A spiritual agency of an opposite character set on foot the patriarchal and Mosaic worship, with all its histories, institutions, and prophecies, culminating in the incarnation and pentecostal baptism. A like agency brought the united descendants of Noah into relations to each other, by the confusion of tongues, to compel their dispersion as the seeding of races and nations, and fixing the bound of their habitation.[1] In these cases trains of influence were set on foot, determining the character and condition of man upon earth, as also the specific form and location of national institutions.

[1] Gen. xi. 1-9; Acts xvii. 26.

Though Babylon was a great outward fact, with a history of three thousand years, yet it had a mystical meaning with the prophets, representing ideas rather than material interests. The ancient cry, that Babylon is fallen, was taken up by John in Revelation, long after the old city had ceased to rule the nations.[1] It was not, therefore, the fall of a material city which was so solemnly heralded, but of errors and delusions corrupting and debasing the nations. It was the breaking up of a nest of satanic powers, called ' Mystery, Babylon the great, the mother of harlots and abominations of the earth.'[2]

Whatever interpretation may be put upon ' the great red dragon, having seven heads and ten horns,' or upon the transfer of ' his power, and his seat, and great authority to the beast with seven heads and ten horns,' and ten crowns, and ' upon his heads the names of blasphemy,' one thing is certain, these are symbols of spiritual power or influence embodied in institutions determining the faith and practice of mankind.[3] Rome pagan and Rome papal are clearly referred to, the former merging its authority, its ideas, and its seven-hilled city into the latter, which it still longs to hold with the same eagerness as ever to subject the nations to its power. Thus the Babylon of inspiration is more than a city,—it is an aggregation of spiritual errors and influences, holding vast masses of men subject to its power, and making war upon truth and its advocates.

The idea of representing unseen forces is not confined to the true worshippers of God,—it is also entertained by idolaters. The apotheosis of the ancient

[1] Isa. xxi. 9 ; Rev. xviii. 2.   [2] Rev. xvii. 5.
[3] Rev. xii. 3, xiii. 1, 2.

heroes consisted in transferring them to heaven and identifying them with the stars, to act as patrons of the nations and institutions with which they were connected on earth. Nimrod, as personating Babylon, became Lucifer the morning star; and several of the planets and signs of the zodiac are still called after these ancient gods and heroes. The Papacy, as inheriting these ancient corruptions, canonizes its saints, and offers them its worship. These deified heroes and saints are no doubt in imitation of the real powers which the Scriptures represent as influencing nations and institutions from the realm of spirits. The divine right of kings is an offshoot of this idea. Governments claim a ghostly origin and authority to strengthen their hold upon the superstition of their subjects; and true patriotism no doubt includes a sentiment of piety to God as well as loyalty to human institutions.

The Bible claims for the cause of truth and righteousness the guardianship of Almighty God. Angels as well as men are its servitors and its advocates. The covenant with Abraham was not only the result of a divine call, but was brought to mind at the burning bush, ages after, when a large portion of the people to whom it related had ceased to hope for its fulfilment. ' I have heard the groanings of the children of Israel, whom the Egyptians keep in bondage; and I have remembered my covenant.'[1] What followed in God's dealings with that people in after ages is over and over again represented as in pursuance of that covenant, the whole extraordinary history being merely the outworking of spiritual forces, the embodiment of heavenly ideas.

When the literal descendants of Abraham finally

[1] Ex. vi. 5.

rejected God in the person of His Son, saying, 'His blood be upon us and our children,'[1] a spirit of unbelief took possession of the nation, ruling them to this day as a malign spiritual power, upon which arguments make as little impression as feathers upon a granite column. Some are indeed plucked as brands from the burning, but not in sufficient numbers to affect the solid framework of unbelief and materialism in which the masses are encased.

It would almost seem as if the dupes of a great delusion on earth, as Paganism, Romanism, Judaism, and Islamism, carried their delusion into another life, to react an influence upon those whom they left behind, confirmatory of their error. If Moses and Elijah interested themselves in our Lord's passion,[2] may not evil spirits still share in the evils among men? Has the light of eternity cured them of the passions and ideas that ruled them on earth? And if cured, why are they still under the wrath of God? No; the idea of continual currents of influence from the spirit-world to make men what they are, or to keep them so, is clearly held forth in the pages of divine inspiration. As a general rule, the greater the number of dead heretics, the greater the power of the living heresy. This is not always so, especially when God vouchsafes a special divine influence to recover men to truth, as under His apostles, under the Reformers, under the zealous spiritual labourers in revivals and missions during the past hundred years, and on like occasions. But even in such cases there is an instant rallying to perpetuate the old delusions, even if they are compelled to take on new forms, as the Paganism of Rome reappeared in the Papacy. Various errors corrupted the Reformers,

[1] Matt. xxvii. 25. [2] Luke ix. 30, 31.

and their work was counteracted by Jesuitism; and even now there are causes constantly at work to vitiate and corrupt our revivals and our missions. How far these counteracting forces are purely earthly, or an emanation of the spirit-world of evil, it is difficult to determine. And one who impartially reads the life of Loyola, and the dark and damaging achievements of his Jesuitical institution, can scarcely fail of being impressed with the working of malign agencies more than human. In such cases it may be well said, 'Woe unto the inhabitants of the earth and sea! for the devil is come down unto you, having great wrath.'[1]

In Daniel the great powers of the world are described as the outworking of spiritual agencies. The Grecian and Roman empires were thus presented to the vision of the prophet long before their establishment. Michael stood up for the chosen people; and Gabriel was delayed in answering Daniel's prayer by the prince of the kingdom of Persia, or by a spiritual personation of that power.[2] Cyrus, the founder of the Medo-Persian monarchy and restorer of the Jews, was foretold, ages before he was born, as destined to fulfil a divine commission of which he was unconscious. 'I girded thee, though thou hast not known me.'[3] His reign and his conquests were in fulfilment of the counsels of eternity and of promptings from the spirit-realm.

The establishment and work of Christianity were more the result of spiritual than of earthly agencies. An angel announced the birth of John the Baptist and of Jesus of Nazareth. Angels hymned the new-born Saviour to the shepherds, and the wise men were miraculously directed to His cradle. An angel strengthened

---

[1] Rev. xii. 12.
[2] Dan. vii. 6, viii. 21, 22, vii. 7, 23, x. 13, xii. 1. [3] Isa. xlv. 5.

Him in the garden, and announced His resurrection. Two angels appeared at His ascension. An angel released Peter from prison, and stood by Paul in his shipwreck. An angel opened the way to the conversion of Cornelius, and the preaching of the gospel among the Gentiles.[1] Besides, from the promise in the garden of Eden, that 'the seed of the woman should bruise the serpent's head,' to the setting up of Christ's kingdom, all the particulars of the event were arranged in heaven. They were made known to the prophets, were wrought into symbol and into history; and thus one institution at least—Christianity—is the cropping out of divine and heavenly powers. The spirit of just men made perfect took part in the work on the mountain of transfiguration; and at the crucifixion 'the graves were opened; and many bodies of the saints which slept arose, and came out of their graves after His resurrection, and went into the holy city, and appeared unto many.'[2] And if nothing exists of the kind on the part of malign spiritual powers, it is the only case, I believe, in which God's genuine working is not counterfeited.

These are great facts in pursuance of the inspired view of the spirit-world as near and in constant communication with men on earth, for good or for evil. When an evil spirit entrenches itself in an institution, how hard to dispossess him! Argument and reasoning are to him what the green withs were in the hands of Samson. Will arguments persuade Niagara out of its course? We call it prejudice, education, habit; but the Bible calls it Belial, 'the spirit of whoredoms,' 'that old

[1] Luke i. 11-35, ii. 8-14; Matt. ii. 1, 2, xxviii. 2-7; Luke xxii. 43; Acts i. 10, 11, xii. 7-10, xxvii. 23.
[2] Matt. xxvii. 52, 53.

serpent, the Devil, and Satan, which deceiveth the whole world: he was cast out into the earth, and his angels were cast out with him.'[1] Here they hold carnival. Their work may be gradual and stealthy, for 'he deceiveth them that dwell upon the earth;'[2] but when once entrenched in the ideas and institutions of a nation or a race, no power but that of God Himself, as one stronger than he, can drive him out.

Christ never contemplated the conversion of the world otherwise than by an organized spiritual force of greater potency and power. 'He that is in you is greater than he that is in the world.'[3] Christianity is not contesting the palm of learning, diplomacy, money, organization, or of worldly power, but of spiritual truth, holy living, heavenly hope, and resurrection power. As the kingdom of heaven among men, it is in conflict with 'the rulers of the darkness of this world, and with spiritual wickedness in high places.'[4]

Jesus, in establishing His kingdom among men, wrote nothing, published nothing, organized neither senate nor army, built no palace, assembled no court, erected neither column nor cathedral, and resorted to no single expedient suggested by human wisdom for the achievement of such a result. What did He do? Why, He simply gathered around Him a few personal followers, of no worldly pretensions, with whom He lived and conversed long enough to thoroughly imbue them with His own ideas, and with His new and heavenly life. Trusting then to divine power to accrue to them at His death, He left them, and returned to His Father. He thus made them what they had no power

---

[1] Rev. xii. 9.   [2] Rev. xiii. 14.
[3] 1 John iv. 4; Luke xxiv. 49; Acts i. 5.
[4] Eph. vi. 12.

to be, and did with them what they had no power to do. The Holy Spirit, restored to His ruling in their nature, according to the original type of man's creation, was the sole efficiency in that institution which we call Christianity. He was joint witness with them of the resurrection; He endowed them for the offices of the Church; He sanctioned the work of conversion among the Gentiles; He qualified Paul for this particular vocation; He descended upon the disciples at Ephesus; He separated Barnabas and Saul; He forewarned the apostles of danger, and directed their preaching in one place, but hindered it in another; He gave power to their words, and wrought mightily in them; He witnessed to their conscience and to believers; He gave them inward joy in all their tribulations.[1] How it is possible that, with such a record running throughout, Christianity should have been regarded as a great worldly organization like the Papacy, or anything of the kind, is passing strange. It only shows how hard it is for human nature to conceive or conserve things spiritual and heavenly.

Are not the laws of Christian progress the same now as ever? Can we hope for a rapid multiplication of conversions, except by means of a sanctified Church? Must it not be by men and women swayed by an influence from above, like fields of grain by summer winds? No other influence can produce conversions worth having. The toys of papal worship may attract an ignorant people, but cannot improve their spiritual condition. Protestant schools, books, tracts, periodicals, learning, science, agriculture, art, civilisation, or statesmanship, may be a means to the work, but never can

[1] Acts ii. 4, vi. 3, ix. 17, x. 44, xix. 6, xiii. 2, xx. 28, xx. 23, xvi. 6-10; Col. ii. 29; Rom. viii. 16, ix. 1; 2 Cor. vii. 4.

be a power for accomplishing it, except as wielded by the Holy Spirit. The Bible itself can do nothing except as 'the sword of the Spirit.' A kingdom of heaven among men can only live and grow by heavenly power.

CHAPTER IX.

SPIRIT IN MORALS.

THE question now before us is as to the effect of spirit and the spiritual upon the theory and practice of morality. Have they anything to do with conscience? This is a question which concerns the connection of morality with religion. That there is a very important connection between them, I believe is generally conceded.

In the Bible view, morality is religion, and religion is morality. The two are not distinguished from each other. All right thinking, feeling, and doing commences with the fear of the Lord, which is the beginning of wisdom. Virtue inheres in piety, and piety in virtue, as light and heat in the sunbeams. Neither can exist in its integrity without the other. A vicious pious man and a pious vicious man are a contradiction in terms.

There are indeed conservative qualities among men which pass for virtues, with which religion has little directly to do. These the inspired writers recognise as a natural conscience, as I have before said, leading men to do without the law things contained in the law.[1] Under their influence civilisation attains in some cases to great worldly pre-eminence, yet it leaves the nations without God, and in a state of great material debase-

[1] Rom. ii. 14, 15.

ment. 'Man being in honour abideth not: he is like the beasts that perish.'[1] His very morality is more bestial than spiritual, more earthly than heavenly. Two classes, the opposite of each other in culture, are especially in this state of abstraction from spiritual truth,— the lowest savages, and some of our most scientific men. It is doubted by some whether the Caffres have any spiritual ideas; and our savans are in many cases so occupied with material cause and effect as to lose sight of God in His universe. They are atheists, pantheists, or anything rather than believers in things spiritual. Still the savages are not without conservative qualities; and our scientific atheists are not without private and patriotic virtues. The Sadducees denied the existence of both angel and spirit,[2] and yet they had an honourable position among the Jews, and were no doubt men of ordinarily good morals for the age in which they lived.

It must be conceded, however, that comparatively few are destitute of spiritual ideas and influences of some sort and to some extent. As in the coldest days there is enough of the principle of heat to preserve vegetable and animal life, so there may be the working of spirit even in those who seem the most destitute of it. The great majority of men, to say the least, are influenced in their beliefs and actions by what they conceive as lying beyond the range of sense or of the natural world. Whether true or false, it is all the same as to the fact of such an influence. The Jews had no conscience against crucifying Christ; but their notions of religious purity restrained them from entering the judgment-hall of Pilate, 'that they might eat the passover.'[3] The Arab would be self-condemned if he

[1] Ps. xlix. 12.   [2] Acts xxiii. 8.   [3] John xviii. 28.

neglected his daily prayers, but not for stealing all he can lay his hands on. The Roman robbers will murder without remorse, but would think heaven shut against them if they did not pay their daily adorations to an image of the Virgin. Who will say that perverted ideas of spiritual realities have nothing to do in such cases?

The most absurd ideas of God and the unseen world are so potent in some cases, as to produce a total disregard to life and its comforts. The Hindoo widow prefers to burn with her dead husband, rather than live a queen in a second marriage. The anchorite starves himself in the midst of abundance, and makes a conscience of living in rags and filth to gain heaven. Who will say that spiritual ideas, such as they are, have no force in such cases? Religion is the great power in shaping our moral convictions, and achieves things impossible to the cold calculations of reason. Moral ideas and impulses, shaped and directed by religion, figure largely in art, architecture, literature, and social organization. They are the greatest forces in history. They direct the expenditure of millions of money. They marshal armies, spirit onward the deadly onset, strew the earth with bones, and rear to the dead their proud mausoleums. The temples and pyramids, surviving the wreck of the ancient world, are monuments to religious convictions of duty and the hope of immortality. The iron caste of India, the savage worship of the red man, who ensures means for the chase in the hunting-grounds of the Great Spirit by burying with his dead brother his bow and arrow, and the undying semi-atheism of the Chinese, have still enough of the spiritual in them to hold the living generations. Such is man in all the phases of his varient life. If doing things as right out of regard to the unseen powers, or posthumous expectations, be religion, how hard to go beyond its influence!

Must not facts like these be accepted as an assurance of objective reality? Are the thousand and one failures of reason and science any evidence against objective truth? Is not the power to fly, to swim, to walk, and the constant endeavour of these exercises, pretty good evidence of air, water, and earth. to perform them in? So, as men take to spiritual ideas of some sort, as birds to air, and fish to water, and quadrupeds to land, how can we doubt the objective reality of a spiritual universe? We may make a thousand mistakes as to its nature, as we do in reasoning, but that cannot unsettle the truth.

But why reason, when we have the safer guide of men divinely inspired? Their theory of morality is, that we exist in the twofold relation of flesh and spirit, connecting us with nature on the one hand, and with a spiritual world on the other, with free powers of action to follow the leading of the one or the other at our option. And as spirit obliges us by its very nature to obey its dictates, or God rather than man, it imposes the corresponding obligation of subordinating the flesh to His ruling. Here is the principle of duty on which all laws of duty are founded; and what is morality but the doctrine of duty? A being with powers so opposite as appetite and conscience, the one to be subordinated, and the other to be obeyed, must of necessity have a battle of temptations for the exercise of his virtue, and the development of his possible excellences. We can conceive no state wherein this necessity does not exist, except that which arises from coming out of the conflict, as our Lord did, to be crowned with glory. Confirmation in holiness is not the first stage in such an existence, as it was not in Adam, but the reward of the conqueror in temptation.

Appetite tends to unrestrained indulgence; and to limit it within due bounds, under the spirit's imperial dictation, is the duty imposed upon man, to put his loyalty and his determination to the proof. Nor is an outward tempter necessary to create the trial. Indeed, a devil could no more tempt a man than a stone, without a basis for temptation in his own nature. With a perfectly holy universe, no race could start into being, under any form of moral agency known to us as possible to creatures, without beginning its career with temptation.[1]

These facts underlie the whole history of temptation, as is shown by the apostle's 'similitude of Adam's transgression.'[2] Adam's transgression had its rise from impulses of flesh and world in opposition to God, of which the serpent took advantage. If there had been

[1] 'The phenomena of man are in part subjected to the laws of the external universe. As dependent upon bodily organization, as actuated by sensual propensities and animal wants, he belongs to matter, and in this respect he is the slave of necessity. But what man holds of matter does not make up his personality. They are his, but not he. Man is not an organism, he is intelligence served by organs. For in man there are tendencies, there is a law, which continually urge him to prove that he is more powerful than the nature by which he is surrounded and penetrated. He is conscious to himself of faculties not comprised in the chain of physical necessity; his intelligence reveals prescriptive principles of action, absolute and universal, in the law of duty, and a liberty capable of carrying that law into effect, in opposition to the solicitations, the impulsions of his material nature. From the coexistence of these opposing forces in man, there results a ceaseless struggle between physical necessity and moral liberty,—in the language of Revelation, between flesh and spirit,—and the struggle constitutes at once the distinctive character of humanity, and the essential condition of human development and virtue.'—SIR W. HAMILTON's *Metaphysics*, p. 21.

[2] Rom. v. 13, 14.

no God and no law circumscribing these impulses, there would have been no sin; 'for sin is not imputed when there is no law.' Still it was in the world as death or inherited depravity, reigning from Adam to Moses even over them who were in no condition to begin their sinful course as Adam began his. They were born under the ruling of the flesh, and therefore in no condition to cast off the spirit's ruling by transgressing an obvious law. Inherited drunkenness is a different thing from that which has been acquired by habit. It is equally pernicious, however guilt in the case may be mitigated. It is death. The rites given by Moses put the Israelites into a condition to sin after the similitude of Adam's transgression,—not by making them actually holy, but as a test of outward loyalty to God. The rest of mankind, as well as those 'from Adam to Moses,' 'having not the law,'[1] were equally incapable of sinning as Adam did, and yet the apostle shows that they were equally in a state of spiritual death. No matter how a people come under the ruling of the flesh, the practical result is the same, as consumption may be equally fatal from a cold as from inheritance. The question of happiness or misery to men here or hereafter cannot be resolved into the benevolence of God, but is to be decided as to whether flesh or spirit rules them, or whether their spiritualism is demoniacal or divine. If the latter is their condition, how is the benevolence of God to make them happy? Will He bring them under the ruling of His Spirit by force in another life, and thus make them happy against their will, since His persuasions had failed with them here on earth? The apostles never reason in this way; never speak of the possibility of happiness to

[1] Rom. ii. 14.

one who does not choose the Lord to be his God; never inquire how he came to choose in this manner, whether from his original impulses after the similitude of Adam, or by an inherited taint of evil; but they accept the fact that sin, as a state of death, rules him, and he can no more be right than a body can be healthy which is diseased in all its organs and processes. Benevolence would dictate that men should not suffer; but will they not, in case they are sick or sinful?

Such is the ruling of the flesh. It begins by rejecting God's spiritual ruling, corrupts the whole nature, unsettles all the foundations of a true morality, and entails the sad inheritance upon posterity. What the law, as delivered in Eden and from Sinai, could not do, because the flesh had induced a weakness to render obedience to it impossible, God sending His own Son in the likeness of this very weakness, and for sin, condemned sin in the flesh; or overcame it in His own person, and provided to do the same in the person of His elect. Hence it is added, as the end to be gained by the great transaction, 'that the righteousness of the law may be fulfilled in us, who walk not after the flesh, but after the Spirit.'[1] Christ put Himself into our nature and circumstances, as the brazen serpent took the form of those that had infused the venom, thus cancelling that venom in Himself by a perfectly spiritual and holy life, and providing the requisite power, by His death and resurrection, to restore the ruling of spirit over flesh in all that obey Him. The object was, the restored dominion of God in the soul of man, which could only be effected by spiritual power. Hence He is said to travel in the greatness of His strength, speaking in righteousness, mighty to save.[2]

[1] Rom. viii. 3, 4.   [2] Isa. lxiii. 1.

Without this divine power restoring to the man a spiritual and heavenly ruling, there can be no true morality, no purified conscience in the world; because nothing else can elevate man above his selfish and worldly life. True, the work may be begun in many cases when it is yet very imperfectly done. The apostle complained of such, that he could not 'speak unto them as spiritual, but as unto carnal, even as unto babes in Christ.' And he adduces their envying, strife, and division, as evidence that they had only partially emerged from the ruling of the flesh.[1] Alas, how large a portion of those in whom we may charitably hope that God has begun a good work, are still held by their old habits and ideas!

The new life from God may indeed take on many different forms, and yet approach perfection, as we find in James, Peter, and Paul some traces of a difference as to their mode of regarding and treating Judaism. Paul blamed Peter's conduct on one occasion, and for good reason.[2] Judaizing ideas, like our habits in evil, had too strong a hold to be exploded at once, even in the most spiritual men. How hard is it for the Spirit of God to totally revolutionize our ideas of right and wrong, and lay anew our foundation of morality! Even Luther had not fully escaped from the disguising influence of a papistic training. Fenelon inveighed against the errors of the Catholic Church, but afterwards recanted, and died in its communion; and yet he was eminently a spiritual and holy man. John Wesley was from youth to old age ruled by his vocation from God, as few others ever have been; and yet he lived and died in a Church establishment exceedingly unlike the societies which he organized, and which

[1] 1 Cor. iii. 1-8.   [2] Gal. ii. 11-15.

grew into one of the most zealous and active of our evangelical denominations. Jonathan Edwards was an equally holy man; and yet he employed his gigantic intellect in reconciling necessity and responsible agency, Calvinism and the freedom of the human will,—points from which both Wesley and Fenelon earnestly dissented.

As inspired men never conceived of a true morality existing apart from true religion, so they never speak of talent or mental culture apart from the Spirit. Abraham, Moses, and David are not called men of talent, but men after God's own heart. Ahithophel's shrewd state-craft made 'his counsel as if a man had inquired of God,' but, having no divine illumination in it, it became 'foolishness.'[1] 'Where is the wise? where is the scribe? where is the disputer of this world? hath not God made foolish the wisdom of this world?' 'The world by wisdom knew not God.'[2]

A mind in which the truth and love of God have no place could not have attainments entitling him to be called wise in the old Hebrew sense. Solomon no doubt had natural capacities above most men, and enjoyed the best culture the age afforded, and yet, when God proposed to give whatever he should ask, he chose 'an understanding heart to judge his people, and to discern between good and bad.'[3] In the original it is a 'hearing heart,' fitted to catch the gentle whispers of heaven, and imbibe truth from God. There is no wisdom in man which is not tempered by love and goodness, and illuminated from above. 'The inspiration of the Almighty giveth him understanding.'[4] The term conscience is not used in the Old Testament,

[1] 2 Sam. xvi. 23. [2] 1 Cor. i. 20, 21.
[3] 1 Kings iii. 9. [4] Job xxxii. 8.

unless the Septuagint is right in rendering *maddá*, *suneidesis*, conscience, in the words, 'Curse not the king in thy conscience.' But even here, I think our common version better: 'Curse not the king, no, not in thy *thought*.'[1] What we call conscience was not made a separate faculty by the old Hebrews, but was regarded as the result of spirit acting upon man to produce his moral ideas, as light in the eye produces seeing.

In the New Testament this spiritual perception is described by our Lord as single or clear, or as evil or unsound, answering to like conditions in the organ of vision.[2] And the apostles describe it as a good and pure conscience, an evil conscience, a conscience seared with a hot iron, a defiled conscience.[3] In all these cases the idea of influence from spirit is kept up, the same as that of light is in all cases of seeing, whether natural or distorted, clear or confused, acute or blunted.

Our moral philosophers generally fail in their theories, because they separate the moral sense from religious ideas and influences. Hobbes regarded conscience as simply a thing of power. A government has power to enforce obedience, and therefore we are bound to obey it. Whatever we are compelled to do, we ought to do; and when compulsion ceases, our obligations cease with it. This is very nearly his statement of the case, though power, as exercised by God over us, he conceives to be the concurrence of motives influencing our conduct, which was determined by a previous concurrence of events, and that by a previous still, and so on, till we reach Omnipotence,

[1] Eccles. x. 20.   [2] Matt. vi. 22, 23.
[3] 1 Tim. i. 5, iii. 9; Acts xxiv. 16; Heb. ix. 9, x. 2; 1 Tim. iv. 2; Tit. i. 15.

whose actions are alike determined by necessity, thus producing what is called Hobbes' doctrine of fate. This of course annihilates all free agency, and reduces moral and physical cause to the same category.

Paley makes conscience the intellect acting on moral subjects, and determining what ought or ought not to be done, on utilitarian principles. We are bound to all actions which seem to us attended by the best results. But does a child wait for results before feeling that it *ought* to obey its parents? No one, I believe, now advocates this theory.

Later writers, as Dr. Wayland, speak of conscience as a 'distinct and separate faculty,' consisting of a 'feeling of the ought or ought not.' It depends neither upon power nor upon reasoning, but stands by itself, and is ultimate and final in its decision of the abstract ought or ought not. This is making man as to his moral feelings a detached item in the universe, or as affected out of himself only by material causes. It makes his mind in its perception of moral obligations what the eye would be if it could see without light. It is true, as I have said, that, as a mere creature of earth, man has, like the beasts, conservative elements in his nature which are a sort of effigy of conscience, but as unlike it as phosphorescence is unlike the sun-beams. That this natural principle accounts for the agony of remorse, the restoring of ill-gotten wealth to those who had not suspected their loss, the confession of concealed crimes, and the extraordinary working of conscience in many ways, no one can for a moment believe. What impulse of man, as disconnected from a higher world, could be conceived as producing results so stupendous? Did nothing else work in Judas when he went out and hanged himself?

Bishop Butler's clear discrimination detected in conscience something more than a separate abstracted human exercise. 'Conscience,' he says, 'is a supreme principle of reflection in every man, which distinguishes between the internal principles of the heart as well as his external actions; which passes judgment on himself and them; pronounces determinately some actions to be in themselves just, right, good, others to be in themselves wrong, evil, unjust; which, without being consulted, without being advised with, majestically exerts itself, approves or condemns him, the doer of them, accordingly; *and which, if not forcibly stopped, naturally and always of course goes on to anticipate a higher and more effective sentence, which shall hereafter second and affirm its own.*'[1]

This is making conscience, what the Bible represents, an influence from the spirit-world affirming the man's own sentence upon himself, and awakening in him a sense of God's authority, and of the retributions of eternity. True, it may be 'stopped' and perverted, as may all our other faculties; but this cannot change the nature of the faculty, nor make it less the response of influences higher than any acting upon the man from himself or the realm of nature.

Revelation is framed to this idea. It reasons out nothing; it offers no scientific facts or principles; but simply presents truths adapted to the spiritual apprehension, with as much confidence of meeting a response, as an artist in holding up pictures to an appreciative audience. True, conscience blends with reason, sometimes to be perverted, and again to find a confirmation of its decisions. But it is so with all our other sentiments. What the eye sees, and the ear

[1] *Sermons on Human Nature*, Harvard Edition.

hears, may be truly or falsely reasoned upon by the mind. All our domestic and æsthetical affections are subject to a like swaying by the intellectual faculties. The radical difference between the conscience-feelings and the intellectual faculties may be seen from the fact, that persons most endowed with the latter are frequently deficient in the former. The muse of Byron, with all its brilliancy, coexisted with the lowest moral debasement. On the other hand, persons without culture in art or science are sometimes distinguished for the piety, purity, and benevolence of their lives. If the eyes are blurred, the seeing is defective, in spite of mental gifts; and if the conscience is seared, defiled, or perverted to intercept true influx from the spirit-world, what can talent or culture do to correct the evil?

CHAPTER X.

SPIRIT IN CONSCIENCE.

THERE are four aspects in which religion or spiritual influence in conscience may be seen :—*First*, as a sense of right and wrong, or of the ought and ought not; *second*, as a sense of a God to enforce the law of right; *third*, a sense of retribution as a means of enforcing the right; *fourth*, as an assurance of immortality, or that we shall live after death, to experience the good or ill of what we do in this life. All these several feelings meet in conscience to account for its extraordinary workings. If conscience is a single or separate faculty, as Dr. Wayland supposes, still it is a river of concurrent streams from distinct and various fountains.

We use the terms sense, feeling, and assurance in this connection for spontaneous impulses, like a little girl's maternal tendencies. She betrays them in affection and care for her doll, long before her reason is informed on the subject of that delicate relation. Instead of being generated by reason, these tendencies rather direct and control that faculty. It is her motherly nature operating in her before she knows the why or the wherefore. The little boy's thoughts go to his whip, his top, and like amusements, because his nature is different. We conceive that the sense of right and wrong, of God, of retribution and immortality, grow up in like manner. They are kindred ideas or impulses, all concurring in the conscience or moral sense.

As a sense of right and wrong, conscience is a sovereign critic upon our internal principles and external actions, as Bishop Butler says, 'majestically exerting itself without being consulted or advised with.' It does not wait for reason, or any other faculty, to affirm its decisions. It says, You ought to do so, and not to do so, and that is the end of the matter. It was this authoritative power, giving its decisions within, that made the murderer of Clarence say:

'I'll not meddle with it, it is a dangerous thing; it makes a man a coward: a man cannot steal but it accuseth him; a man cannot swear but it checks him. 'Tis a blushing, shamefaced spirit, that mutinies in a man's bosom: it fills one full of obstacles. It made me once restore a purse of gold, that, by chance, I found. It beggars any man that keeps it.'[1]

This passage truthfully represents conscience as an impulse reasoned against, opposed, or 'stopped' in its course, as Butler says, as we oppose any one or anything that interferes with our prevailing choice. This accords with the Bible truth of sin, as resisting the Holy Spirit, as forsaking God, as contemning God, as forgetting God, and as casting off fear, and restraining prayer before God.[2] It is not God as appearing to us in any outward form who is thus dealt with, but God working through the principles of that nature which He has given us. His voice is heard in those impulses to right acting which we call conscience.

---

[1] *Richard III.* Act i. scene 4.
[2] Acts vii. 51; Deut. xxxi. 16; Ezra viii. 22; John xvi. 13; 2 Chron. xxi. 10; Ps. x. 13.

This view is sustained by what we see in real life. The wrong is distinctly perceived by many who have no dread of committing it except the fear of courts, or of being disgraced among men, or of suffering some other worldly inconvenience. The certainty of not being found out puts them at rest in their course of crime, so far as an evil-disposed mind can be at rest. The naked sense of the wrong has no force to deter them from its commission. But where this sense of the wrong is seconded and affirmed by anticipations of a future world and a coming judgment, how different the result! A man in England, after having been twenty-two years an unsuspected murderer, lately gave himself up to justice, to relieve his conscience, and was hung on his own self-impelled confession. Cranmer, at the stake, held in the flame the hand that had written a recantation of his principles, saying, 'That unworthy hand.' Death, in its worst forms, has been freely accepted by millions, rather than refuse the voice of conscience speaking in the depth of their nature. Something more than a bare sense of right and wrong is present in all such cases. Even animals show signs of having this sense; and a thieving dog lops his tail and ears, and sneaks from the presence of his master. It is a higher impulse in the human soul, no doubt, than in any animal; but still, detached from spirit, God, eternity, it has not the requisite force to insure a virtuous life.

Many persons have a distinct perception of the wrong they have done, but feel no remorse. 'Fools make a mock at sin,'[1] and consider themselves nobler, more courageous, and more manly than those timid souls who are deterred from their own wild career by

[1] Prov. xiv. 9.

scruples of conscience. Said a boy who heard the fearful oaths of another, 'I wish I dared swear so.' This is the daring of a conscience relieved of all spiritual ideas and restraints. The sense of the wrong remains, but unchecked by the fear of God or man, like the unjust judge.[1]

Others have God much in their thoughts, and believe in a future retribution, or profess to do so, and yet these seemingly spiritual views do not make their sense of right and wrong at all more acute and reliable. They will do things manifestly wicked without seeming to know it, or having any sense of guilt or shame. How self-complacent were the Pharisees in praying at the corners of the streets, and wearing passages of the law upon their garments, and yet using those very pretences of extraordinary piety to ensnare widows to entrust them with their substance, that they might devour it![2] Their religion was divorced from the sense of right and wrong, as that sense in the former class was divorced from religion. In our day, how many become intensely devout, praying and praising night and day, and yet their word 'is not to be trusted in the ordinary transactions of life! These may be exceptional cases; still they exist, showing the effect of detaching soul from spirit, or morality from religion, on the one hand, or, on the other, of making religion consist in ceremonies, emotions, or anything else, when it does not act as an executive force in conscience, to rectify and enforce its decisions. The true working of spirit in this faculty is illustrated in the case of Zaccheus, rendering him both just and generous.[3]

These facts show that there are distinct and distinguishable elements in conscience, soul, and spirit, or man's

[1] Luke xviii. 2-5.   [2] Matt. xxiii. 14.   [3] Luke xix. 1-9.

natural sense of right and wrong, sustained by worldly or prudential considerations, and spiritual ideas or influences from God and the realm of spirits. These two elements may be likened to the nerves of sensation and motion in the human body, one of which may be paralyzed, and not the other, so that the diseased member acts while it does not feel, or feels while it does not act. Their united contributions are necessary to muscular health and vigour. So soul and spirit, the natural conscience and spiritual truths and influences, must commingle within us, in order to a sound, true, and vigorous state of our moral nature. A conscience evil, defiled, cauterized, and encumbered with dead works, is not annihilated, but is spoken of by the apostles as still existing, though incapable as perverted reason or vitiated feeling of doing its proper office. A paralyzed arm is still an arm, however it may have lost its cunning. No matter how a man may disconnect himself from God, he has still a nature that concerns itself about right and wrong, though it be only 'deceiving and being deceived.'[1]

Nothing is plainer or more generally conceded than that this faculty, as it exists among men, is intimately connected with the idea of God. However this idea may have originated, it is still a great fact in human nature. And our concern is with what is, or with what the Scriptures teach, and not with how it came to be. Sir William Hamilton thinks that the idea is derived from our moral, and not our intellectual nature. 'If there be no moral world, there can be no moral governor of such a world,' he says; 'and we can have no ground on which to believe in the reality of a moral world, except so far as we are ourselves moral

[1] 2 Tim. iii. 13.

agents.'[1] This is no doubt very true, but it is a truth far more conclusively affirmed by inspired vision, which throughout recognises man as accountable to God for what he is, and what he does, and affected by influences from a higher world as really as from this.

The idea of God is not a thing reasoned out, any more than the fact that we exist. No man ever reasoned himself into the belief of his own existence. That comes to him spontaneously, like the little girl's maternal feelings as manifested in her care for her doll. They gush up from her nature; and so it is with our sense of the divine existence. It comes up spontaneously, to shape our ideas, and to impel us to worship, if it be nothing better than gold, silver, brass, or wood; wind, water, storm, or stars; fowls, four-footed beasts, and creeping things. Some convert their atheism into an object of adoration, and are willing, as Lord Bacon says, to die for it. The African vents his spiritual instincts upon his fetish, the American Indian upon his Great Medicine, the old Greeks upon Jupiter, as the Hebrews found scope for theirs in Jehovah, the Maker of heaven, earth, and sea, and all things therein. Each conceived of his god as the rewarder of what to him seemed right, and the punisher of what to him seemed wrong. However gross and corrupting the idea, still, to the devotee, it is spirit and not matter,—as it is spirits that a boy fears in a graveyard, and not dead men's bones. It is the idea of supernatural power of which animals are incapable, because theirs is a world of sense, while ours is a world of spirit, especially in what concerns right and wrong. We feel that we must be right with the world above as well as that below.

[1] *Metaphysics*, p. 23.

> ' 'Tis greatly wise to talk with our past hours,
> And ask them what report they bore to heaven,
> And how they might have borne more welcome news.'

Reasoning against such a tendency of thought may confuse our ideas, but cannot pacify our sense of a God above to supervise our actions. Can we reason ourselves out of the sense of pleasure and pain? Even reason is prone to stumble upon the question of a great First Cause, as well as conscience upon that of amenableness to God. Both parts of our nature, the intellectual and the pathemic, are under a like necessity of stepping out of the range of the natural to find the groundwork of its convictions and its moral feelings. No absurdity of worship, no monstrosities of theology, no perversions of the moral code, have ever effectually cured men of their tendency to worship, and to feel that there is a God above to take cognizance of their actions. As our family ties survive in spite of all the corruptions and abuses of the sexual and conjugal relations, so our moral feelings, as centring in God, have outlived ten thousand errors in duty and theology.

The Bible acts advisedly, therefore, in keeping God ever before us as our Sovereign, and His spiritual laws as our rule of conduct. In heaven, the place of His throne, service is done to Him day and night. There the beams of His throne fall so directly and so radiantly, that the angels cover their faces to soften the insufferable brightness. Moses veiled his face, and Paul 'sobered' or moderated his language, after being admitted to visions of heaven, for the sake of those who could not comprehend all he thought and all he felt.[1] Can we wonder that the sun of such a system, however obliquely shining and darkly obscured by error and

[1] Ex. xxxiv. 33; 2 Cor. v. 13, xii. 2; Matt. xvii. 2; 1 Cor. ii. 12.

passion, should have its effect in the coldest moral climes of this sin-cursed world? What may not be hoped to man from the restored idea of the true God? 'This is life eternal, to know Thee, the true God, and Jesus Christ whom Thou hast sent.'[1] Right affections towards God are the only corrective of conscience, the sole basis of a good and happy life. The whole Bible is framed to the idea of restoring God to His proper seat in human nature. The seers and the law of Moses represented this in prediction and by symbol; 'but we all, with open face beholding as in a glass the glory of the Lord, are changed into the same image, from glory to glory, even as by the Spirit of the Lord.'[2] The more we know of God, the greater the purifying influence. Familiarity here breeds reverence and not contempt, as handling electricity increases our sense of its power. 'Oh that Thou wouldst rend the heavens and come down,'[3] is a prayer that contemplates the removal of all obstructions between our souls and God, that infinite truth and love may flow in upon us from above, to illumine our darkness, to exalt our aspirations.

How terrible to the guilty is the sense of the speaking Divinity!

> 'Methought I heard a voice cry, "Sleep no more!"
> Macbeth does murder sleep.'[4]

Even the *purpose* of a wrong robs the soul of rest:

> ' Between the acting of a dreadful thing
> And the first motion, all the interim is
> Like a phantasma, or a hideous dream.'[5]

Conscience, as a mere calculation of earthly consequences, could hardly be supposed to attach any such

---

[1] John xvii. 3.   [2] 2 Cor. iii. 18.   [3] Isa. lxiv. 1.
[4] *Macbeth*, Act ii. scene 2.
[5] *Julius Cæsar*, Act iv. scene 1.

significance to an evil design. The wound goes deeper than the external rind of our existence; it strikes to the secret core where centre the nerves and fibres of our spiritual being, connecting us with God. It is a cut in the great arteries, through which we feel that our life-blood of purity and peace is oozing out. Conscience, as connected with God, takes the alarm at the first motion to crime, and, as a householder the thief in his open window, seizes us by the throat to deter us from its commission. Its opposition is feebler as we advance, because our hold upon God and right is relaxed, and we come in the end to do with glee what at first we could not think of without horror. Then we are God-abandoned, as a sick man is given up by his friends, when disease has corrupted all the springs of life within him, and left no hope of his recovery. 'It is a fearful thing to fall into the hands of the living God.' 'For our God is a consuming fire.'[1]

Retribution is another aspect in which conscience is to be viewed. We are not to think of this as the result of an outward threatening, as a child under the rod, or a state criminal at the bar of his sovereign, but as inherent to the man, and a part of his conscience. The feeling of retribution begins in the unrest of a criminal purpose. A glutton needs no flagellations to punish him. His repleted stomach, and overcharged blood-vessels, and dizzy head, and shaking limbs, and torpid digestion, are his stocks, his thumbscrews, and his whipping-post. 'Dying thou shalt die.' No overt act can increase its certainty. It comes as the inevitable working of the moral forces which made the sin possible, as breathing carbon ensures death. The guilty one feels that he is

[1] Heb. x. 31, xii. 29.

> 'cabined, cribbed, confined, bound in
> To saucy doubts and fears.'[1]

Retribution dominates him from the working of his own nature, and without interference by others. Insensibility, like cauterized flesh, may afford momentary alleviations; but this is only deadening the sense of a less by means of a greater pain. Nemesis cannot thus be baulked of her purpose.

Guilty purposes are formed at the instigation of avarice, voluptuousness, ambition, revenge, or other dark impulses, and are usually sustained by any amount of fallacious reasoning. We come to doubt whether we ought to forego the good within our reach or the redress of our wrongs. The more we turn over the matter, the more our reasons for doing the deed grow upon us, and at length, our scruples cancelled, we rush upon the act, throwing our doubts to the wind. Then comes the recoil. The wind of the day has cooled our hot blood, as in the case of Adam,[2] and conscience collides against eternal truth and justice. The spirit-world opens upon us its terrors. Medusa shakes pestilence from her horrid hair. We 'flee when no man pursueth.'[3] Thus Lady Macbeth, on looking at her murder-stained hands, cried out with an infinite depth of woe:

> 'Here's the smell of blood still: all the perfumes
> Of Arabia will not sweeten this little hand. Oh! oh! oh!'[4]

Such is the outworking of spirit as a retributive element in the wrong-doer. He cannot feel as careless as a beast in doing a deed of blood till he has reduced himself to a bestial condition, and extinguished from his soul all the inbreathed attributes of the divine at

---

[1] *Macbeth*, Act iii. scene 4.
[2] Gen. iii. 8. 'Wind' is the literal rendering.
[3] Prov. xxviii. 1.   [4] *Macbeth*, Act v. scene 1.

our creation. Retribution is in the criminal himself. It is a part of his nature. It rewards him with inward approval when he is right, and with condemnation when he is indeed criminal. This, therefore, is an element in conscience, and not something extraneous to it, and is an essential constituent of those deep, profound, and terrible exercises of the man which we ascribe to this faculty. There is no being in the universe that the criminal has so much reason to dread as what is in himself,—'the demon thought.'

Another element in conscience is the sense of the *permanency* of rewards and punishments. This involves *immortality*, the belief of which among all nations is far in advance of the intellectual evidences of the doctrine. The greatest reasoners of heathen antiquity, Socrates, Plato, Cicero, Cato, Seneca, were strong in their hope of immortality; but when we examine the grounds on which they founded it, we cannot but feel their insufficiency. Cicero makes much account of the younger Scipio's dream, that his dead father appeared to him, saying, 'Do not consider yourself, but your body, to be mortal; for you are not the being which your corporeal figure evinces; but the mind is the man, and not that form which may be delineated with a finger. Know, therefore, that you are a divine person.' This dream, which is long, and well told, shows the tendency of thought among educated pagans just prior to the introduction of Christianity, in which 'life and immortality are brought to light through the gospel,' without which we have no available hold upon a life to come, as a thing of intellectual belief.

Immortality, like the existence of God, moral liberty, and other like truths, we are, as it were, necessitated to believe, though we cannot reduce them to any such form of certainty as that two and two make four, or the whole of a thing is greater than its parts. It is a part of our moral nature to feel that, however punishment of wrong may be delayed, it will come in the end,—if not in this life, in one that is to come. If we could feel a certainty of dying like the beasts, it would lead us to say, 'Let us make the most of life while we have it. Let us take our fill of its pleasures. "Let us eat and drink; for to-morrow we die."[1] Very few men can really feel this at their death, however they may have acted upon it in life. They still have lingering doubts as to what is to come after death. The question is ever obtruding upon the rustic, as well as the poet and philosopher:

> 'Has man within him an immortal seed,
> Or does the tomb take all? If he survive
> His ashes, where? and in what weal or woe?—
> Knots worthy of solution, which alone
> A Deity can solve.'

This assurance of immortality, like the eye, though unable to originate light on the subject, is quick to feel its impression when it comes. It fancies it sees it in things very dark and uncertain, as the confidence felt in ghost-seeing, spirit-rapping, and the like, clearly shows. There is in most men a longing after immortality, as the infant appetite longs for its yet untasted food, which leads them to seize on the first evidence that comes within their reach. And a certain unreasoning confidence enters largely into the working of conscience, which is thus graphically depicted by Shakespeare in the oft-quoted passage:

> 'To be, or not to be, that is the question,—
> Whether 'tis nobler in the mind to suffer

---

[1] 1 Cor. xv. 32.

> The stings and arrows of outrageous fortune,
> Or take arms against a sea of troubles,
> And, by one opening, end them ?   .   .   .
> To sleep ! perchance to dream,—ay, there's the rub;
> For in that sleep of death what dreams may come,
> When we have shuffled off this mortal coil,
> Must give us pause !   .   .   .   .
> .   .   But who would fardels bear,
> To grunt and sweat under a weary life,
> But that the dread of something after death,—
> The undiscovered country, from whose bourne
> No traveller returns,—puzzles the will,
> And makes us rather bear those ills we have,
> Than fly to others we know not of?
> Thus conscience does make cowards of us all.'[1]

This is a true picture of our anticipations of a coming life in the workings of conscience. They give a significance to what we are and do, which is quite out of the question to a mere creature of earth. Even Xenophon felt this. 'That person,' he says, 'who is conscious to himself of having neglected his oaths, in my opinion, can never be happy; for whoever becomes the object of divine wrath, I know no swiftness can save him, no darkness hide him, no stronghold defend him; since in all places, all are subject to the power of the gods, and everywhere they are equally lords of all.'[2]

This idea of immortality, acting with a sense of God and retribution as a spiritual element in conscience, is precisely what the seers saw in man. How else can we 'have respect unto the recompense of the reward' in a coming life, in refusing the pleasures of sin for the trials of duty? How else can 'a certain fearful looking for of judgment and fiery indignation' attend a course of sin? Morality in the Bible and in real life is a joint influence of two worlds,—that of nature and that of spirits.

[1] *Hamlet*, Act iii. scene 1.   [2] *Cyrus*, Book II. sec. 4.

CHAPTER XI.

HISTORY AN OUTGROWTH OF SEED-TRUTHS.

WHEN we consider the Bible record of man in his several stages,—in his innocence, in his transition to guilt, and in his progress towards restoration as conducted by divine love and power,—we find it every way adjusted to the views which the inspired writers give of his creation and the elements of his nature. The history of animals, as in water, on land, or as amphibious, is not more suited to their organs, than the moral and spiritual developments of our race to its constitution. If the Bible were a fiction, it would be more extraordinary, in the harmony of its various and complicated statements, as a work of human genius or invention, than it is even as a supernatural revelation. How are we to account for the fact that documents written by so many persons, in ages and countries remote from each other, and in such varieties of social condition and educational training, should so uniformly adhere both to one type of humanity and to one theology, except on the principle of truth in the sources of their information, and in the objects which they describe? Their views of man contain no such discords of opinion as we see in the metaphysicians, and their doctrines of God are not varient and conflicting. The first chapters of Genesis and the last of Revelation are as singular in their adjustment to each other, as in their imagery of the river, the tree of life, and of paradisiacal beatification.[1] Does this look like fiction?

It may be well, at this stage of our subject, to condense into one view the seed-truths of man considered in the previous chapters, that we may enter on our further inquiries with a clear idea of the race whose record we would follow up in its principal bearings.

The existence of two distinct worlds, the spiritual and the natural, is clearly set before us in the word of God. The spiritual world vastly transcends the natural in its position, power, and variety of parts, in reference to which Jehovah is called 'the Lord of hosts;' 'thousand thousands ministering to Him, and ten thousand times ten thousand standing before Him.'[2] Great as the material universe seems to us, the inspired writers made little account of it compared with what opened upon them in the realm of spirits.

The modes of conceiving truth or of knowing are radically different in the spirit-realm from what they are in the natural man, on account of which, symbols and peculiar forms of representation, such as we meet with nowhere out of the Bible, become necessary to convey spiritual truths to men in the flesh. They must be embodied as seed in soil, before they can yield a harvest of ideas to minds so subject to material laws as ours are. It is a process of spiritual incarnation.

The Hebrew language grew up, to a great extent, from an effort to express through it spiritual ideas; and hence it has discriminations between soul and

---

[1] Gen. ii. 8-17 ; Rev. xxii. 1-5.
[2] 1 Sam. i. 11 ; Ps. lix. 5 ; Isa. xlvii. 4 ; Jer. xlvi. 18 ; Dan. vii. 10.

spirit which are indigenous to no other language. In other respects also, as well as from the ritual worship, the peculiarities of Hebrew history, and the messages of prophets, it became before all other languages the vehicle of heavenly truths, and the most fitting organ for bridging the gulf between natural and spiritual modes of conception and of thought.

The mind of the flesh and the mind of the spirit are both proper to man as uniting in his soul,—body on the one hand, and spirit on the other; though the one becomes carnal-mindedness when it rules him as now in his carnal state, and the other spiritual-mindedness when he is ruled by the Holy Spirit.

The type of man is in God as seen in this, that God unites in Himself both the spiritual universe and material nature; so man unites in himself body on the one hand, through which he communicates with matter, and spirit on the other, through which he is fitted to communicate with the realm of spirits. 'God created all things by Jesus Christ, who is the image of the invisible God, the first-born of every creature;' 'the Word in the beginning with God;' the characterized or expressed Divinity; who is both the Son of God and the Son of man, and therefore the archetype of humanity.[1] He is the temple in heaven; and man was created to be such on earth, thus uniting in the adytum of his being the Holy Spirit with his outer life as his ruling power in all things. God would rule the world by man, as He rules heaven by His 'Son, whom He has appointed heir of all things,' saying, 'Let all the angels worship Him.'[2]

This twofold connection of man with spirit and

[1] Heb. i. 2-4 ; Col. i. 15 ; 2 Cor. iv. 4 ; John i. 1, 14.
[2] Heb. i. 2, 6.

with flesh is the hinge on which his whole development turns. It is set forth in a variety of ways by inspired men, as that of using the outer organs of his body for his earthly life, and the inner organs for his interior life,—ground, mortal, flesh, skull, on the one hand; and heart, kidneys, bowels, and inward parts, on the other. These two classes of terms show the duplicate view which the seers took of man.

Spirit, soul, and body are also used for a like distinction. They are not three distinct natures, as some incautiously express themselves. The nature is a unit in the soul or conscious selfhood, but a unit with the capacity of fleshly communication on the one hand, and spiritual on the other. The soul in Hebrew is the personality as distinguished from his capabilities of being either a beast, an angel, or a devil. What a man is and what he is capable of, are distinct views of his nature as a unit. The soul is not flesh, though it may be fleshly; nor is it spirit, though it may be spiritual,—that is, not spirit in the sense that God is so. It is receptive of spirit, and is sometimes called such; though Dives in hell was not spirit in the sense of being spiritual, any more than he was flesh, however fleshly he seemed still to be in his ideas and feelings.[1] The soul is substance, not matter; not an ethereal essence exhaled from God, to be melted at death into the expanse, as some foolishly talk, but the basis or substratum of powers rendering it strong to will, to act, and to enjoy or suffer throughout the ages of eternity.[2] Such is the *nephesh* of inspired men. It lives in flesh by breathing air, it lives in God by prayer and holy aspirations.

[1] Luke xvi. 19-31.
[2] Matt. xxv. 46; Dan. xii. 2; John v. 29; Rom. ii. 7.

Man's spiritual relations occupy the chief attention of inspired men. Their visions, doctrines, laws, ceremonies, histories, sketches of character, and their whole range of thought, are in this respect unlike all other writers, except as ideas have been derived from them. They dwell in the unseen world. Spirit in revelation is what the life is to the body. The all-pervading presence, holiness, and glory of God are their great idea. They are the inspiration of those who cry Holy, holy, holy, in heaven, as they are of our Christian doxology upon earth.

The realm of spirits is related to our faculties of spiritual apprehension precisely as nature is to our minds, through the bodily senses. And nothing prevents our conscious and happy connection with it, except the preoccupation of our minds with things material and earthly. A fleshly life bars communion with God. The petitions which Jesus teaches us to offer,—'Thy kingdom come, Thy will be done in earth as in heaven,'—contemplate our restored connection with the spirit-realm, and no doubt the ultimate commingling of God's family in heaven with His family on earth, as in the primitive life of the race.

The great-organizations, politico-religious, are the outworking of spiritual forces, beneficent or malign; and it is this blending in them of seen and unseen agencies that accounts for their hold upon men, and consequent perpetuity. The war spoken of in Revelation between 'Michael and his angels' and 'the dragon and his angels,' seems to be a conflict between the good and evil of these institutional forces.[1]

Morality and conscience owe their chief power to this connection with the spirit-world.

[1] Rev. xii. 7-9.

Such are the leading principles at the foundation of all human development, and they shape the course of history. Diet, climate, peculiarities of race, and like causes, have no doubt a modifying influence, just as a river is tinged by the soils over which it flows; but, like the river, these contributions from a higher world are still an element distinct from all their surroundings. They are the powers which connect man with immortality. They work in us; they pervade our life, like the unseen magnetism acting upon our bodies; sometimes concealed, and again revealing themselves to our faith; and in them we live and move and have our being. They have no necessitating power over our wills more than the air we breathe; and yet, like the air, they are a motive-power with us, and the result upon our character and our destiny depends entirely upon how we use them. Such is the teaching of inspired men on this important subject.

That the principles thus developed in the preceding pages are the modifying forces in history, who can doubt? Were not the antediluvians deluged with vice before they were with water? Did not their whole history turn upon their twofold relation to God and the world? Were not the Noachian tribes dispersed as the seeding of nations, to check the mad project of using their united strength to scale heaven and attain to the state of gods?[1] Indeed, we have only to look at the world as it now is to find abundant evidence of the Bible view of man and his relations. Millions of the race are so entirely detached from God as to lead wholly a material life. They are savages, and sunk to the level of nature. And yet, to show their inherent fitness for a higher life, they are super-

[1] Gen. xi. 6, 7.

stitious; they practise witchcraft; they have, in fact, a sort of perverted spiritualism, that as clearly evinces higher elements than those of a merely animal nature, as the faith or the devotion of Christians. They are an illustration of what comes from detaching the race from God as Spirit, or from His spiritual worship. This is the view which the apostle gives of the heathen world, in that celebrated passage in which their vices and abominations are said to have arisen from their ignoring the 'eternal power and Godhead,' which are so 'clearly seen' and so easily 'understood from the things that are made.' 'Because that, when they knew God, they glorified Him not as God, neither were thankful; but became vain in their imagination, and their foolish heart was darkened.'[1] Thus heathendom as a history, including its worship of devils and its vices against nature, is an outgrowth of the seed-truths of man and his relations on which the inspired writers so largely insist.

And when we turn from this degraded class to the great actors in history, what do we meet with but men expending upon ambition, or schemes of personal power and aggrandisement, the attributes of their nature which fit them to aspire after glory, honour, and immortality? But for a soul that only heaven was made to fill, how could there have been so wide a grasp upon earthly glory, in their perversion, as we see in Alexander, Cæsar, and Napoleon? Why the miser's far-reaching plan for acquiring what he can never enjoy but in imagination, unless born for a wider field of action and possession than earth can afford? Indeed, the whole life of man, and his history from the beginning, clearly affirm the inspired ideal of

[1] Rom. i. 20, 21.

a being born to be acted upon by two worlds, but by his own act detached from the greater of the two, to expend his energies upon the inferior and to satisfy himself with its husks.

In tracing our principles to their results, however, it is not our purpose to follow in the track of general history, but to notice only a few of the states and transitions to which they have given rise, together with the circumstances, agencies, and powers which God has set on foot for our redemption. The whole process of innocence, guilt, and punishment, as well as the means of restoring the race to holiness and heaven, is studiously adjusted to its nature and its inalienable prerogatives. To deal with man otherwise than as a free moral agent, would disqualify him alike for virtue and for vice, for sin and for holiness. Do trees grow by persuasion, or moral excellence by enriching the soil? The treatment must correspond to the nature,— a rule in nothing more rigorously adhered to than in God's dealings with men.

The great burden of our subsequent chapters lies in the direction of the fleshly life which we have fallen into, and its demoniacal possessions, and of God's plan for breaking it up, by destroying the works of the devil and re-establishing His kingdom here below. Redemption is not an abstraction nor a doctrine, though doctrines are used in prosecuting it; not an organization, though, like life, it cannot well subsist without it; but it is a great fact of human history and experience. The Grecian and Roman annals are not more a history. It is a power set on foot by Heaven, which has gone on advancing from age to age, gathering momentum as it advanced, and adding to the elect family an innumerable host out of every kingdom and nation and people under heaven, over whom Christ is enthroned 'King of kings and Lord of lords; who only hath immortality, dwelling in light which no man can approach unto; whom no man hath seen, nor can see: to whom be honour and power everlasting. Amen.'[1]

[1] 1 Tim. vi. 16.

CHAPTER XII.

HAPPINESS OF BEING RULED BY SPIRIT.

THE right use of a thing is the happy use of it. A machine with all its parts in their place, and doing their office, is in its highest state of efficiency and usefulness. And our bodies are in their greatest health and comfort when their organs and fluids and processes each performs its function and ministers its due share to the general result. So of our minds. When those powers are in the ascendency which have an inherent right to control, we have repose; but when we are borne away by blind impulse, misery is sure to ensue. Even in the natural man reason is a safer guide than appetite, and conscience than passion; because that is their office, and the more our impulses are subjected to their ruling, the greater our success in all that concerns our worldly affairs. But when God, a spiritual world, future retribution and immortality, are brought into consideration, what madness to ignore them, or to subordinate them to our momentary lusts and pleasures!

It is not of spiritual ruling as truth to the reason that we now speak, but truth wrought into the affections by the Holy Spirit. If the whole subject-matter of divine revelation were before a man's mind in his natural state, and he were required to shape his life by it as a merchant his, by figuring up the results of his business, could he do it ? Is not something more than spiritual truth as an idea necessary to make it a power in the soul ? A critic in art may be no artist. One who writes beautifully on the domestic affections may be morose as a tiger in his own family. So one may expatiate eloquently on the doctrines of the Bible, and yet be destitute of their real power. Spiritual ruling is like natural ruling in this, that it is not a thing of mere calculation, but of affectional influence and soul-power. The natural world acts upon thousands through their senses, who know very little of it as a matter of science. Maternal love is out of all proportion to the theory of it existing in the mind. Indeed, affection in human nature at large, is, like a mill-pond to its narrow confined flume, a vast reserved force of which but a little escapes through the vent of logical ideas or intellectual truths. It is the great ruling power in history.

So, in speaking of a spiritual ruling, we include much more than truths from the spiritual world. Truths are indeed the flume through which 'the water that springeth up into everlasting life'[1] flows in upon our souls; but that water is a fountain of holy affections flowing out in love to God, good-will to men, and spreading fertility and beauty over a landscape otherwise arid and waste. Grace as a ruling power in the soul is this added affectional influx from God, by which He accompanies His truths to our minds; and our Lord has it in view when He prays, 'Sanctify them through Thy truth: Thy word is truth.'[2] The truth is here contemplated as the means by which the purification of the affections was to be reached. It is the sword by which the Spirit cuts off God's enemies of

[1] John iv. 14. [2] John xvii. 17.

lust, unbelief, malignity, and worldliness in our souls, and prepares the way for His army of graces and holy affections.[1]

Nearly all attempts to treat theology as a science are a failure, as in painting fire you can get everything but the heat. That wanting, and what have you in the picture to convey an idea of fire to one who had never seen or felt it? Grace as favour, grace as a theory, grace in the schools,—what is it as compared with grace in the heart? It is the life that escapes the surgeon's knife in his attempts to search it out. As men can do nothing without affection, and that is the great power that binds them to their sins, so how are they to be detached and brought under spiritual ruling, except by the counteracting force of divine and heavenly affections? Now grace is this counteracting power in the soul. 'It reigns through righteousness unto eternal life.'[2] That is, by restoring spiritual ruling over the fleshly nature, and thus setting us right with God, right with conscience, and right in all our relations, it produces a new sense of joy and delight, that so satisfies our craving, that we freely accept it in exchange for the pleasures of sin. Darkness may be pleasant to one who never knew anything better; but let him have light, and how will he exult at the exchange! A fetid atmosphere may be agreeable to vitiated olfactories; but, after being rectified by inhaling pure air, how they loathe the former stench! Such is the reign of grace in the soul. It is the corrective of vitiated desires, thus reigning through righteousness, or giving a new and right bent to the soul's pursuit of happiness. Grace came with truth by Jesus Christ, or He provided, by His mission,

[1] Eph. vi. 17.   [2] Rom. v. 21.

Happiness of being ruled by Spirit.

to impart to us a new affectional bent as well as a new order of belief, and thus to make us altogether new.[1]

We stand related to a spiritual the same as to a natural universe, but had lost a due sense of the former, and were solely occupied with the latter. So far as spirit acted upon us at all, it was that of 'the prince of the power of the air' exercising dominion over the disobedient. And to be restored, we must not only know spiritual truths, but we must accept them by a 'faith working by love'[2] as our chosen guide in all things; and they must become even more real to us than anything in our outward life; and not only more real, but infinitely more desirable. Was not the spiritual world infinitely greater to our Master than this earthly world? Were not His joy and His peace from this higher source? And if we are in conjunction with heaven, will it not be the same with us? 'He that findeth his life shall lose it; and he that loseth his life for my sake shall find it.'[3]

We will not here stay to describe the process by which a soul comes into this state of deadness to the world and life in God, but proceed at once to consider the ineffable blessedness of it. 'Take my yoke upon you, and learn of me; for I am meek and lowly in heart: and ye shall find rest unto your souls.' 'Peace I leave with you, my peace I give unto you.'[4] 'We which have believed *do* enter into rest,' that is, as a matter of present experience. 'Thou keepest him in perfect peace, whose mind is stayed on Thee; because he trusteth in Thee.'[5] Passages of this kind might be

[1] John i. 17; 2 Cor. v. 17.　[2] Gal. v. 6.
[3] Matt. x. 39.　[4] Matt. xi. 29; John xiv. 27.
[5] Heb. iv. 3; Isa. xxvi. 3.

multiplied, showing the sense of profound repose which arises from feeling ourselves restored to God's ruling within us. 'It is a peace that passeth all understanding,'[1]—too deep to be fathomed, too expanded to be measured, too enduring ever to end, and too high to stop short of the throne of God. It is God's peace. This peace which Jesus had under all His sufferings, He bequeathed to us at His death; and the inheritance is sure to all who learn of Him lessons of meekness and lowliness, to all who wear His yoke or live under the ruling of His Spirit.

With what gladness and singleness of heart did the disciples eat their meat, when they came at Pentecost under God's own dominion! It was not a kingdom of meat and drink; not of exactitude in the matter of external rites; not of creeds and definitions; not of sacerdotal orders or sacred vestments,—but of 'righteousness, and peace, and joy in the Holy Ghost.' Heaven drops down the dews of grace, and all beautiful flowers and fruits respond with fragrance and with joy.

> 'To humbleness of heart descends
> This prescience from on high,
> The faith that elevates the just
> Before and when they die;
> And makes each soul a separate heaven,
> A court for Deity.'—WORDSWORTH.

'I will greatly rejoice in the Lord; my soul shall be joyful in my God.' 'The fruit of the Spirit is love, joy, peace.' There was great joy among a people with whom the Spirit was working in power, as in the revival at Samaria.[2] Such expressions in a great variety

---

[1] Phil. iv. 7.
[2] Phil. iv. 4; Isa. lxi. 10; Rom. xiv. 17; Gal. v. 22; Acts viii. 8; 1 Pet. i. 8.

of forms and circumstances constitute a noticeable future of revealed religion. The Lord was a sun and shield in the view of its writers, giving them grace and glory, and withholding no good thing; to whom it was ever in their hearts to say, 'Whom have I in heaven but Thee? and there is none upon earth that I desire besides Thee.'[1] Their faith was a fountain of happiness.

It gave them songs even in the night of their calamities. The inflowing of God's spiritual influence to the soul is like the form of the Fourth walking unharmed in the midst of the fiery furnace, and giving protection to those entrusted to His care. As we have seen, Jesus, though a man of sorrow, had no brighter jewel to leave with His Church on earth than His peace. His holy soul, like the sea, was quiet at bottom, however tossed by winds on its surface. So the apostles were joyful in all their tribulations, confidently saying, 'Who shall separate us from the love of Christ? Shall tribulation, or distress, or persecution, or famine, or nakedness, or peril, or sword? Nay, in all these things we are more than conquerors through Him that loved us.' Their trials made their graces only the more illustrious, producing patience, experience, and hope, and thus intensifying their joy in God. It acted as heat upon gold, to render them purer and more brilliant, fitting them for 'praise, and honour, and glory, at the appearing of Jesus Christ.' The prophet's song is a celebration of this joyful influence from heaven under the privations of this life. 'Although the fig-tree shall not blossom, neither shall fruit be in the vines; the labour of the olive shall fail, and the fields shall yield no meat; the flocks shall be cut off from the fold, and there shall be no herd in the

---

[1] Ps. lxxiii. 25, lxxxiv. 11.

stalls: yet I will rejoice in the Lord, I will joy in the God of my salvation.'[1]

Millions since the ages of inspiration have testified to the happy effect of coming under the Spirit's ruling. Says Augustine, 'By a light, as it were of serenity, infused into my heart, all darkness and doubts vanished from my mind.'[2] Edwards, about twelve hundred years after Augustine's time, bears similar testimony. 'I found from time to time,' he says, 'an inward sweetness that would carry me away in my contemplations. This I know not how to express otherwise, than by a calm, sweet abstraction of soul from all the concerns of this world; and sometimes a kind of vision, or fixed ideas and imaginations, of being alone in the mountains or solitary wilderness, far from mankind, sweetly conversing with Christ. This sense of divine things would often of a sudden kindle up, as it were, a sweet burning in my heart—an ardour of soul that I know not how to express.'[3] These two men were giants of intellect as well as of faith; and their testimony, though no truer than that of millions of others before and since their respective ages, may be thought to have the greater weight.

Now these facts accord with Moses' account of man's primeval Eden, showing that the same law obtained as to the effect of the Spirit's ruling in the first innocence of the race, as in its redemption to holiness by Jesus Christ. So far as the garden of God was a scene of fountains, flowers, fruits, and shady groves, or of external beauty, it was so, not for its own sake, but for the man for whom it was provided, or as a reflec-

---

[1] Job xxxv. 10; Dan. iii. 25; 2 Cor. vii. 4; Rom. v. 3, 4, viii. 35-37; 1 Pet. i. 7; Hab. iii. 17, 18.
[2] *Memoirs*, p. 167.   [3] *Complete Works*, vol. i. p. 19.

Happiness of being ruled by Spirit. 123

tion of his blissful life in the companionship of God and angels. It was the abode of heaven upon earth, and a symbol of heavenly life. Wherever there is a human soul in which God has set up His throne, there is a garden of Eden, there flows the water of the river of life, and there is the tree of life in the midst thereof. The secret of his paradise is in being right with God, right with himself, and right in all his relations. The spirit rules the flesh, and not the flesh the spirit.

'The Lord God planted a garden eastward of Eden; and there He put the man whom He had formed.' The place was made for the occupants, and without them it could not have existed. A material garden, great as may be its delights, would come utterly short of Moses' description. Spiritual men have always regarded Eden as more than an outward fact. It sets forth the infinitely varied and beautiful truths, the accordant feelings, the heavenly joys, and divine communion, which, in the person of man, had been dropped among the elements of this earthly world. It is the light in which pictures are seen that brings out their beauty. It is the spiritual medium through which things are contemplated that sheds upon them the glories of heaven. The earth, the mountains, the wilderness, the visible heavens, the course of providence, and even the judgments of God, become to one in the spirit of Edwards a scene of transporting contemplation. 'Alleluia: for the Lord God omnipotent reigneth,'[1] is a pæan of praise that finds thence its inspiration.

Had no mind or moral forces been reflected from Eden, but only brutal instincts or material delights,

[1] Rev. xix. 6.

think you it would have found a record in God's word? No; an inner man, with his immortal powers, capabilities, and associations, must have looked out upon nature and read the Divinity in all its lines, and felt Him in all its events, to make it a scene of joyousness and of beauty, and a field for spiritual expatiation, or Eden would have been what the golden age is in the dreams of the poets,—a thing of imagination, the mirage of a sentimental hallucination skirting the horizon of the past. What a poor representation of man's primeval abode are the groves, fountains, and voluptuous delights by which the Oriental monarchs sought to reproduce it! The cottage is often more an Eden than the palace, because it is the seat of love and devout affections, while malignity, hatred, and hell are found in many a gilded hall and flowery garden. The rustic couple, living in piety and faith, are truer successors of Adam and Eve than those who dwell in kingly and queenly state.

This glorious planting of God, so far as it was outward, was the seeding of truths far more vital than anything in itself. Every tree, every leaf, every ripening fig, orange, grape, apple, and pomegranate, glowed with the sunlight of heaven. It was a record of God, and could be read by the spiritual primeval man without book or reasoning. God spoke through it to his heart. The divine love, truth, holiness, and all-pervading presence were revealed to him in everything. In this respect Adam's experience was but the prototype of that of every truly spiritual man: God in everything, God everywhere, God always delightfully near,—this is the feeling. This feeling made Eden what it was, and obtained for it a place in the inspired record. It shows what man was and is under the ruling of the Holy Spirit. With no nature to be thus ruled, material beauties enough could not have been brought together to invite the visit of angels, or to have sat for the picture of man's primeval innocence. A golden age is a delusion of the past, except as realized in the human soul radiant with heavenly light; and with that it is equally a reality of the present.

Hence the paradise of the New Testament is a reproduction of the Eden of the old. It is applied to that heavenly world into which Paul was caught up, where he 'heard unspeakable words, which it is not lawful for a man to utter.'[1] This was wholly a spiritual scene, and so far exceeding all material representation, that it is not lawful to attempt to utter or depict it in that form. Moses' imagery of Eden, in the first chapters of the Bible, is applied by John, in the last chapters of Revelation, to the New Jerusalem, which also had its 'pure river of the water of life proceeding out of the throne of God and the Lamb,' answering to that which watered Adam's garden, and which 'became into four heads.' 'In the midst of the street of it, and on either side of the river, was there the tree of life, which bare twelve manner of fruits, and yielded her fruit every month: and the leaves of the tree were for the healing of nations.'[2] Thus the earliest and latest records of inspiration contain like thoughts and like imagery, showing that they were united in the same immutable and eternal spiritual truth; that the beatification of man in his original innocency, of man in a state of sanctification on earth, and of man as glorified in heaven, has one basis,—the absolute enthronement of God in his soul. This is the holy of holies where God has His throne, where

[1] 2 Cor. xii. 4.   [2] Gen. ii. 9, 10; Rev. xxii. 1, 2.

His laws are deposited, and His rod of authority ever buds and blooms. The same fountain of truth and love flowing from God refreshes the inhabitants in each of these states, and the same tree of life supplies them with its fruits.

God's spiritual reign over man is as much a fact of primeval Eden as of New Jerusalem. As Cousin justly says, 'When affection has conquered selfishness, instead of loving its object for its own sake, the soul gives itself to its object, and—miracle of love!—the more it gives the more it possesses, nourishing itself by its own sacrifices, and finds its strength in its own self-abandonment. But there is only one Being worthy of being thus loved, and who can be thus loved without illusions, and without mistakes, at once without limits, and without regret,—to wit, the perfect Being who alone does not fear reflection, who alone can fill the entire capacity of our hearts.'[1]

'The tree of knowledge of good and evil'[2] points to a state wherein ideas, reasonings, aspirations, and self-consciousness abate the simplicity and entireness of our love and devotion to God, and which, without questioning and without doubt, give Him the first place. Knowledge is of the outer man, divine love of the inner man; and the triumph of the former at the expense of the latter as a motive-influence with us, ruling our wills, is the inlet to evil, the opening of hell to the soul of man. As, in the experience of the most of us, the period of undoubting filial love and confidence was the golden period of our life, as compared with the succeeding distrust which followed from our own waywardness or the discovery of parental defects; so unreasoning faith in God does infinitely

[1] *Lectures*, p. 108.   [2] Gen. ii. 17.

more to make our lives golden and beautiful, than any of the inventions of our self-reliant reason or impertinent speculations. Seeking to know from the pride of knowing, exercising our intellects with a view to worldly pre-eminence, or to make ourselves independent of divine guidance, is 'the tree that brought death into the world and all our woe.'

The word of God can never have its proper effect upon us, while we think of its sketches merely as things of the past, and remote from us as events of another planet. We must feel that they apply equally to ourselves as to any preceding generation. The laws of animal life are not more identical to every generation than those of spiritual life. Adam lived by eating and drinking, the same as we do. He was not more bound to follow God's leading than we are ; nor was its abandonment to enjoy forbidden gratifications more fatal to him than to us. All seed-truths are the same to us as to him. He was happy in right living, and miserable in wrong living; and so are we. His harmony with God and holy angels made his Eden; and if we love and trust 'Him whom we have not seen, we also rejoice with joy unspeakable and full of glory.'[1] Our modes of coming into these blessed relations with God are different, and so is our nature as affected by sin ; but our happiness equally has a spiritual, holy, and heavenly foundation. It comes from the ruling of God in our souls.

[1] 1 Pet. i. 8.

CHAPTER XIII.

HOW HEAVEN IS LOST.

THE reign of God in the soul constitutes its heaven, in reference to which our Lord speaks of Himself while on earth as 'the Son of man who is in heaven.' He brought with Him heavenly life in the perfection of His character, and imparted it to His devoted followers, insomuch that 'the kingdom of God was said to be within them.' It was a state of grace and salvation, in which is realized the answer of the prayer, 'Thy kingdom come; Thy will be done on earth as in heaven.'[1] God's kingdom comes in the sanctification of the Church as a means to its glorification. It is the reign of heaven in individual souls of which we now speak.

Now this heaven of the soul consists alike of submission to God in the primeval man, in the sanctified on earth, and the glorified above. It has its subordinate varieties, but the principle is the same. In the primeval man it was innocence; in the saints it is growth in grace; in the glorified it is grace perfected. It is a heaven in which God is the sun ruling all the planets, satellites, and asteroids of thought and desire, and all the active powers, whether of the outward or inward man. This is the only source of their harmony,

[1] John iii. 13; Matt. v. 3, 19, 20, vi. 10, xi. 11, 12; Luke xvi. 16, xvii. 21.

and a necessary condition of heaven. 'The meek shall inherit the earth,' 'Godliness has the promise of the life that now is,' and 'the hundredfold more in the present time to those who forsake all for the gospel,' are promises which have their fulfilment, not in the abundance of the things of this life, but in the heaven of divine love, educing the greatest good from earth, and ending in 'a far more exceeding and eternal weight of glory.'[1] Such is the Bible representation of God's ruling in the soul; and it must be accepted, however it conflicts with the experience of those who claim to be subjects of the divine kingdom. This is God's truth, already realized in the faith of some, and not to be invalidated by the unbelief of others.

In all these cases of beatification, the state of the soul in relation to God, and not its location, is the great point insisted upon by the inspired writers. The mansions of our Father's house are 'prepared' for those who are suited to them, and they are 'many,' as adapted to all their specific varieties or degrees in glory.[2] They are a paradise of redeeming love, as Eden was of primeval innocence,—the occupants determining the character of the dwelling, and not the dwelling that of the occupants. The mind shapes the body, and not the body the mind; and hence, in idiocy, the body loses its comeliness. No greater error can be imagined, than that of conceiving of heaven as a place to go to to make one happy, who has not heaven already in his own soul. Millions of deluded men, who are living in vice and wickedness, feel sure of heaven, on the ground of extreme unction and priestly absolution. Or they have once had certain religious experiences, which,

[1] Matt. v. 5, 19; Mark x. 29, 30; 1 Tim. iv. 8.
[2] John xiv. 1, 2; 1 Cor. xv. 41, 42.

though now dead, and unsustained by anything in their lives, awaken in them the fallacious hope of going to a heaven of which they have not a single element in their souls. Alas that fictions should take the place of facts on so grave a subject, or that heaven should be for a moment thought of as anything but God the all in all of our being!

How much logic has been from first to last wasted, to explain how it is that beings in the heaven of God's ruling should of their own accord abandon it, and accept hell in its place! And yet do we not see much that is analogous to it in real life? How many a son and daughter, husband and wife, abandon a happy and honourable home for a career of infamy and woe! Such defections proceed by a gradual process of specific pleasures, with eyes blinded to the result, which comes as a final retribution. These cases in men already depraved are, indeed, unlike those wherein a heaven of perfect innocence and bliss is abandoned for the guilt and misery of hell; though the latter, too, will be found, on examination, to be a choice of specific pleasures, rather than of the final result. Temptation has arisen and prospered even among innocent beings, if the Bible is to be believed. How could this have happened?

The difficulty is to accept the scriptural view of the soul, as independent in the production of effects, or in originating acts of praise or blame. The soul's responsibility ends where necessity begins. From this remark, however, must be excepted the incapacity which arises from previous acts of wrong, just as a criminal, though incapable of being innocent, is still responsible for his guilt. The incapacity of a sinful state is both our guilt and our punishment. But how can a first transgression in one previously innocent be extenuated on any such ground? The question is not as to the incapacity of one already guilty to become innocent, but how an innocent being could originate a sinful act? It seems to be thought by some, that a necessity of some sort, such as that of the strongest motive, for instance, must have ruled him. As Sir William Hamilton says, 'Though an unconquerable feeling compels us to recognise ourselves as accountable, and therefore free agents, still, when we attempt to realize in thought how the fact of our liberty can be, we soon find that this altogether transcends our understanding, and that every attempt to bring the fact of liberty within the compass of our conceptions only results in the substitution in its place of some more or less disguised form of necessity.'[1]

Reasoners on this subject, a hundred years ago, thought to escape the difficulty by inventing the distinction of natural and moral necessity. Though both are alike absolute and irreversible, yet, since motive is cause in moral necessity, and physical agencies in natural necessity, therefore the actor is responsible. If I do a wicked thing, I do it from motive, and am guilty; but if a malarious atmosphere gives me a fever, it is my misfortune, and not my crime. The motive as cause is not blame or praiseworthy, but only the effect, or the act resulting from the motive. Hence God could decree a motive to be the cause of sin, without being implicated in the sin itself. Hopkins and Emmons[2] were not satisfied to stop here, but held that God creates all sinful volitions as well as all good ones, in the same sense that He created the world.

[1] *Metaphysics*, p. 24.
[2] Celebrated American divines in a past age.

Still He is not implicated in their guilt, because guilt is not in the creator of a sinful volition, but in the one who exercises it. The absurdity of the conclusion has exploded the reasoning; and though many hold moral necessity as an incontrovertible axiom, very little use is made of it in our religious discussions. We have drifted away from it into the currents of modern thought, and are out at sea, while we suppose ourselves still moored to the doctrine of necessity.

The moment we look beyond the soul itself for the cause of its responsible actions, and ascribe them to God, to the strongest motive, or to some influence acting upon the will to necessitate its determinations, we stumble upon 'the supposition that acts of volition are results of the same iron necessity which determines the phenomena of matter,' and thus 'we subvert the foundations of religion, natural and revealed.'[1] The freedom of the will is as sure to us as our own existence, and yet it is one of those things which we cannot formulate in thought; nor can our volitions be reasoned about as effects, like those produced by ordinary causes. They have their cause in the man, and that is the end of it. 'Lo, this only have I found, that God made man upright; but they have sought out many inventions.' 'Let no man say, when he is tempted, I am tempted of God; for God cannot be tempted with evil, neither tempteth He any man: but every man is tempted, when he is drawn away of his lusts, and enticed. Then, when lust is conceived, it bringeth forth sin; and sin, when it is finished, bringeth forth death.'[2] No more reliable account of the origin of evil than this can be given.

Men are called gods, in reference, no doubt, to their

[1] Sir W. Hamilton's *Metaphysics*, pp. 21, 22.   [2] Jas. i. 13-15.

resemblance to the Divine Being in this moral freedom of originating volition. 'God standeth in the congregation of the righteous; He ruleth among the gods;' that is, among those whose prerogatives were like His own. 'Worship Him, all ye gods.' 'Thou shalt not revile the gods,' or those to whom the word of God came, as interpreted by our Lord, who justifies this application of the term. It was also said by the prophet to the idols, 'Do good, or do evil, that we may know that ye are gods,' involving the idea that to act voluntarily constituted likeness to the freedom of the Divine Mind.[1] This likeness of the soul to God in the freedom of action is our sole clue to the divine character; for we can have no conception of Him as an Almighty Intelligence, except as we take the idea from the attributes of our own mind. We never think of our acts as necessitated by something going before or apart from our voluntary agency; but the sense of responsibility as the sole originators of them, inheres in us in spite of all our reasonings to the contrary. And as we cannot feel *our* acts to be necessitated except by ourselves, so we cannot think of *God* as necessitated in what He does, except by His own sovereign pleasure. If it were otherwise, and we could think of any prior cause as necessitating our own acts, we should think the same of God; and the result would be a ruler of the universe ruled by Fate as the highest source of power, the real Divinity, to which the homage of all hearts is due. Thus moral necessity, by imperious laws of logic, ends in natural necessity, and Pantheism or Positivism is the unavoidable issue.

In Scripture, all ideas of moral responsibility terminate in the soul itself as an independent cause-pro-

---

[1] Ps. lxxxii. 1, 6, cxxxviii. 1; Isa. xli. 23; Ex. xxii. 28; John x. 34, 35.

ducer, and not in anything outside of itself. Within the limit of its free voluntary agency it is absolute and supreme, as we have already seen; no power being able to trespass upon it against its will. Within that limit lie all its moral responsibilities, as the inspired writers abundantly teach. 'It is accepted of a man according to what he hath, and not according to what he hath not.' 'For unto whomsoever much is given, of him shall much be required.'[1] 'It is only as man is a free intelligence, a moral power, that he is created in the image of God; and it is only as a spark of divinity glows as the life of our life in us, that we can rationally believe in an Intelligent Creator, a Moral Governor of the universe.'[2]

Still, absolute as man is in his own domain, he is subject to a law which cannot fail to hold him under God's authority,—if not by precept, then by penalty. The precept and penalty are both alike inseparable from man's nature. They are a part of his constitution as a free moral agent. A man is free to take poison, but will not the penalty of the wrong act be sure to follow? If the precept enjoining or interdicting an act fails to secure our obedience, then the penalty takes effect to hold us still under God's authority. Both are a sweet savour unto God, the one of life unto life, and the other of death unto death. God's authority is maintained in both cases; and so He does not lose His power of control over us by reason of our freedom. It is not a control, however, which consists in arranging the causes of crime, nor in creating the sinful volition, as some have supposed, but in leaving our nature to work out its own destiny. In that the divine authority is suffi-

---

[1] 2 Cor. viii. 12 ; Luke xii. 49.
[2] Sir Wm. Hamilton's *Metaphysics*, pp. 21, 22.

ciently secured. Moral freedom, therefore, does not involve a power to escape from under the government of God, who reigns as absolute in hell as in heaven, and by the same love too; though in the one case it is commuted into wrath, and in the other into unspeakable bliss and glory. The difference is not in the authority, but in the soul-powers of those upon whom it is exercised, just as the excellence of a government is as fatal to the disobedient as it is happifying to the obedient. God needs no fines, imprisonments, or overt punishments, because His laws work out their appropriate results by the very constitution of a moral agent.

Now, temptations to evil in holy men, or in a state of primeval innocence, are, like rewards and punishments, the outworking of their faculties while in a state of trial. They arise from specific impulses which are perfectly innocent in themselves, each tending towards undue indulgence, in which alone the wrong exists. These specific impulses impose upon the man the duty of duly balancing one against another, and of subordinating all to God's spiritual reign in his soul. This is therefore the duty, and this the law of duty. Animals are led by instinct to regulate their faculties, —eating, sleeping, and living as their condition and the necessity of their nature require. But reason and conscience supply in man the place of instinct in animals, wherein God reveals His spiritual truths as 'a light to our feet and a lamp to our path.'[1] Our souls are open to God and the realm of spirits on the one hand, supplying a peculiar and distinct law of thought, feeling, and action; and to the realm of nature on the other, from which we derive ideas and impulses

[1] Ps. cxix. 105.

equally peculiar, but requiring always to be subordinated to the former. We converse with the first through faith, and with the other through sense; in the one case acting as seeing invisible truths, and in the other as affected by the visible and the tangible. Spirit in conscience, and flesh in appetites, passions, and worldly ideas, are the two forces that unite in our moral agency to constitute our duty and our law of duty. These are the facts, beyond which we cannot go, any more than we can go beyond properties and attributes in our natural sciences.

A moral agent could no more exist without these conditions, than pleasure and pain without sensibility. Reason is nothing without occasions for its exercise. Conscience is nothing, except as connected with something to be regulated by it. A metallic hand is a watch-regulator, only as part of a watch to be regulated by it. The authority of God could be nothing to us, except as the enforcement of a law of duty in our own nature. Can His authority as a moral ruler act upon a stone or a beast? The right and wrong is not in the faculties to be regulated by God's law of duty, but in the use we make of them. In the power to see, hear, smell, taste, or feel, what evil is there, till we have used it for an evil purpose? Or what evil is there in the love of food, light, sound, odours, or agreeable sensations, till we have in some way indulged them at the expense of conscience or of the divine law? Where is the evil of loving wife, children, houses, lands, money, merchandise, bank-stock, or any other good, so long as it is subordinated to God and the best interests of mankind? The crime is not in the sense, affection, or impulse, but in exercising it criminally, or out of due proportion to other affections or claims upon us. I am now speaking of the faculties in an uncorrupted state, and not as vitiated by inherited or habitual sins. Every one will see the difference between sin as a judicial corruption of nature, and sin as a first act; nor did this difference escape the notice of an apostle, as we see from his comparison between those who had and those who had not sinned after the similitude of Adam's transgression.[1]

How could a nature with so many specific impulses work out its destiny without temptation? No matter how innocent, it could make no difference, till by exercise and habit it had attained to the strength and consistency of holiness. Innocence does not repress the onward tendency of an impulse, when it has reached its proper limits, as a fly falls with singed wings when he touches the flame. No, it may be more active than ever as it approaches the boundaries of wrong, which God seems to have had in view when He prohibited not only the eating, but also the 'touching,'[2] to suggest that we should stop short of the boundaries of wrong, and thus let our moderation be known.[3] To dally with temptation is the next step to committing sin. Here, on the extreme boundaries of right, comes the temptation to take one step more into wrong. With no evil, and no extraneous malign influence in the universe, a being with the nature of man could not act without occasional inward conflicts in checking specific desires; nor could his innocence become virtue and holiness without such conflicts. Victories are not to be won without battles, nor praiseworthiness without a resolute resistance to becoming blameworthy. The very laws of moral development involve temptation, so far as we know the history of God's universe. This is as much

[1] Rom. v. 14.   [2] Gen. iii. 3.   [3] Phil. iv. 5.

a fact as a theory. How was it with Adam? how with Christ? how with those who have come out of great tribulation, and washed their robes and made them white in the blood of the Lamb? That those who overcome will wear crowns and palms of victory, as denoting exemption from further conflict, rather confirms than unsettles the principle of temptation as the law of moral and spiritual progress, at least in that part of God's moral government which is subjected to our inspection.[1]

We look into the Bible, and what do we find? Was it not an impulse right in itself that betrayed the man after God's own heart into sin? God Himself concedes the right of David's desires; and enumerating how much He had done for him, He adds, 'If that had been too little, I would moreover have given unto thee such and such things.' That is, all his desires had their limits, within which gratification was lawful. So Moses, in his highest state of spiritual power, became provoked at the people's obstinacy, or into undue consciousness of what he could and must do to confound the 'rebels;' and these specific impulses betrayed him into sin, and closed against him the promised land. Self-reliance and panic urged Peter forward into a very wicked act, though the core of his piety remained intact and unchanged.[2] In each of these cases the specific impulse came in an exalted state of spiritual power and faith, laying 'the foundation for repentance from dead works,' but not ending in permanent apostasy.[3]

Moses' account of the first sin is more to our pur-

---

[1] Rev. vii. 9, 14.
[2] 2 Sam. xii. 8; Num. xx. 10-12; Mark xiv. 66-72.
[3] Heb. vi. 1.

pose, because it shows the working of specific impulses in producing temptation to those who were in a state of perfect innocence. 'And when the woman saw that the tree was good for food, and that it was pleasant to the eyes, and a tree to be desired to make one wise, she took of the fruit thereof, and did eat, and gave also unto her husband with her, and he did eat.' Prior to this she had listened doubtingly to the serpent's denial of God's authority as to the effect of eating the fruit of that tree.[1] We have here five specific impulses in the tempted to create an internal struggle, of which the serpent took advantage; to wit, doubt, appetite, taste, the desire of knowledge, and ambition. It was to develope these inward powers of man, or his faithfulness in subordinating them to the God-ruling in his soul, that this prohibition of one of the trees of the garden was no doubt given. His internal faculties imposed a duty and a law of duty; and the prohibition was a test of his obedience. The act of eating or not eating of that particular tree was of little consequence, except as a test of his obedience to the higher truths and laws of his being.

The first element in the temptation was *doubt*—in itself a right exercise when rightly directed. All advance in knowledge and virtue begins with a doubt as to whether there is not something better for us than we have yet attained to. Doubt is the parent of investigation and of growing knowledge. It is holding the mind in an attitude of waiting for more evidence before coming to a decision. But where the question of maintaining our moral purity becomes a matter of doubt, it is a first step to sin. Such it proved to Eve. She listened hesitatingly to the serpent's charge of false-

[1] Gen. iii. 4-6.

hood upon God, saying, 'Ye shall not surely die; for God doth know, that in the day ye eat thereof then your eyes shall be opened, and ye shall become as gods, knowing good and evil.' Herein her defection began, in giving a wrong direction to an innocent and important impulse.

Appetite for the fruit was a subsidiary impulse, to increase the doubt whether it was not best on the whole to eat of it. This, too, is not only innocent, but necessary; for how can we live without eating? It was not appetite that constituted the wrong, but only exercising it towards a forbidden indulgence. 'When the woman saw that the tree was good for food,' and dwelt upon the idea, then 'the lust was conceived which bringeth forth sin.' She thought with herself, no doubt, Why should so innocent a gratification be denied? It is unworthy of God. The serpent must be right.' Thus doubt and appetite mutually strengthened each other.

Taste, or the love of the beautiful, added its current to the evil impulse. The fruit was 'pleasant to the eyes.' There is certainly no wrong in being delighted with what is beautiful. Beauty is akin to holiness.[1] But when used as an impulse to things wrong in themselves, or which God has forbidden, it becomes a sublimated licentiousness; and the more we feel it, the greater our danger. All the most voluptuous and damning pleasures are embellished with every charm to the eye, to increase their attractiveness and multiply their victims. Thus one of the noblest impulses of our nature may be easily converted into our strongest temptation, to demand a vigorous resistance on the part of a virtuous mind.

[1] Ps. xc. 17, cx. 3.

The *desire* of *knowledge,* one of the noblest passions, also lends its attractions to that which is evil, when it contravenes truth and right. But when conjoined with love and goodness, it acquires a new and higher character ; it becomes wisdom. ' The wise shall inherit glory.'[1] It is only when knowledge puffeth up, when it robs us of our simplicity, and renders us crafty, cunning, and impertinent in our investigations and our character, that it is an offence to God, and a curse. The worst heresies of the world began with men gifted in everything but truth, holiness, and the love of God. ' The world by wisdom knew not God,' for the good reason, that another element than simple knowing, that of faith, is necessary to apprehend God.[2] An eager curiosity concurred with other innocent impulses to create the first temptation. ' A tree to be desired to make one wise,' came to Eve's mind in a way to corrupt the simplicity of her trust in all that God required.

The *ambition* to be ' as gods, knowing good and evil,' had also its charm to Eve. Who can set limits to the aspiring of the human soul ? And is it not quite right when it seeks perfection in goodness, and in the power of good to others ? Did not our Lord mount the cross to reach the throne of the universe ?[3] Ambition thus directed is godlike. But when it is a selfish desire of pre-eminence, that seeks its gratification by over-riding millions, or in claiming infallibility for fallible men, and the viceroyalty of God on earth, what can be conceived of more absurd or blasphemous ?

' If, aspiring to be gods, angels fell,
Aspiring to be angels, men rebel.'

Such are the specific impulses which Moses repre-

[1] Prov. iii. 35.   [2] 1 Cor. i. 21 ; Isa. xxix. 14.   [3] Heb. ii. 9.

sents as working in an innocent being to produce temptation and a fall. They would have operated in man without an outward tempter, as they seem to have operated in the race to which that old serpent the Devil and Satan belonged, to produce its relapse into evil. The laws of moral action, as consisting in specific desires to be regulated and controlled out of a regard to our duty to God, are no doubt the same in all the intelligent and responsible races; as it is found by the spectroscope that matter has the same elements in the sun and stars as in our earth. Beings may be created innocent; but to acquire virtue and holiness, they must exercise their moral faculties under temptation in a way to ensure praiseworthiness. But for this elementary condition of man himself, the lies and seductions of the serpent would have fallen upon him as persuasion upon a stone, or arguments upon a shrub.

Moses' record of the fall of man is a perfect prologue to history, bringing to light and anticipating the great forces which have from first to last been most active in shaping events. What has done more than scepticism, or the extinction of faith in God and the spiritual world, to produce this universal earthliness and impiety for which the race has been distinguished? What has proved a greater power in history than the fleshly appetites? Beauty, natural and artistic, how has it in all ages ministered to voluptuousness! Art, architecture, priestly robes, gorgeous processions, and various æsthetical contrivances, hold millions in error and wrong, as the serpent's eye the charmed bird; and all argument and persuasion fail of bringing them to the knowledge of the truth. Science falsely so called, as well as the abuse of much that is true, is it not now, as it always has been, a great antagonist of faith, and the source of fatal and damning errors? How extensive the materialistic tendency of denying all truth, except what may be formulated to the reason, or reduced to the conditions of a defined conception or axiom!—whereas nothing within the range of our knowledge can be so defined, the simplest forms of matter always including things which our reason cannot embrace in its idea of them. And yet, because spiritual truths are addressed to our faith rather than to our reason, therefore in the pride of our knowledge we deny them altogether, and come to the monstrous conclusion that mind is merely a secretion of matter! And ambition inflating us to the state of divinity, and arrogating honour due only to God, has created nine tenths of the gods which still claim the homage of mankind. Who can imagine a greater power in history than ambition?

Nor has demon influence been less active in human history than it was in the first sin. How potent was it in the time of our Lord! How has it associated itself in the form of witchcraft, necromancy, magic, and astrology, with nearly all the false religions of the world! Corrupt spiritualism is even more prevalent than the true, and thousands believe in it who have no faith in God or His word. Thus the events of Eden are singularly adjusted to human nature, as it has proved itself to be in its career of nearly six thousand years. Why then speculate about the fall of man as a distant and doubtful event, when the same elements are active in us all, and the same event is transpiring in all our experiences? The causes which lost heaven to Adam may lose it to us.

CHAPTER XIV.

THE SPIRITS IN PRISON.

TO profit by the Bible, we must read it as applying to our present experience, and not merely to that of the dead generations. The search for a cure of our actual diseases is very different from that of an amateur student or of a professional man. It is as a record of man's unchanging characteristics, imposing the same duties and laws of duty, the same rewards and penalties, and the same hopes and fears, that it becomes a book alike for all ages. The seed-truths of man, like the acorns of the first and last generation of oaks, have an undying life. What God enacted for Adam and all previous individuals and nations, has the same significance for us as for them. Those who receive the gospel in power as well as in word, and those who preach it with a personal application, are those who get from it the greatest good to themselves, and do with it the greatest good to others. And our object in these pages is to set forth a few of the underlying truths, which, from being universal to our race, are as useful and as essential to us as to any going before.

We have seen what it is to have heaven in our souls, and what it is to lose it; and we come now to consider what follows from so great a loss.

There are few subjects on which we deceive ourselves more than upon this. We think of the death penalty inflicted upon Adam as bodily dissolution, or as a great physical fact like a public execution, in which not only man, but the beasts and the elements of nature, alike participated. We suppose that death, as an extinction of organic life, then began its reign over everything that hath breath; that brutes had else been immortal; and, if brutes, why not trees, foliage, fruit, and every product of the soil? Why not ascribe to sin vegetable as well as animal death? Milton represents the animals as then changing their nature, the hitherto docile lion now beginning to growl, and the placid skies to be overcast and weeping sad drops upon the face of the earth,—a sort of weeping, by the way, that no form of life can well dispense with. But we fail to find in the prologue of Moses anything of all this. The day succeeding man's sin opened with just as sweet a dawn; the teeming earth exhaled as delightful a fragrance, and has to this day scenes that might be copied for a picture of Eden; the landscape was sown with pearls and gold; and Eve was no doubt outwardly as beautiful, and Adam as majestic in form and stature, as before the fatal deed was done. The birds warbled melodious notes from overhanging branches; the lambs disported themselves in luxuriant pastures; and the heavenly bodies poured radiant light upon the joyous scene. These blessings have been attendant upon the human race in its subsequent career, and how should they have been suspended on the occasion of the first sin? The avenging angel did not strike down the guilty pair, nor inflict upon nature any sudden convulsion. The bowers of Eden were still their hiding-place.

To get round these facts, and still preserve the idea

of bodily death as the threatened penalty, various schemes have been devised, such as a reprieve of threescore years and ten, or death *in posse* if not *in esse*, or assured if not at once inflicted; and thus much special pleading has been resorted to in accounting for the fact that the penalty threatened was not inflicted on the day of the sin. But, after all, *was* it not inflicted in manner and form as intended in the threatening? Was not the changed state of man's soul, from the moment he came voluntarily under the ruling of his fleshly nature, an infinitely greater death penalty than a thousand bodily dissolutions, or any imaginable amount of physical disaster? When shall we learn that God's revelation is a thing of mind, and not of matter? Its rewards and punishments infinitely exceed all our ideas of a paradisiacal millennium amid the groves and material delights of a restored world, or of a lake of literal fire and brimstone. No outward scene of horror can compare with the loss of God's sensible favour, happy communion with heavenly beings, or the inward peace and joy of a rightly regulated soul. These made Eden; and the loss of them was succeeded by a hell whose anguish no outward alleviations could effectually mitigate. Who can estimate the amount of woe of which the soul of man has been the seat? It is a boundless, bottomless sea of agony.

The divine word contemplates our state under a variety of figures,—imprisonment, bondage, servitude, impotence, death. Deliverance from it is 'liberty to captives, the opening of the prison to them that are bound, proclaiming the acceptable year of the Lord' as a year of release from debt and enslavement.[1] 'Whosoever committeth sin is the servant of sin; and the

[1] Luke iv. 18, 19; Isa. xlii. 7, xxxv. 5, xlix. 8, 9; Zech. ix. 11, 12.

servant abideth not in the house for ever,' but is cast out of the family as no part of it; while 'the Son abideth ever,' as homogeneous with its members, and an inheritor of their privileges.[1] Such is our Lord's interpretation of this bondage. It is the extinction from the soul of that which constitutes its free life in God. But He adds: 'If ye continue in my words, then are ye my disciples indeed; and ye shall know the truth, and the truth shall make you free.' 'If the Son therefore shall make you free, ye shall be free indeed.'[2] What can be intended by these words, but the freedom of a soul under God's ruling, or guided in all things by the true and the right; and the enslavement of one in whom lust, and appetite, and ambition, and malignity, and every dark passion, reign unchecked and uncontrolled? 'The liberty wherewith Christ maketh us free' is deliverance from this hell within.[3]

The impotence and death of this state are set forth in terms equally graphic: 'The heart of this people is waxed gross,' or fleshly and brutal, 'and their ears are dull of hearing, and their eyes have they closed; lest they should see with their eyes, and hear with their ears, and understand with their hearts, and be converted, and I should heal them.' 'God has given them the eyes of slumber;' or torpidity and insensibility to spiritual things have ensued from giving themselves up to the flesh and the world, and they are as impotent as if born without eyes. And to complete the dark picture, they are represented as 'dead in trespasses and sins,'—a deadness that consists in 'walking according to the course of this world, according to the prince of the power of the air, the spirit that worketh in the children of disobedience,' and therefore purely

[1] John viii. 34, 35.   [2] John iii. 31, 32, 36.   [3] Gal. v. 1.

the result of coming under a fleshly dominion. No power but that which raised Christ from the dead can recover them from this state.[1]

Peter took a like comprehensive view of the condition into which the race relapsed at the fall: 'For Christ also hath suffered for us in the flesh, the just for the unjust, being put to death in the flesh, but quickened by the Spirit; by which He went also and preached to the spirits in prison; which sometime were disobedient, when once the long-suffering of God waited in the days of Noah, while the ark was a preparing, wherein few, that is, eight souls, were saved by water. The like figure whereunto, baptism, doth also now save us (not the putting away of the filth of the flesh, but the answer of a good conscience toward God), by the resurrection of Jesus Christ, who is gone into heaven, and is on the right hand of God; angels, and authorities, and powers being made subject unto Him.'[2] We quote this passage, not for critical disquisition, nor to attempt the settlement of its disputed points, but to call attention to a few points which bear directly upon our subject. First, that the antediluvians were spirits in prison, not in the sense of being outwardly locked up either in a future hell, in the heart of the earth, in Hades, or in any such confinement; for there is a total lack of evidence that Christ ever preached in any such prison. Second, that still it is Christ's mission to preach to the imprisoned spirits spoken of. Third, their imprisonment is in some way connected with the filth of the flesh, from which they are relieved by Christ's resurrection power as represented in a baptism which denotes a conscience or spiritual purification. Fourth, that in heaven, as head of those thus raised up

[1] Eph. i. 17-21, ii. 1; Rom. vi. 4-11.   [2] 1 Pet. iii. 18-22.

with Him, He will have the supremacy of angels, authorities, and powers. Here we have a comprehensive view of the state into which the human family relapsed, as an imprisonment in the flesh and the world, so dominating them as to deprive them of their free life in God,—a freedom never more to be enjoyed till the Son makes them free, and they become spiritual men.

The apostle here writes of sin as a physician of a disease which is alike in all ages, taking his example of it from aggravated cases thousands of years ago, to show its symptoms and its malignity. In the next chapter he changes the figure from preaching to spirits in prison to 'preaching to them that are dead, that they might be judged according to men in the flesh, but live according to God in the spirit.'[1] Their fleshly state is arraigned, condemned, and executed, as it were, by gospel truth brought home to the conscience; but out of their death comes forth the new man in Christ, whose life is 'according to God in the spirit.'[2] A like comprehensive view of the remedy preached as the same in all ages, is presented in the first chapter of this epistle: 'Redeemed by the precious blood of Christ, as of a lamb without blemish and without spot; who verily was fore-ordained before the foundation of the world, but was manifested in these last times for you, who by Him do believe in God, that raised Him from the dead, and gave Him glory; that your faith and hope might be in God.'[3] The blood of Christ here represents a spiritual power working in all the

---

[1] 1 Pet. iv. 6.
[2] 1 Pet. iv. 6, with which compare Gal. ii. 19, 20, Rom. vi. 11, 2 Cor. v. 15, etc.
[3] 1 Pet. i. 19-21.

ages, to relieve the imprisoned, and the dead in fleshliness and worldliness, and to raise them up to 'faith and hope in God,' or to a spiritual and heavenly life.

What was this imprisonment of the antediluvians which the apostle employs to represent that of men in all ages? It was fleshly lust intensified, killing out every devout and noble sentiment, and becoming the worst of imprisonments and deaths. 'They ate, they drank, they married and were given in marriage.'[1] The sons of God even were ensnared by the voluptuous daughters of men, repressing and extinguishing their small remains of spiritual vitality, and rendering it unavailing to their children, who became the *nephilim*,[2] giants, 'strong of appetite,'[3] only the more skilful in wickedness for what few religious truths they inherited. Every imagination of the thoughts of their heart was evil continually; all flesh was corrupted by this beastly life; violence too, as usual, went hand in hand with lust, of which the deluge was a fitting catastrophe.[4] The ten generations preceding the flood, having few arts, giving limited attention to government, and to a great extent without armies, courts, diplomacies, organizations, or other means of diversified interest, such as grew up among the descendants of Noah, would seem to have lived merely a bestial life, with a few rare exceptions. This was their imprisonment. After the flood it was otherwise, and men became warriors, hunters, builders of cities and states; thus finding channels for their teeming activity, which rendered them no less worldly, no less dead in sin, but still more conservative, and therefore not so fitting an illustra-

---

[1] Matt. xxiv. 37-39.
[2] The word *nephilim* means monstrous births.
[3] Isa. lvi. 11.   [4] Gen. vi. 1-13.

tion of Peter's idea of sin as a state of imprisonment to fleshly lusts, and death to all spiritual and holy affections.

'The spirits in prison,' like men in whom slavery has extinguished all manly aspirations, had lost the idea and the desire of spiritual freedom. Such ideas and desires were dead in them, constituting the worst feature of their imprisonment. Children stolen by the Indians from the border settlements of America, have in some instances lost all notions of civilised life, and become savages in their feelings, predilections, and habits, to the extent of being irreclaimable by their sorrowing friends. Attempts to change their nature after finding them, by introducing them to the customs and usages of civilisation, have proved a failure, and at the first opportunity they would escape again to the freedom of their wilderness life. In such cases, something more than a knowledge of the contrast between savagery and civilisation is necessary to reclamation. They must in some way be brought to view their condition from a civilised standpoint, just as, in the fabulous doctrine that human souls transmigrate into animals, a man who has become a dog, for instance, must be made to feel as a man before he can know the degradation of a dog's life. While the nature of a dog is still in him, how can he aspire to anything better? So men must have a changed nature, or must in some way be made to conceive the degradation and misery of being carnal, and the excellence of a spiritual and holy life, before they can know what they are, and what they must become in order to be saved. This is the great point to be gained by preaching to the spirits in prison, and to men that are dead, that the quickening power of the Spirit attending the word may bring them to a sense of their lost estate, and of the only way of salvation.

The idea of the prison, of the death, or of 'the sin, the most mysterious and the most sorrowful of all ideas,' as De Quincey says, must be infused into a man's soul, before the work of reclaiming him to holiness can commence. 'Sin is a taint in the individual, not through any local disease of its own, but through a scrofula equally diffused through the infinite family of man.' Conviction of sin is not merely the feeling of specific wrongs, as theft, lying, murder, or drunkenness, under the remorse of which men's consciences sometimes rankle,—though this may be included; but beyond all this, it is a feeling that our nature is corrupt, and that when we 'would do good, evil is present with us.' 'We are shapen in iniquity, and conceived in sin,' are 'the degenerated plants of a strange vine,' and our 'whole head is sick, and our whole heart faint.'[1] Our nature is dominated by the flesh, or by natural ideas and interests; and there is no redemption for us, except that which consists in re-establishing the spiritual ascendency over us in which the race was originally created. Sin is a constitution, a body, an organism, called 'the old man,' 'the natural man,' and 'the body of the sins of the flesh,' and as such is propagated from father to son, the same as any other quality of our common manhood.[2] This is as much a physiological fact as a doctrine of divine revelation. It is the ascendency of the outer nature, causing us more anxiety as to what we shall eat, drink, wear, how we shall rise to wealth and power, and

---

[1] Ps. li. 5; Jer. ii. 21; Isa. i. 5.
[2] Rom. vi. 6; Eph. iv. 22; Col. iii. 9; 1 Cor. ii. 14, 15; Col. ii. 11; Rom. v. 15-21.

transcend others, than how we shall lay up treasure in heaven or be rich towards God.[1] Man, as made to be ruled by spirit, could not become wholly earthly, without entailing a nature and circumstances upon his posterity to make them so too.

The account given by Moses of the manner in which man glided into this carnal state is worthy of particular notice. Though all at once, or on the day of the sin, according to the threatening, it was by successive stages. In symbolizing them to us, acts are ascribed to God which were His only in the sense of their being wrought out by those laws which He had established in our nature, as the architect whose mind supplied the model is said to build a structure on which he never struck a hammer. Thus God drove out the Canaanites, and He drove the Jews into captivity, when the first was effected by the hard-fought battles of Israel, and the other by the Chaldee invasion.[2] So the sufferings of the church are Christ's sufferings, and those who despise His servants despise Him, because His Spirit is in them as the moving power.[3]

'God walking in the garden in the wind of the day,' as in the original, or when the evening breeze had tempered the heat, denotes the subsidence of those passions which had impelled to the sin, and preparing the sinner to hear the voice of God as formerly; but O how different the impression! What had been his heaven, was now his hell. He skulked; he hid himself among the trees of the garden; he resorted to a

---

[1] Matt. vi. 19, 20; Luke xii. 21.
[2] Josh. xiii. 14, 15; Jer. viii. 3.
[3] Col. i. 24; 1 Thess. iv. 8; Luke x. 16; Acts ix. 4, 'Why persecutest thou *me?*'

subterfuge to cover his naked deformity; and thus reflection put him upon an escape from evils which he felt to be impending.

> 'Well, I'll *hide* the body in some hole,
> Till that the duke gives order for his burial:
> And when I have my meed, *I will away;*
> For this will out, and *I must not stay.*'

Did this murderer wait for a pursuing executioner before making his escape? No, there is a law through which God more speedily and more effectually works out His ordeal of trial; and that took effect in Adam the moment reflection succeeded to the vehemence of passion, and he sought concealment. Moses and Shakespeare agree as to this feature of human nature.

The adjudication equally reflects principles common to mankind. It began with Adam, who charged the blame on Eve, and she on the serpent, who accepted the charge in silence. The hopeless criminal, instead of casting the blame on others, glories in it as all his own, and relates with gusto his hardihood and bravery in doing the deed. He asks no partner to share his hellish honors; nor did Satan on this memorable occasion. In the judgment the order is reversed, and the demon is first to be doomed to dust as his home and his meat, and to final destruction under the heel of the woman's Seed; the woman is next given over to sorrow and subjection; while the man is last assigned to toil and sweat in extracting bread from a thorn and thistle infested soil, and to the dust from which he was taken, as his only road to that immortality into which his nature had else been commuted by a process as happy as it would have been glorious. Our change from mortal to immortal is now painful, and we are all our lives in bondage through fear of death. But with a sinless race, it would no doubt have been anticipated as the nuptial or coronation day of the soul; and it becomes so even to us in the full exercise of a faith enabling us to say, 'O death, where is thy sting? O grave, where is thy victory?'[1]

The expulsion from Eden resulted from a necessary separation of spiritual life from one in a carnal state.[2] No power could perpetuate such a life as that of Eden in those who have assumed an attitude of hostility to God. The fall of man is not an abstraction, but a great fact of history. It is indeed represented to us by imagery to a certain extent symbolical, but it is none the less a matter of fact. Even this imagery is suited to the idea of imprisoned convicts, or to criminals under restraint. What is uppermost in the minds of men thus situated? Is it not the dread of justice and of the executioner, and also a desire to escape? The dread of justice is a silent, sullen feeling, which is rarely expressed, as to acknowledge a fear of justice would be a confession of guilt. In conversing with criminals, I have found the claim of innocence almost universal; but the desire of escape is an active loquacious principle, ready for any subterfuge to elude justice. Plea of innocence, turning State's evidence, breaking jail,—nothing comes amiss on which hangs the least hope of deliverance. These two ever-present forces in a guilty mind are, no doubt, brought to view by the symbols of the cherubim and the flaming sword at the eastern gate of Eden to guard the way to the tree of lives, the representative of spiritual freedom and life in God. 'So God drove out the man; and He placed at the east of Eden cherubim, and a flaming sword which turned every way, to keep the way of the

---

[1] 1 Cor. xv. 55.   [2] Gen. iii. 23; Rom. vii. 14.

tree of life.'[1] To Adam, Eden was liberty; expulsion, slavery: he and his posterity were thenceforth spirits in prison.

The cherub, the symbol of a retributive Providence, denotes power, majesty, and avenging justice. Those at the gate of Eden are no doubt a symbol of the forces in criminal natures which indispose them to innocence, and which therefore render it impossible for them to resume their free life in God. They cannot, because in their vitiated state they will not. The idea of God is repulsive to them, and how then should they be attracted towards Him? 'God riding upon a cherub' denotes rapid execution in His works of power and punishment.[2] Ezekiel's vision gives a graphic idea of the various agencies executing God's decrees. The whirlwind, the flame like amber, the variously formed living creatures, the man, the lion, the ox, the eagle, with wings having hands under them, all moving with wheels touching the earth, or connected with man's material life, and impelled by one mind,—these are some of the features by which God's infinitely diversified providence over a guilty and imprisoned race are set forth in prophetic vision.[3] The great power in this complicated mechanism was the unseen but living soul, showing that in nature as well as in man mind is the supreme force.

The cherubim, as God's all-comprehending providence, are a terror to guilty men. They are never represented as speaking, except in the language of events. Those of the Jewish temple were gigantic human figures,

---

[1] Gen. iii. 24.
[2] 2 Sam. xxii. 11; Ps. xcix. 1.
[3] Ezek. i.; Heb. xi. 27. [In view of this invisible providence Moses endured.]

standing in the darkness of the holy of holies, where God had His throne and His law, unseen to mortal eyes, continuing from age to age as conservators of the divine government against the impotent opposition of men and devils. At the gate of Eden they sat, too, in solemn silence, as time notched its centuries. No word proceeds from their lips; no emotion agitates them amid the wrecks of generations or of empires passing under their view; no vacillation of purpose disturbs them in executing the eternal decrees.

It is a fact worthy of note, that the winged bulls exhumed at Nineveh stood to the living generations who chiselled them out of stone as guardians of their gateways; that the Egyptian and Grecian sphinxes, and, I believe, the Scandinavian griffins, and also the fabulous animals of India, performed a like office. They were invested with attributes of terror to interlopers; and, from the Grecian story of Œdipus and the sphinx, there can be no doubt that they were among heathen nations a type of man's fears in the hand of an inexorable Providence. Œdipus as the murderer of his father, the husband of his mother, the father of his brothers and sisters, the persecuted of his sons, and then voluntarily blinded to hide from him these evils, sets forth a pagan's idea of the malignant influences working in providence. I suppose there are no visible links to trace this idea as represented by these fabulous animals to the same source with the cherubim of Moses; and yet one cannot but feel, from the use made of them to guard gateways, and the general dread with which they were associated, that they must have had the same origin. The feeling of not being right with God is alike prevalent among all nations; and can we wonder that it should be expressed under a like symbolism? Is it not as a law-work essential in redemption?

The sword of flame appeals to the universal desire of imprisoned criminals to effect their escape. It supposes the gateway still open, but guarded by the cherubim against those who had no right to enter; while the sword denotes authority and illumination, to assist those who come in the right way. They were to 'keep' the way of the tree of life, not to close it. This sword suspended over the gateway, and 'constantly turning itself,' as Gesenius renders the passage, 'reflects light not only within the garden, but to those without who would enter. It is a light to assist the spirits in prison to effect their escape, and to return and eat of the tree of life, and live for ever.' This is a gospel for the imprisoned and the dead—'a light shining in a dark place'—the voice of the Son of God calling the dead to life, arraigning and condemning them, as 'men yet in the flesh, that they may live according to God in the spirit;' and thus the sword of flame can mean nothing but God's truth preached 'in demonstration of the Spirit and of power' to men in their fleshly state, to restore them to a heavenly life.[1] The gospel is a sword, not only as spoken with authority, and unlike the scribes, but as being an executioner to kill as well as to make alive, to 'crucify the flesh, with its affections and lusts,' as the only mode of a sinner's escape from impending wrath. We must die to sin before we can live unto God; we must leave our worldly life before we can enter into the strait and narrow gate, and thus find our way back to 'the tree of lives,' and eat, and live for ever.[2]

[1] 2 Pet. i. 19; John v. 25; 1 Pet. iv. 6; 1 Cor. ii. 4.
[2] Matt. vii. 29; Gal. v. 24; Rom. vi. 6; Matt. vii. 13, 14; Luke xiii. 24.

This idea of the gospel as a killing power as well as a power to make alive is too obvious a feature of revealed religion to need further comment.

The word of God is often represented as a sword.[1] In this application of the symbol of Moses, therefore, we are not fanciful, but are fully sustained by the interpretation which inspired men put upon their own symbols. It is a two-edged sword, to signify, no doubt, that it cuts towards the interests of man as a citizen of this world and of heaven. It asserts our duties towards men and towards God, and cuts off our vices as well as our impieties. The same idea seems to be included in the 'tongues' of fire being cloven which sat upon each of the apostles on the day of Pentecost. Each tongue darted jets of flame in opposite directions, to indicate not only a power to propagate truth, but truth of man in his embodied as well as disembodied relations. Though some critics give a different interpretation, this to the writer seems more analogous to the use of the term in other places, as well as to the contents of the divine word as bearing upon two worlds. The sword of flame turning every way opened the dispensation of symbol; the cloven tongues of flame, the dispensation of power. The one reflected a measure of light upon all the nations, their pagan ideas variously perverted being borrowed from it; while the other has reflected some truth over the whole area of human civilisation. 'That was the true Light, which lighteth every man that cometh into the world.'[2] 'Its turning itself continually' is like the flame of a lighthouse shining far off on the

[1] Eph. vi. 17; Heb. iv. 12; Deut. xxxiii. 29; Rev. i. 16, ii. 12, xix. 15.
[2] John i. 9.

ocean expanse, to guide the passing marine of all nations.

Among the thousand religions and inventions devised for the soul imprisoned in fleshly lusts and worldly ideas to effect its escape, this is the only one that accomplishes the object. This goes direct to the root of the evil in a heart alienated from God, and teaches us that we must be born again in order to enter the kingdom of heaven. Ceremonies, priestly absolution, the cattle on a thousand hills, the first-born of our flesh for the sin of our soul, are without avail here. As our bondage is enslavement to the flesh, our freedom is in the spirit of adoption, crying, Abba, Father.[1]

[1] John iii. 4-7; Ps. l. 8-15; Mic. vi. 7, 8; Rom. viii. 15.

CHAPTER XV.

DOCTRINE IN HISTORY.

THE Old Testament! what can we find in that suited to our present civilisation? Who can live as Abraham did, or utilize Moses' obsolete laws? Who would not abhor to kill off a whole race, as Samuel the Amalekites; or to hang sons for the sins of their father, as David did the house of Saul? Who dances in worship except fanatics, or observes ox-killing ceremonials except at a political barbecue? Are such stories fit to read to our families or congregations?. Such is the language and feeling of many, and we have heard like feelings expressed even by Christians of intelligence and piety. The Old Testament out of date since the New came into vogue! Indeed, why then did the Son of God and His apostles make it the text of so many sermons and epistles?

The error of this reasoning is in conceiving that a doctrine could exist without a history, or in failing to consider that history, in working its way into doctrine, necessarily allies itself to what accords to the thought and usage of the living generations. Thought in a child is evolved from sensations, and not sensations from thoughts. It is several years before a thought becomes so grooved into a child's mind as to be a memory of his after life. Why did not the plough idea start up into its present perfection thousands of years ago? Why this long history of clumsy constructions of that useful implement running through so many ages? Why did not some statesman a thousand years ago invent the British Constitution, and thus prevent the wars of the Roses, and Henrys, and Stuarts, and Georges, and Long Parliament—this infinite flow of human blood? Why did not Pastor Robinson put the American Constitution into the hand of the Mayflower Pilgrims, to be worked up to in the New World?

The truth is, a doctrine without a history is like a constitution without national development,—a thing to dream over, as Plato over his ideal republic, or as the French savans over their *ne plus ultra* governments in the time of their Revolution; but not a thing to walk on all fours in this matter-of-fact world. Creeds, like constitutions, become a fixed fact only as they are shaped by history. The Nicene Creed embodied ages of philosophical discussion; religious controversy, national war and diplomacy, and the great interests of Christendom, giving it birth, and form, and perpetuity. The Westminster Confession was backed by Presbyterian history; and the Thirty-nine Articles by an English National Church which, under Rome, had had a thousand years' growth and formation. The Methodist Book of Discipline took form from a widespread and powerful religious movement, and from a series of antecedent events involving the action of thousands of earnest minds. History, and usage, and the Bible, answer to the Baptists, Quakers, and some other sects, all the purposes of denominational cohesion without a general creed, showing that standards of faith and practice are quite as dependent upon fact as upon doctrine. What would Rome be without her history, her material forms, or her vast accumulations in money, cathedrals, sacred foundations, and priestly orders, vestments, and prestige?

So of revealed religion as contained in Holy Scripture: as an abstraction, it would have but a feeble hold upon us, if any at all; but as a history flowing onward with the actual current of human events, it has grown to a power wide as the world. But if it had been given to man in scientific definitions, or in the carefully-worded articles of a creed, or in the essay-style of those who object to the barbarous record of the Old Testament, it would have been as incomprehensible and unavailing as Emerson's lectures to a congregation of Digger Indians. The Bible as it is shows the outworking of the real forces in human nature from the beginning of time, together with God's various modes of supernatural illumination, to point out its wanderings and direct it in the way it should go. The causes producing the history are the antecedent forces in the case, just as the plough idea is grounded in the necessities of agriculture, constitutions in the demand for social organization, and religion in a spiritual faculty, which, however repressed, will for ever assert its claims in one way or another. And as the history follows the causes producing it, so doctrine comes after the history, and supposes an age of reflection and of ripe intellectual culture, like that of the man in working up into poetry, philosophy, or instruction, the feelings and fancies of his childhood.

Thus of Christian doctrine. Up to the time of Moses there was no prescribed creed or ritual. Sacrifices were merely free-will offerings, prompted by devout minds, but required by no recorded commandment. The patriarch who had special tokens of God's presence, or an abundant harvest, gave expression to his grateful or glad emotions by the killing of animals, or the offering to God of fruits and libations, the same as when he was made happy by a friend's visits or benefactions. Thus Cain and Abel, on some such special occasion— the one from a receipt of worldly good, in which his heart was bound up, and the other in view of spiritual truths opening upon him with unusual clearness, and kindling his devout emotions—brought each his freewill offering. The different result to Cain from what it was to Abel arose, I think, not from *what* they sacrificed, as many suppose,—for the offerings which both brought were alike required under the law of Moses,—but from the different spirit and character of the two men. 'By *faith* Abel offered unto God a more acceptable sacrifice than Cain,'—faith not as a doctrine of the reason, but faith as the power for a spiritual and heavenly life.[1] But the history of Cain shows him to have been as worldly in his religion as in his malignity, and that, like the son of the bond-woman, he was born after the flesh, and not by promise.[2] This difference of character made the history of the two men so different, their offerings being alike spontaneous, but from dissimilar motives.

That sacrifice arose rather from God's laws working in human nature than from specific enactment, would appear from other remarkable cases. Thus Abraham, at his tent-door in the plains of Mamre, hastened to prepare a feast for the three heavenly messengers by whose presence he was made happy. The 'calf, tender and good,' the hastily-baked cakes of Sarah, the butter and milk, the water of purification, those usual accompaniments of a sacrifice, were soon in readiness, and

[1] Heb. xi. 4; Gen. iv. 4–7.   [2] Gal. iv. 23.

the patriarch stood under the shade of his oak to wait and tend while the meal was served to his guests.[1] All was spontaneous, gushing up from a fountain of spiritual delight in the soul, and in obedience to no other law. Such was Gideon's sacrifice, when he besought his celestial visitor not to depart till he came bringing a present, and set it before him. He, too, 'brought unleavened cakes, and meat in a basket, and broth in a pot,' which the angel dissolved into flame by fire coming out of the rock, when he took his departure.[2] And Manoah, when made happy by the promise of a son, 'took a kid, with a meat-offering, and offered it upon a rock unto the Lord; and the angel did wondrously; and Manoah and his wife looked on,' 'for he ascended in the flame of the altar.'[3] Though there be no divine command originating sacrifices, with so many like examples before us, how can we doubt that God instituted them through the convivial principle of man's nature, called into exercise in celebrating special visitations from heaven?

The patriarchal history is full of these gracious visitations from God, filling devout souls with ineffable delight: they gave expression to their feelings in the universal language of such occasions, by the killing of animals, by offerings of fruits and libations, by solemn assemblies, sometimes by music and dancing, much the same as when they were made happy by the visits of their earthly friends.[4] The paschal supper and the Jewish feasts were provided for by law, not as originating sacrifices, but as reducing to form and doctrine the results of a spontaneous impulse which had wrought in holy men from the beginning of time.

[1] Gen. xviii. 1-8. [2] Judg. vi. 11-21. [3] Judg. xiii. 19, 20.
[4] Lev. iv. 15; Judg. xxi. 21; Deut. xvi. 14-17; Ex. xv. 20, 21; 2 Sam. vi. 12-14.

The corrupted ritualism of heathen nations had doubtless a similar origin, being either derived from the early patriarchs or from their own imaginary visits from their gods. Agamemnon feasted his heroes in honour of the gods to celebrate his victories. The gods of Olympus had their feasts, when they were excited to laughter by limping Vulcan acting as cup-bearer, which were no doubt types of the royal celebrations in Homer's time, rather than of anything occurring among the celestials. Heathen offerings were largesses given to the malignant divinities, such as those with which they bought the favour of their tyrants, and sometimes consisted of human sacrifices.[1] They hoped thus to commute with Heaven for the punishment of their crimes, and buy the privilege of sinning, like the Catholics, in paying for priestly dispensations. These tendencies of human nature are universal; and can we wonder that sacrifices should have arisen without an express command? They have a history in the workings of the human soul, just as every thought in a child's mind has a long series of antecedent sensations, sympathies, and endeavours.

Jesus took advantage of this feature of human nature, in giving us His last supper as a perpetual memorial of Himself. As in the old dispensation redeeming truths, in anticipation of their fuller revelation by the Messiah, were symbolized by sacrifices, feasts, and various ceremonials, so we celebrate them as accomplished facts which we would ever keep in mind. Our memorial is simple, deriving its significance from the greatness of the facts, and not from the imposing character of the ceremonial. The whole

[1] 2 Kings iii. 27.

ritual worship of holy men from Adam to Christ, however, had in view the reality of redemption as a recovery from the world, the flesh, and the devil, to walk with God as Enoch[1] did. They had the truth as an experience of inward power, though not as a symbolized doctrine. Abel, Noah, Abraham, and others, were priests of the Most High each in his day, who resorted to sacrifice in the exercise of their function, and to express their joyful fellowship with heavenly beings. 'God had respect unto them;' the witness of it they had in their inmost being; it was like the smiles of grace still felt in believing souls, the Lord testifying of their gifts;[2] and they constitute an order of events which are the most potential facts of history. They are God's tokens, not by creeds and laws, but in what is antecedent to both, except the creed and law of supreme love and obedience to God. They are the white stone with a new name, which no man knoweth, saving he that receiveth it; a token of hospitality which gives unfailing access to the hidden manna that really comes down from heaven.[3] Abel's experience was that of Bunyan's Pilgrim at a view of the cross, when his burden left him; it was the same with Jacob's in Luz, and of Augustine and Edwards, which have before been noticed. A like experience in the Mayflower Pilgrims took them to New England, to realize among nature's wilds and savage men their own exalted ideal of spiritual life in God. It wrought powerfully in Luther, and Knox, and Calvin, and others, to precipitate the great Reformation. It was fire in their bones, and they could but speak and act in setting forth God's truth to an ungodly age.[4]

[1] Gen. v. 22.
[2] Heb. xi. 4.
[3] Rev. ii. 17; John vi. 32, 33.
[4] Jer. xx. 9; Ps. xxxix. 3.

God's power in the soul will find expression, as by the sacrificed lamb in Abel, the ladder in Jacob, the Reformation in Luther and his coadjutors; in the religious settlement of the New World by earnest men; in the field preaching of Whitfield and the Wesleys; in the missions of Brainerd, Martyn, and others. 'All these worketh that one and the same Spirit.'[1] Who will say that these are not potential facts of history?

Though piety before Abraham's time, a period of about two thousand years, was without organization or symbolized doctrines, yet its spirit was the same as now; in reference to which our Lord no doubt speaks when He says, 'Before Abraham was, I am,'—a thought that refers, I think, not merely to eternity of being, but to His working in the earliest times, in reference to which Jesus says, 'Abraham rejoiced to see my day; and he saw it, and was glad.'[2] Under that patriarch the doctrines of the gospel took form; and 'the Scripture, foreseeing that God would justify the heathen through faith, preached before the gospel unto Abraham, saying, In thee shall all nations be blessed.'[3] Justification to Abraham was precisely what it had been before to pious men, consisting in no outward form, but in the restored life of God in the soul. To call anything short of this justification, or to speak of a man under the power of his lusts as right with God, is to call slavery freedom, and hell heaven.

The doctrine of the *new birth*, as consisting in a separation from our carnal state to live and walk in the Spirit, is the first doctrine set forth in Abraham's history: 'Get thee out of thy country, and from thy kindred, and from thy father's house, unto a land that

[1] 1 Cor. xii. 11.   [2] John viii. 56-58.   [3] Gal. iii. 8; Gen. xii. 3.

I will show thee.'[1] What Abraham's life had previously been we are not told, except that he lived among ancestors who 'served other gods,' having their household divinities, and therefore the unfitting associates of one solely devoted to Jehovah.[2] The historical fact of his transfer to Canaan was the symbol of a great truth—that no man since the fall can become a servant of God, without a separation from his old life in the flesh, and becoming a new man in Christ Jesus. It was an acted, not a written, doctrine with Abraham, and yet is the same with that so often expressed by the apostles: 'Ye see your *calling*, brethren;' 'that ye may know what is the hope of your *calling*;' 'ye are *called* in one hope of your calling;' 'the prize of the high *calling* of God in Christ Jesus;' 'we pray always that God may count you worthy of this *calling*;' 'make your *calling* and election sure.' 'Come out from among them, and be ye separated, saith the Lord, and touch not the unclean thing; and I will receive you, and will be a father unto you, and ye shall be my sons and daughters, saith the Lord Almighty.' Indeed, the acted principle of the Hebrew polity, as well as of the Christian church, was one of detachment from other nations, or from a fleshly life and worldly men, to signify a difference of origin, like being born of spirit and being born of flesh.[3]

Abraham's first step, therefore, symbolized a great doctrine, the lack of which seems to have caused the retrocession of his ancestors into idolatry, as it had the sons of God before the flood into voluptuousness. Though in spirit separated from the world, they were

[1] Gen. xii. 1.   [2] Josh. xxiv. 2; Gen. xxxi. 30-35.
[3] 1 Cor. i. 26; Eph. iv. 4; Phil. iii. 14; 2 Thess. i. 11; 2 Tim. i. 9; Heb. iii. 1; 2 Pet. i. 10; 2 Cor. vi. 17, 18; John iii. 6, vi. 63.

not in fact, but lived intermixed with the carnal and worldly, and hence their apostasy. Abraham lived a life of separation, or of consecration, and thus symbolized a doctrine which has become a permanent article of the true faith.

Another doctrine brought out in his life is that of a *divine call*, as the source of all true godliness. True religion is not intellectual culture, nor a change of opinion, nor a new status of the outward life; but it is an infusion of grace, or a new life, from God. 'Ye have not chosen me, but I have chosen you.' 'We love Him, because He first loved us.'[1] Why should God interest Himself in recovering us from our natural state, if there was any possibility of our doing it for ourselves? Can the guilty make themselves innocent? Theology is prior to the church, as seeding is before the harvest. Abraham might have emigrated to Syria from Mesopotamia, as thousands of others in all ages have changed countries; and it would have had no significance beyond the improvement of his worldly condition. But doing it in obedience to a call from God gave a religious character to the act, and made it to all subsequent ages the symbol of a life directed by the Spirit of God instead of our natural impulses. As a man must live before performing the functions of life, so a soul dead in sin must be quickened together with Christ before beginning his pilgrimage to the New Jerusalem. The outward shaping of the church in any particular age is somewhat like the course of a river, which meanders through valleys, rushes in cascades, or winds around mountains, according to the country through which it flows. Abraham's life was nomadic, like that of the

[1] John xv. 19; 1 John iv. 19.

tribes among whom he lived. The institutions of Moses were a revision of many previous customs, adapting them to sacred uses, and the subsequent career of his nation became a part of general history, being more or less mixed up with the ideas and doings of other nations; while the Christian church took form from the synagogue worship, and was more or less modified by the state of civil society. Thus the heavenly call or power wrought out its results like leaven in meal, not to convert barley into wheat, but to assimilate both the one and the other class of mind and culture into its own forms of spiritual thought and feeling. It melts Jew and Gentile into one spirit, not into one form of civil government, nor into the same social customs, modes of dress, or general usage. Those who think to accept Christian doctrine as something dropped into them directly from heaven will be disappointed. 'Search the Scriptures,' said our Lord; 'Compare spiritual things with spiritual,'[1] taught an apostle; neither of which can be done without going over the inspired documents from Moses to John the evangelist. This is the channel through which the pure river of doctrine comes from God to us; and let no one demur at following up this river because it flows upon rocks, around headlands, over sands, and through regions so much more barbarous and inhospitable than our own. Truths from God must be sought in the writings which He has dictated in histories, and institutions moulded by His own hand.

Covenant relationship to God is another doctrine lived by Abraham. It is 'avouching the Lord to be our God, to walk in His ways, and to keep His statutes, and commandments, and judgments, and to hearken unto His

[1] John v. 39; 1 Cor. ii. 13.

voice;' and it is to have 'God avouch us to be His peculiar people.'[1] This is a personal matter between God and our own souls, and cannot be done by proxy. It admits of no sham, but is a great fact of the inward life, in which God alone reveals Himself. It is admitting God to the throne of our hearts, in place of that world by which we have been so long and so disastrously ruled. A man under the oath of allegiance to a government is bound in all things by its laws and institutions. And when God said to Abraham, 'My covenant is between thee and me,' and the agreement was ratified by mutual consent, there was no disannulling it, or avoiding its responsibilities: 'It was an everlasting covenant.'[2] Whatever God should require, the soul under such bonds is bound to do.

But could he do it without *faith?* How could a soul be justified or right with God, without implicitly relying upon all that God told him? Unbelief unsettles confidence and annuls the contract. God has no outward police to compel submission in a refractory spirit. When our will rebels, the flesh is supreme in us, and how can we serve God and the world at the same time?[3] How can we be in covenant with hostile forces? The compact with God takes effect primarily upon our souls, and is an individual and not a community transaction.[4] The nation of Israel did indeed stand for a time in that relation; but it was for the special purpose of representing outwardly the spiritual compact between individual souls and God. They lost their position, however, through unbelief, and the apostles explicitly show, that 'only they which are of

---

[1] Deut. xxvi. 17, 18.   [2] Gen. xvii. 3-7, 13.   [3] Luke xvi. 13.
[4] It becomes a community influence, by 'baptizing those who feel it into one body,' the church. 1 Cor. xii. 13.

faith are the children of faithful Abraham.'[1] Our faith, like that of Abraham, must have its trials; and 'by works it must be made perfect,' as his was when he offered up his only son of promise, and thus became heir of the world, and the father of all that believe.[2] Who does not see that the significance of this transaction is in elevating faith to its true position, as that exercise by which spiritual truths are made real and potential to us, and which alone makes us pleasing to God and in union with Him? This is everywhere the doctrine of faith in the New Testament.[3]

The *Divine Incarnation* is another doctrine included in Abraham's history. 'He saith not, To seeds, as of many, but as of one, And to thy seed, which is Christ,' is the apostle's reasoning on the subject.[4] The Incarnation in the person of Christ was in order to the indwelling of the Holy Spirit in the church; as He Himself says, 'I in them, and Thou in me, that they may be made perfect in one;' or as the apostle expresses it, 'that we might receive the promise of the Spirit through faith.' 'This promise is to you and your children, and to all that are afar off, even as many as the Lord our God shall call,' as He called Abraham to a spiritual and holy life.[5] All these passages are founded in the old Hebrew idea of the *nephesh* or soul as open to two worlds, the spiritual and the natural, and the destined sanctuary and throne of the Most High in establishing His kingdom here below. It had been lost by man's rejection of God in order to come

---

[1] Gal. iii. 7-9; Rom. iv. 9-13, ix. 8.
[2] Jas. ii. 21-23; Gen. xxii. 9-12.
[3] Heb. xi. 6; John xi. 25, 26, iii. 36; Mark xvi. 16; Acts xvi. 31.
[4] Gal. iii. 16; Gen. xii. 3, 7.
[5] John xvii. 23; Gal. iii. 14; Acts ii. 39.

under the ruling of the flesh, and is now restored in the faith of Abraham and in his promised seed as the re-enthroned Divinity in all that believe. This is the doctrine of Abraham's seed.

Circumcision also was more a doctrine than a fact. As a fact, it was a mark of distinction between Israel and other nations; but as a doctrine, 'it is of the heart, in the spirit, and not in the flesh.' 'We are the circumcision, who worship God in the spirit, and rejoice in Christ Jesus, having no confidence in the flesh;' it is 'made without hands, in putting off the body of the sins of the flesh, by the circumcision of Christ,' or by the excision of worldly desires by His grace operating in our souls.[1] Even the prophets deduced from the rite a like significance, calling upon the people to circumcise their hearts, to put away their worldly appetites, and come under God's spiritual dominion.[2] Here we have the same ideas brought to view as in our baptism, in which we are buried and raised with Christ, as the apostle shows, and are 'sanctified and cleansed with the washing of water by the word, that we may be presented to Christ a glorious church, not having spot, or wrinkle, or any such thing; but that it should be holy and without blemish.'[3] Thus in all the rites and histories of the Old Testament come to view underlying doctrines of man's spiritual state, and the changes which it undergoes in redeeming him to God out of every kingdom, and tongue, and people under heaven. All are founded in the fact of the soul's twofold relations to spirit and to matter.

Another doctrine of Abraham's career is that of

---

[1] Rom. ii. 29; Phil. iii. 3; Col. ii 11.
[2] Deut. x. 16; Jer. iv. 4.
[3] Col. ii. 12; Eph. v. 26, 27.

heaven as an aggregation of kindred spirits. 'In a good old age, an old man, full of days and satisfied, he was gathered to his people.' 'Satisfied,' as the word means, or happy to go, like a man from a long journey reposing again in the bosom of his family, he took his place in 'the better country, that is, an heavenly; wherefore God is not ashamed to be called their God: for He hath prepared for them a city.' And our Lord adduces the fact that God called Himself 'the God of Abraham' as evidence of the soul's immortality; 'for He is not a God of the dead, but of the living.'[1] Abraham never owned a foot of the land in which he sojourned, except a burial-place for his dead, showing how entirely his hopes centred in the promised seed and in his heavenly home. In Abraham's history, therefore, fact is doctrine, and doctrine is fact.

[1] Gen. xxiii. 3, 4, xvii. 20, xxv. 8; Heb. xi. 16; Matt. xxii. 32.

CHAPTER XVI.

DOCTRINE IN WORDS AND SYMBOLS.

AS doctrinal truths were inward experiences or intuitions to the early patriarchs, and history in Abraham so under Moses they took on the form of words and symbols. The process reminds one of growth in a child's mind from sensations to ideas, and from ideas to words and symbols. The endeavour of sensation is towards thought, and of thought towards expression. Thus, twenty-five hundred years of detached revelations and experiences among holy men at length found embodiment in the ceremonial law. And they were still further chiselled out in the Israelitish history. The redemption of that people from Egyptian slavery by power and a stretched-out arm symbolized our escape from the bondage of the flesh by the power of grace; their wilderness life of forty years, and partial conquest of Canaan, where many enemies remained as 'pricks in their eyes and thorns in their hands,'[1] is a type of our earthly warfare and partial sanctification; their apostasy and subsequent captivity but too faithfully resemble our backsliding and its sad consequences; and thus the whole outward life of that nation put into form and expression the inward working of antagonistic forces in Christ's church.

Our purpose is not to expound these symbols, but

[1] Num. xxxiii. 55.

to show their position and necessity in redemption, or in recovering a people to God's praise out of this corrupted and enslaved world. The ceremonial law and Jewish history will be found singularly pertinent to what the seers saw in the nature of man.

Truths are realities, and words the expression of them. Words and symbols are the soil which the seed must take on in order to a harvest. They do not originate truths nor change their nature, but put them into a form to be understood and used by men in the flesh. Multiplication and interest tables do not make or alter the relation of numbers, but they are a great convenience to learners and business men. So spiritual truths existed in full force before they were expressed in terms to be apprehended by us. But now that they are so expressed, our business is to search for them in words and symbols as for hid treasures. 'Search the Scriptures;' 'Hold fast the form of sound words;' 'Having the form of knowledge and truth in the law;'— these are passages that clearly show where saving truths are to be found, and our duty in reference to them.[1] The practice of Christ and His apostles, of casting their ideas in the symbolical mould of the Old Testament, is an example for us; and those who follow it the most closely make the most effective sermons, and have the greatest spiritual power. The essay style of our modern pulpit is mere moonshine in comparison. Books to melt the truths of the Bible into the fashionable literature of the present day are a dead failure. We can scarcely better dispense with Bible words and symbols than with Bible truths themselves. 'The form of sound words' is as much a revelation from God as the doctrines which they contain.

[1] Prov. ii. 4; 2 Tim. i. 13; Rom. ii. 20.

God's plan of symbolizing His truths proceeds on the principle that the world was as destitute of appropriate modes of expressing them as of the truths themselves. Indeed, how should it be otherwise? How can men invent words to express ideas which are not in their minds? Ideas must precede and create a necessity for language before language can exist. And as spiritual truths had perished from the human mind, except in detached cases, and natural ideas alone remained, how could the languages that took their rise from Babel under these circumstances be a fitting vehicle of a revelation from heaven? As well use a Hottentot dialect to express Locke's work on the Understanding. In all languages, the etymology of words shows that they had their origin in material ideas. Soul was breath; spirit, wind; understanding, standing under; circumspect, looking around; circumvent, coming round: and thus words, even most abstract and spiritual in their present meaning, began with a material idea. There are a few exceptions in words used by inspired men; as Jehovah, for instance, made from the verb to be, and meaning Being or Eternal, which is a special invention to denote an idea utterly lost to the nations.[1] They had their *Elohim* or local gods,—a term often applied to Jehovah, but in a very different sense from their use of it.

Greek is confessed to be the most finished language in the world, and was deeply imbued with poetry, philosophy, and oratory; and yet it had no terms to express a single New Testament doctrine, except as Hebraized or accommodated to its new use. De Quincey says justly, that 'the ancients (meaning the Greeks and Romans before the time of Christianity) had no idea, not by the faintest vestige, of what in the scrip-

[1] Ex. vi. 3.

tural system is called *sin*. The Latin word *peccatum*, and the Greek word *amartia*, are translated continually by the word sin; but neither one word nor the other has any such meaning in writers of the pure classical period. When baptized into a new meaning by the adoption of Christianity, these words, in common with many others, transmigrated into new philosophical functions. But originally they tended towards no such acceptations, nor could have done so; seeing that the ancients had no avenue opened to them through which the profound idea would have been even dimly intelligible. Plato, four hundred years before Christ, or Cicero, more than three hundred years later, was fully equal to the idea of *guilt* in all its gamut; but no more equal to the idea of *sin*, than a sagacious hound to the idea of gravitation or central forces. It is the tremendous postulate upon which this idea reposes that constitutes the initial moment of that revelation which is common to Judaism and Christianity.' He then adds, in words before quoted: 'Guilt, in all its modifications, implies only a defect or wound in the individual. Sin, on the other hand, the most mysterious and the most sorrowful of all ideas, implies a taint in the individual, not through any local disease of his own, but through a scrofula equally diffused through the infinite family of man. This idea was utterly and exquisitely inappreciable by pagan Greece or Rome.'[1]

The race of man from Adam to Moses, a period of twenty-five hundred years, was so occupied and dominated by natural or fleshly ideas, as to completely lose the sense of its moral and spiritual status. Though infinitely removed from the spiritual life of Eden, they were as insensible of it as we of the millions of miles

[1] Am. ed. of his works, pp. 238, 239.

intervening in absolute space between our location in summer and winter, because we have no faculties by which to detect the earth's daily movement in its orbit. Men had no landmarks by which to tell what holiness is, or how far they had wandered from it. How, then, should they have any words or symbols to express a true idea of either sin or holiness? To impart to them spiritual truths was even a greater task than to elevate the lowest and most beastly race of savages to the highest state of civilisation.

The words and symbols of doctrine were created to meet this great necessity. It must be an outward process, of course, because there was no chance of developing the requisite truths and ideas from within, as thoughts spring from sensations, and words from thoughts, in the growth of a child. 'Who can bring a clean thing out of an unclean? Not one.'[1] As the human mind had become closed to all but natural ideas, in order to reach it at all, it must be through that channel in reference to which God is said to 'come down to deliver,' to 'come down upon Mount Sinai,' to 'bow the heavens and come down.'[2] There is no change of location in God, but only of His attitude in dealing with us, which was originally through the spiritual or higher faculties of our nature, but now through our natural or lower faculties. He condescends to us, since we cannot rise to Him. He knocks at the outer gateway of the soul, seeing that the inner is closed. We meet with God by attending prayerfully to the outward word, and opening to Him that door, that He may 'come in and sup with us, and we with Him.'[3] The apostle expresses a like idea, when he speaks of

---

[1] Job xiv. 4.   [2] Ex. iii. 8; Num. xi. 17; Isa. lxiv. 1.
[3] Rev. iii. 20.

talking as with babes to those who were too carnal to be spoken to as men. He condescended to their low apprehensions.[1] The material forms of the ceremonial law grew out of this necessity of reaching men through this carnal channel, and thus educating them to the effigy of spiritual truths, preparatory to their ultimately receiving those truths in their own nature, or as 'spiritually discerned.'[2]

But why not do all this at once? Why protract the process through two thousand years? Was not God able to do it for all men, as He did it for Abraham and Moses? No, not in accordance with His own laws of moral agency and development. These inspired men had been prepared for their mission, not only by their own training, but by ages of previous divine illumination descending from their forefathers, and centring in their minds. Is it not easier to induct into science one born of scientific ancestors, than one born in a savage condition, and of savage forefathers? The writer claims no ability to explain the motives of God's conduct, but only to interpret obvious facts. The fire from heaven must have wood and a victim to light upon; and also it must work its miracle of burning among minds attent and anxious for the settlement of great moral questions, as with Elijah on Mount Carmel; or how could a spiritual result be expected to ensue? The whole nation was 'halting' between the worship of Jehovah and that of Baal, and the fire came to settle their minds. A band of savages might have stared at the burning, but it would have conveyed no lesson to their minds, for lack of previous preparation.[3]

But why did not God create among men the requisite preparation, so as to complete the whole work in a

[1] 1 Cor. iii. 1.   [2] 1 Cor. ii. 14.   [3] 1 Kings xviii. 17-40.

single generation? The answer is obvious: it would have withdrawn them from the moral category, and reduced them to a government of force, like the changes of the seasons. Man's free moral selfhood cannot be influenced in a way to invade its prerogatives, without making him merely a thing to be disposed of by natural laws; and the result would be neither spiritual nor moral. Within its castle of free-will the soul is absolute, and no being in the universe more carefully respects its authority than God Himself, as His dealings with an untoward and rebellious race from the beginning of time fully show. If it were in our power, as in His, to annihilate the things which we deem giant wrongs, how long would they hold out? The Pope's Œcumenical Council would be deluged with ashes from Vesuvius, like Pompeii and Herculaneum, if our policy were to prevail instead of His, who 'suffereth long, and is kind.'[1] Man's freedom would have perished, and his hope of spirituality with it, had God acted on our narrow policy in governing the world. When the Spirit's baptism came on Pentecost, it came to men extraordinarily prepared, not only by their intercourse with the Son of God, but by a two thousand years' previous history, shaping their thought and their language, and preparing the world for their message. Scarce a province could be found on which the religion of Abraham and Moses had not reflected its light.

Look now at a few of the truths chiselled by the ceremonial law into relief upon the granite surface of human nature. Take, for example, the distinction between clean and unclean, in beasts, persons, utensils, garments, places, and everything pertaining to daily life. It was sure death to a person deemed unclean

[1] 1 Cor. xiii. 4.

to obtrude within the sacred precincts of the temple. More than once, Paul's intercourse with the Gentiles well-nigh cost him his life among the Jews. Peter could be persuaded only by a miracle to enter a Gentile's house.[1] To eat with unwashen hands was an enormous crime.[2] These and a thousand other things, perverted no doubt, yet even in their perversion showed how deeply Moses' law had ploughed the distinction between clean and unclean into the Jewish mind, and through that people into a wide area of Gentile thought and feeling. When, therefore, this thought and feeling were turned from ceremonial to moral pollution, as consisting in the general depravity of the race and in all wrong-doing, how tremendous were the ensuing throes of conviction! Under Peter's sermon three thousand suddenly awoke to such a sense of their utter moral corruption, as to cry out at once, 'Men and brethren, what shall we do?'[3] Their participation in our Lord's crucifixion no doubt wrought in their minds; but their training under the law, giving them an intense horror of being considered unclean before God, no doubt had its effect. The time had come, foretold by the prophet, when they should discern the real distinction between clean and unclean—that it was not ceremonial, but in being righteous or wicked, serving God or serving Him not.[4] They now first understood what it is to be unclean.

The ceremonial law reduced to symbol truths that became power under the gospel, as the building of the tabernacle provided a seat for the theocratic government. Without some such embodiment to the idea of men, or upon which their materialized thought

[1] Acts x. 28.
[2] Matt. xv. 2.
[3] Acts ii. 37.
[4] Mal. iii. 18.

might take hold, spiritual truths could have gained no foothold in human nature. They must be seen acting in outward life, or they would be, like numerical abstractions or unexpressed geometrical relations, utterly inaccessible to minds without spiritual apprehension. And now that these truths are expressed in the altar service of the Jewish tabernacle, the terms and forms of thought thence derived have become essential to the understanding and propagation of them. A latitudinarian missionary, who, in disgust of Hebraistic forms of thought, should invent some other vocabulary with which to graft Christian ideas upon the pure reason of the literary Chinese, for instance, would live and die in a nightmare. It would be an agonized effort to speak without a voice, and to be heard by those who have no ears. The forms of thought supplied by the law of Moses and Hebrew history are as much a part of Christianity as a man's body is of himself.

It may be difficult to illustrate our precise idea of the position of ceremonial law and Hebrew history in the plan of redeeming mercy. Suppose, however, that there was no civilisation in the world, no such nations as London, Paris, and New York represent, but all mankind were Caffres and Patagonians, and an attempt were made to introduce civilisation, how should it proceed? Suppose the more favoured denizens of another planet were to engage in the work, could they do anything with words explaining a condition of civilisation; its advantages over a savage state; its sciences, arts, and exquisite refinements in thought and manners? No, for the languages of earth would have no words for such ideas. And how could they teach by example, when no model community could be offered to their consideration? and if there were, a savage mind would deem his own state vastly preferable. What could be done in the case, but to introduce law and order into things pertaining to daily savage life? These they understand; and by enacting under severe penalties that they must wash themselves every day, to recover them from their filthy habits, you come within the range of their comprehension. They are cannibals, or they eat the vilest animals; and by putting them upon a specific diet on pain of death, you give them some notion of clean and unclean, or of the food fit for a civilised people. They have no standard of right and justice among themselves, and this must be enacted and enforced. And so of everything relating to their enjoyments. Law and order are essential elements of civilisation, as well as truth, justice, and intelligence; and these can be enforced in reference to the lowest things of life equally with those which are highest, and the one may be made to reflect the other. And the term law as used by the apostles, though it has respect to the ceremonies required by Moses, manifestly includes, by representation, something far higher and more spiritual than the outward acts in which they consisted.[1] So of the civilising process which we have supposed: though beginning with the things on a level with a savage, still it would be to represent law in a higher sense, as pertaining to greater intellectual advancement.

Now the foregoing case is an approximate statement of the position of the ceremonial law, 'which stood only in meats and drinks, and divers washings, and carnal ordinances,' 'a figure for the time then present,' but 'imposed until the time of reformation,' or till men

[1] Rom. ii. 15, 20, 25, iii. 19-31, v. 13-20; Gal. ii. 16-21; Heb. vii. 11.

could be educated up to something better.[1] The holy place, or outer sanctuary, where the priests performed their daily ministrations, being open to the comers and goers in the surrounding courts, gives an idea of the natural faculties of man illuminated by divine truth as represented in the candlestick,[2] showing that those activities which are concerned about the affairs of this life, are to be guided by the law of God. These ministrations in outward things had thus a spiritual significance, just as laws regulating a savage life would be with a view to something higher. Separated from this room by a thin veil was the holy of holies, where were the ark, the tables of the law, the cherubim, and the earthly throne of Jehovah, who administered there by visible tokens the government of His people. It was then a kingdom of symbols; it is now a kingdom of grace; but hereafter it is to be a kingdom of glory. The way into the holy of holies is our medium of access to God through the human nature of Christ, who says, 'I am the way,' and 'No man cometh unto the Father but by me.'[3] The clean animals, as alone fit for sacrifice, are the purified affections and the holy life, which God can alone accept as offerings from us. The universal sprinkling of blood shows the necessary inflowing spiritual current of life from God, of which blood is the emblem, to render our prayers and offerings, and everything pertaining to our activities, acceptable to God. As the inbreathed life from God made Adam spiritual, and put a heavenly impress upon his whole outward life, so with us, it is 'the spirit that quickeneth, the flesh profiteth nothing;'[4] and our whole

[1] Heb. ix. 6–12.   [2] Heb. ix. 2.
[3] Heb. ix. 8; John xiv. 6; Eph. ii. 13.
[4] Lev. xxii. 20, 21, 25; John vi. 63; Eph. v. 27; Heb. xiii. 15.

being is thus purified by what blood represents.[1] The burning of the refuse without the camp, and the escape of the duplicate goat, denote a total annihilation of our fleshly impurities, or their 'separation from us as far as the east is from the west.'[2]

These are a few of the points which show the general spirit of the Mosaic ritual, as reflecting a character purified from fleshly ruling, and restored to God's dominion in the soul. How clearly do they contemplate a state of perfection far in advance of the present attainments of professing Christians! We have an example of the sort of life contemplated by the law, in Him who came to fulfil all righteousness, and to magnify the law and make it honourable.[3] He fulfilled and magnified it, by converting its doctrine into fact, its shadow into substance. This He did, not as John the Baptist, by leading an ascetic life, but by attending weddings, feasts, and mingling in all the affairs of men, and subjecting them to the absolute ruling of the 'Spirit which God gave Him without measure.'[4] There are ideas of power in God's appointed symbols of faith which have never been fully reached except by the God-man.

Thus altar, sacrifice, holy place, holy of holies, the tabernacle and its ceremonial, with God's administered government over Israel from Dan to Beersheba, were to the material age for which they were instituted, what object-teaching is to our children. This is a sort of teaching to which the infant is committed as soon as he opens his eyes upon the world; and it would be vain for us to attempt anything for him higher than

---

[1] Ex. xxiv. 5-8; Lev. xvii. 11; Heb. ix. 22; 1 John iii. 5, i. 7.
[2] Lev. iv. 11, 12, xvi. 8-10; Ps. ciii. 12; 2 Cor. vii. 1; Eph. v. 4.
[3] Matt. iii. 15; Isa. xlii. 21.   [4] John iii. 34.

sensible impressions, if these had not first supplied him with a fund of ideas as the basis of a more intellectual life. We show him sheep, oxen, lions, trees, triangles, squares, parallelograms, circles, cones, and tell him that they are called so and so, and have such and such natures and uses, and by this process it was that the greatest minds rose to power and pre-eminence. By a like process, God has educated a materialized race to spiritual truth and heavenly life. Words would be an empty sound, without truths in the mind for them to represent.

CHAPTER XVII.

WORDS AND SYMBOLS IN POWER.

THE power of words and symbols is not in arguments to convince the reason, nor in imposing scenes to impress the senses, nor in eloquence to move the feelings, but in an energy from God acting through them to restore our consciousness of His presence, and of our amenableness to Him. As there is a spiritual universe of which our race had lost the view by reason of sin, and it must regain its place in our minds in order to the due balance of our characters, nothing can avail with us which does not effect this object. No one who reads the Bible can fail to see that it was penned by men to whom the realm of spirits was as much a reality as that of nature, and its truths and facts transcendently the greater of the two. The one is mind, the other body; the one imperishable, the other perishable; and as every voluntary muscular movement is an act of the mind, so all material events, from the feeding and falling of sparrows, the numbering of our hairs, and the painting of lilies, to the ordering of the heavens with their luminaries, are acts of an infinite and everywhere-present intelligence. Viewing things thus is the habit of all spiritual men.[1]

The general state of thought and feeling among men,

[1] Matt. vi. 26-30, x. 29, 30; Ps. viii. 3.

it must be obvious, is quite otherwise. 'God is not in all their thoughts,' and they prosecute their enterprises with indistinct and unavailing conceptions of anything above and beyond their earthly life.[1] Or if they give attention to church-going, Sabbath-keeping, or other exercises implying a higher world, it is more with regard to the decencies of society than from any inward feeling of their relationship to God and immortality. Many have great talent with little conscience, 'ever learning, but never able to come to the knowledge of the truth ;' growing rich perhaps, but not 'towards God;' having a wide intellectual grasp, but no wisdom to give it a beneficent direction.[2] They are paralytic on the side towards God and the spiritual universe, turning all their force upon the world-side, which is, however, encumbered, misdirected, and unavailing. Is it not easy to see, that the first thing in healing them is to restore this paralyzed side to its sensibility to God and spiritual truths? Can a conscienceless man have his other powers improved, without danger to himself and society?

Much is said of setting men right with their condition; a necessity which all parties concede, though they differ widely as to how it is to be done: Some speak as if education and civilisation were the only panacea; others think the cure must be effected by exploding all ghostly ideas, and bringing men to the positive and the tangible, or to live according to what they call nature; and others still insist upon submission to a worldly hierarchy and its rites, in order to ensure present peace and future salvation. But the inspired writers have but one idea on the subject,

---

[1] Ps. x. 4, xiv. 1, liii. 1.
[2] 2 Tim. iii. 7 ; Luke xii. 21 ; Ps. xciv. 11.

which is, that as God and spiritual truths have lost their hold upon us, and this is the primary source of our evils, there is no setting us right but by re-establishing their dominion, and bringing us to the faith that acts as 'seeing Him who is invisible.' This is a separate transaction between every soul and God; and words and symbols are the intermediate means of carrying on the negotiation. Training is not the thing; civilisation is not the thing; a priesthood is not the thing; words and rites are a dead letter, in themselves considered; but it is to be 'quickened together with Christ,' in the sense of having our lost spiritual connection with God and His throne re-established within.[1]

This sensible connection with God, as the only perfection for human nature, is the thought with which the Bible begins, and it is that with which it ends. The divine inbreathing opened heaven to the first man; he talked with God; and with the clear vision of a seer he no doubt 'saw the Lord sitting upon His throne, and all the host of heaven standing by Him on the right hand and on the left,' his purity of heart fitting him for such a vision; and he lived the life of heaven here below.[2] But when he fell under the ruling of fleshly impulses and natural ideas, all this was lost; and God, even to those who are restored to Him, is seen not by a vision, but by faith. 'The just shall live by faith;' and 'believing, we rejoice with joy unspeakable and full of glory.'[3] Faith with us takes the place of vision with Adam and the inspired prophets, in giving reality to the spiritual world. It

---

[1] Eph. ii. 5; Col. ii. 13; Matt. vi. 10.
[2] Gen. ii. 19, 20; Matt. v. 8; 1 Kings xxii. 19.
[3] Matt. xi. 27; Heb. xi. 27; 1 Pet. i. 8; Hab. ii. 4; Heb. x. 38; Gal. iii. 11; Rom. i. 17.

is as if lightning and thunder had at first made electricity visible to men, but afterwards ceased; so that though now, as ever, animal and vegetable life is pervaded by this fluid, and subsists by means of it, yet it can only reveal itself to our faith from an electric battery, and not, as formerly, by flashes to the eyes and intonations to the ears. To do this, the battery must be more than mechanism; it must be charged with a power wholly unlike itself, of which it must act as the medium to our nerves and muscles. Electricity gives us the shock, not the battery; and that shock becomes the basis of our faith in what we have not seen. So of words and symbols; unless charged with a spiritual power totally distinct from themselves, they can produce no faith, and no salvation. Is not faith the gift of God?[1]

Words and symbols, then, are the battery, but spirit is the power. We must be in some way assured that God is speaking to us, and that the spiritual world is no delusion. Preaching and ceremonials unattended by this cannot be the power of God unto salvation. The process is not one of education, but of *regeneration*; not a development of what was before in us, but a 'creation in the image of Him that created him;' and it is the work not of the Adam who was 'a living soul,' but of the Adam who is a 'quickening spirit.' All these truths of the divine word concur in this, that though God's dominion over us is re-established, it is different from the old, in being one of faith rather than of open vision.[2]

Can we wonder, therefore, that a Book of such aims should deal largely in the supernatural? Whether its

[1] Eph. ii. 8.
[2] Matt. xix. 28; Tit. iii. 5; Col. iii. 10; John iii. 3; 1 Cor. xv. 45-48.

miracles are true or false is not the point for us to consider in these pages; but whether, admitting that there is a spiritual world, to which our minds had been closed, it can be reopened to us, except by means which are out of the order of nature? As our minds had been dominated by things in that order, to the extent of losing the consciousness of anything beyond, how can what is beyond be opened to us otherwise than by miracle? If the miracles of the Bible fail us, we must look for them elsewhere, to put us into communication with a higher world. The supernatural claims of the Bible are what most of all fit it to our necessities. Signs and wonders attested the mission of Moses, of our Lord, and of all the prophets. God maintained His position on the mercy-seat of the temple, giving responses to the people out of the order of nature, so long as its ritual retained its efficacy. The Holy Spirit is represented as the sole efficiency in the Christian church, in reference to which our Lord says, 'Without me ye can do nothing,' and, 'Lo, I am with you always, even unto the end of the world.'[1]

It is a favourite idea with some, that miracles are of no force except in an age of infancy and credulity. They ask, What effect would miracles have among a scientific people, who can do things with their sciences which would have been regarded in the ignorant Bible generations as even more wonderful than anything done by the prophets? 'WE depend upon logic and an induction of facts, not upon magic and necromancy.' With how good a grace such a boast comes from an age in which spirit-rappings and Joe Smith's revelations have obtained such foothold, let truth and can-

[1] Ex. iv. 8, 17, xxv. 22; Deut. xviii. 21, 22; Acts ii. 19; John xv. 5; Matt. xxviii. 20.

dour determine. Does this look like the emancipation of the human mind from the influence of miracles? The truth is, men have a natural aptitude for such manifestations; and when cut off from the true spiritual universe, is it wonderful that they should betake themselves to lying miracles? They may be harder to convince of those recorded in the Bible than some former generations, but in reference to all others they are sufficiently gullible.

The truths and events of the Bible are claimed to be by supernatural attestation, as much as English history claims to be a record of the English people. Beings not embodied in flesh are the principal actors, speakers, and dictators from beginning to end. We can hardly read a page without having our thoughts directed to something not in the order of nature. This is a necessity of the case; for how can spirits otherwise reveal themselves to our consciousness? If the burning bush had not been a 'great sight,' and out of the order of Moses' previous experiences, how should he have turned aside to inquire into it? And the voice speaking to him out of the bush, calling him by name, and entrusting with him a great commission, assured him of the miracle, and that he stood on holy ground, and in direct communication with the God of Abraham, of Isaac, and of Jacob. A like attestation was given to Jacob when he said, 'The Lord is in this place, and I knew it not.'[1]

But it may be said, If miracles were ever necessary, why not now? Why do not heavenly beings thus manifest themselves in all ages, and to all men? Because they would then become ordinary events, and would lose the effect of miracles. A single sunrise

[1] Ex. iii. 2-6; Gen. xxviii. 16.

occurring out of the order of nature once in thousands of years would be the greatest of all supernatural manifestations; but coming as it does every morning, it makes little impression. Besides, miracles no more contain in themselves the power to make us spiritual men, than words and symbols. They are a part of the battery through which the requisite power reaches us. They are not educators, but confirmations of the truth, by means of which the Holy Spirit calls us from our death in flesh to spiritual life in God. If God had come down upon Sinai in the wonderful manner described, in the midst of thunder, and lightning, and tempest, and yet no law had been given, and no truths affirmed thereby, what more would it have been than the passing wonder of a day? Men would have gazed, and wondered, and perished.[1] The seemingly supernatural manifestations of modern spiritualism call attention from wondering crowds; but having no great truths of faith and duty to enforce, they fail of the required effect. Nobody is made truly spiritual and holy by their means. But the miracles of Moses established a polity which lasted fifteen hundred years, and exerted a widespread influence upon the affairs of mankind. The Jews exist to this day as a monument of its moulding power; while Christianity, as the realization of its highest ideal, is at the head of our civilising agencies. If miracles contained in themselves the power to raise men to a heavenly life, then they would be alike necessary to all. Our Lord recognises the difference between them and the truths they confirm, in the saying, 'They have Moses and the prophets, let them hear them;' and, 'If they will not hear them, neither will they be persuaded though one rose from the dead.'[2] Those

[1] Ex. xix. 16; Heb. xii. 18-21.   [2] Luke xvi. 29-31.

whom truths fail to reclaim are in no state to be benefited by miracles.

The Old Testament is throughout a miracle. As one has said, 'its prophecies are so numerous, and so closely connected together, that one might regard the Old Testament, considered as a whole, as forming one great prophecy. As soon as sin had entered into the world, it announces, under the name of "the Seed of the woman," a Restorer who will destroy the work of the tempter, and raise fallen man. From this passage, which is found in the third page of the book, the Old Testament is but, as it were, a pre-existing history of the Restorer, and of a certain kingdom which He will found on earth. The country and people of the Messiah are already indicated in the twelfth chapter of Genesis. He was to be born of the seed of Abraham, in the land of Canaan, which God gave to Abraham for this very purpose. It was this well-known promise which led Abraham to Palestine; which brought back his descendants after an exile of four hundred years; in short, which formed the Jewish nation. It is this which leads Pascal to say, that "there is a great difference between a book made by a private individual and sent forth among a nation, and one which makes a nation itself." ... Take from the Jewish history the promise of a Messiah, and you annihilate it. You can no longer account for the origin, nor the religion, nor the manners of this singular people, whose distinctive characteristic has always been, and still is, the expectation of a Messiah.

'After the call of Abraham you may trace the course of prophecy throughout the whole of the Old Testament. You will see it unfold and display itself from age to age, from prophet to prophet, during an interval of two thousand years, till at length it is accomplished in

Jesus Christ, whose name signifies Jesus-Messiah. Each prophet in his turn seems only to have been sent to bear witness of Him, and to add his link to the chain of narrative, in which we find clearly indicated the people descended from Abraham, the tribe of that people, the family of that tribe,—the time, the place, in which the Messiah should appear, with all that He would do, and all that would be done to Him. Hence this profound expression in the Apocalypse, " The testimony of Jesus is the spirit of prophecy."[1] Besides all these prophecies, or rather this perpetual prophecy, the Old Testament contains a succession of facts and institutions which bear reference to the Messiah and to His work. I allude especially to those sacrifices which prefigured a sacrifice to come, and to which, according to Daniel, the Messiah would put an end.[2] And, wonderful to relate, Jesus Christ did indeed put an end to them. They were constantly offered till His appearance, but ceased almost immediately after His death; yet the Jews have the same reason for offering them now which they had before the Christian era, since they are still in expectation of the Saviour for whom their fathers waited.'[3]

A well-attested miracle, as evidence of a power superior to nature, is the same to those who do not witness it as to those who do, the same to every other age as to the one in which it occurred, provided the proof of its existence is well authenticated. But in the case before us there is an unbroken series of proofs from Adam to this day, if the present condition of the Jews be regarded. For if the miracles themselves be not repeated as specific signs and wonders,

[1] Rev. xix. 10.   [2] Dan. viii. 11, xi. 31, xii. 11.
[3] *Lucilla*, by Adolph Monod, pp. 49-51.

what but the veritable record of their existence, as we find it in the Bible, can account for the oneness of idea among that peculiar people in their eighteen hundred years' dispersion among all the nations of the earth,—an idea still so potent among them, as to keep them distinct from those among whom they have so long lived? And when we add to this the influence of Christian truths of a Jewish origin, or as a fulfilment of the Old Testament rites and prophecies, in moulding the present civilisation of Europe, or as the source of its best ideas in religion, morals, civil and common law, personal freedom, institutional charity, and public education,—an influence which no one can deny;—when all these things are considered, I say, the miracles of the Bible become as great a reality to us as to those who witnessed them. Indeed, they are even more potential, just as the life of Christ, as expatiated on by the apostles, made many more converts among those who had never seen Him, than were made by His personal presence among the witnesses of His extraordinary power in word and deed. Quite another process is necessary to make us spiritual men than the surprise and commotion of seeing a miracle. It is a process by which our faith is secured to the truths affirmed by miracle, and our hearts are won to a spiritual and heavenly life.

God's ordinary working in the temple of old, and at present in the Christian ministry, though supernatural, is not, strictly speaking, miraculous; for the good reason that it is ordinary, and follows a fixed connection of cause and effect. 'How shall they call on Him in whom they have not believed? and how shall they believe in Him of whom they have not heard? and how shall they hear without a preacher? and how shall they preach, except they be sent?'[1] These questions reveal an order beginning in miracle, and sustained by influences above nature, though quite in another line from the signs and wonders of inspired men. So, God's daily responses from the mercy-seat, in administering the theocracy of old, were according to a fixed arrangement like the order of nature, though of a character to keep before the minds of the people a power above nature, and of a continual efflux from the spiritual world. It is so under the ministry of the word: when it is in power, we feel that God is speaking to us, and eternal realities open upon us with extraordinary clearness and pungency.

It is proper to add a remark as to the particular rites selected, and the particular miracles wrought in attestation of them. How often are these things thought or spoken of as puerile, and unworthy of God! 'Suppose a man were to do the same things now-a-days, what would be thought of him? If it were known that he was desolating a country or drowning a whole army, the innocent with the guilty, would he not be remonstrated with by every humane society in the world? Why kill a whole herd of defenceless swine in recovering a lunatic to sanity? Would not the Society for Preventing Cruelty to Animals immediately take it up?' Though it is not our mission to apologize for God, or explain the motives of His conduct, we cannot shut our eyes to the fact that rites and miracles, though having one object in all ages—re-establishing God's spiritual authority over man—yet were of a character suited to the particular people for whom they were designed. The ceremonies sanctioned on Sinai, though different in their combina-

[1] Rom. x. 14, 15.

tions and uses from all others, were made of things with which the people were familiar, such as a religious house with its adytum, altars, sacrifices, priestly orders and ceremonies, incense, intercession, and the whole paraphernalia of the tabernacle worship. The demand of Moses for a three days' journey into the wilderness, to do sacrifice with his people, was an idea familiar to Pharaoh and his court, in reference to the surrounding tribes, who worshipped different gods, and in their own chosen sacred places. The nomadic life of Israel in Arabia for forty years was an idea familiar to that country, and is so to this day. The plagues of Egypt were suited to impress a Nile-worshipping, agricultural-loving country; and the escape of Israel through the Red Sea, and the returning tide to overwhelm their pursuing enemies, were best of all fitted to make the Egyptians and surrounding peoples feel that there was no God but Jehovah, and to 'declare His name in all the earth.'[1] What can be conceived more impressive than the scenes of Sinai, occurring as they did among the most jagged peaks and broken ledges in all the world, and in the view of a people from the Nile valley who had hardly seen a mountain before in all their lives?

Whether such rites and miracles are best adapted to us is not the question; but whether they were not most effective in that and subsequent ages under the theocracy, to impress upon a fleshly and brutalized race the idea of an Infinite Intelligence dwelling in a spiritual universe, whose laws and operations are entirely apart from and above anything in this earthly world. The only question of interest to us is, whether they are well-attested manifestations from such a

[1] Ex. ix. 14-16; Rom. ix. 17.

Being and such a universe? I maintain that *we* have the means of settling this question, which no Jew under the theocracy ever had, unless he was divinely inspired. We have the accumulated evidence of thousands of years, and can well afford to say with Peter, that we have followed no cunningly-devised fables in giving our faith to divine revelation, but have been witnesses of its majesty in the later events of the world.[1] Though the words and symbols adopted in embodying celestial truths are an appropriation of things previously known and in use, as they must be to graft them upon human nature, we see in them something higher, holier, and more divine. No people can greatly anticipate the ages before them; and one of the greatest evidences of divine inspiration is, that it blends in with the current of human thought and language, as a river shapes its course by the features of the land through which it flows, and not by the topography of an imaginary or an unknown country. Moses not only sprinkled with blood the people and all the utensils of divine service, but the book of the law; not because the *law* needed purifying, but the language in which it was recorded had been so exclusively devoted to worldly and material ideas, that, without being purified or adapted to its new use, it could not be the vehicle of truths so spiritual and holy. A new language was not created, but one already spoken and understood received a new and heavenly deposit of ideas and meanings.[2]

This is the policy throughout—the use of common things for sacred purposes. The Christian church is modelled on like principles. It is not a society of angels living on earth, but a purely human institution,

[1] 2 Pet. i. 16.   [2] Heb. ix. 9.

conforming in its order, ordinances, ministrations, and discipline very much to the synagogue worship of previous ages, and its social surroundings in the ancient Roman world. The point was to open heaven to a materialized race, and not to organize a great worldly power like Judaism or the Papacy, and to do it with as little interference with the political ideas and social order of the people as consisted with the accomplishment of its main purpose. Spiritual worshippers were the object of pursuit, not monarchists nor republicans, not the social forms of Judaism nor those of heathenism. Not only Jerusalem and Gerizim lost their position as the necessary seats of acceptable worship, but the whole paraphernalia of priestly robes, orders, sacrifices, and ceremonials lost their significance, or became the expression of heavenly truths. They passed into spiritual meanings, or words in power.[1] Power,—power to open a closed heaven to a race imprisoned in worldly ideas and carnal lusts,—this is the mission of revealed religion; this alone gives value to its words and symbols.

[1] John iv. 23 ; Heb. viii. 1-13.

CHAPTER XVIII.

LAW THE BASIS OF GOD'S RULE IN THE SOUL.

WHAT law or religion is it that God uses the power of miracles, of inspiration, and of the Holy Ghost, to establish among men? Let the reader earnestly and prayerfully follow us in our inquiries on this subject. Is what you realize of heavenly life in yourself, or in the ecclesiastical order to which you are attached, *the* thing which God employed so many ages of supernatural manifestation to establish? Is it the Papacy, with its vast worldly appliances? Is it any existing organization, religious or civil? Is it our modern civilisation, with all its pretensions? Alas that so many should look outward for 'a kingdom that cometh not with observation!'[1] So absorbed are they in material ideas, that the real domain of humanity, which needs to be reconquered to God and occupied by the Holy Spirit, is lost sight of. The province from whence alone must come the civilisation which is of lasting value to the world—the soul-province in its relation to spirit—is put last, as a thing to be reached by education, science, social culture, or that hollow-hearted thing which we call refinement. These absurd ideas are in many cases fostered by mistaken views of the ceremonial law established at Sinai, as if that demanded a great worldly realization in some form,

[1] Luke xvii. 20.

either of creed, organization, ritualistic show, or of Church and State administration, when the apostle expressly teaches that 'God found fault' with that order of things; that it 'made nothing perfect,' but was merely 'the bringing in of a better hope;' and that it was a dead failure as a means of making men just and righteous before God.[1] And yet what are our great ecclesiastical organizations, but attempts to galvanize into life this ritualistic carcase?

The law of God in Scripture is, directly or representatively, a spiritual force acting in the domain of the soul, to regulate its faculties, or to bring its inward life into harmony with God, and from that vantage-ground to extend the kingdom of heaven over all the outward affairs of this world. It is therefore by its very nature individual, and not organic or corporate, except as it affects communities, nations, and governments, by improving the spiritual character of the individuals composing them.[2] The spiritual universe where God is enthroned, but to which men are to a great extent dead, is infinitely greater than the natural; and the divine law is given to restore their consciousness of it, and re-enthrone God in His dominion within them. It is that heaven may rule them, not earth. This is the cardinal idea of the divine law. Love is the sum of the law, a spiritual and not a natural affection, as is shown both by Moses and by our Lord. On this hang all the law and the prophets.[3]

The law is a force, not an ideal to be lived up to, as a philosophic sect make it a point of conforming to cer-

---

[1] Heb. vii. 19, viii. 8; Rom. iii. 20; Gal. ii. 16; Heb. ix. 9, xi. 40.
[2] In what sense it works itself out organically in 'the body of Christ' will be seen hereafter.
[3] Deut. vi. 5; Matt. vii. 12, xxii. 37-39.

tain rules. To one who obeys the law, God is a power everywhere present, everywhere supreme, as air is everywhere and always alike necessary as a life-force. We live, move, and breathe in God; and there can be no moral law which has not the sense of God, or the exercise of supreme love to Him, for its basis. Where that is wanting, the god of this world is the ruling and legislating divinity in the formation of laws and institutions. Selfishness in such a state of things is the sole basis of individual action and of social order. Is not this clear from the policy of governments, and from the whole life of man upon earth? There is no repose, but all is 'like the troubled sea which cannot rest, but casteth up mire and dirt;' and to men in this state it is that our Lord addresses the invitation, 'Come unto me'—*me*, the law of God personified; 'take my yoke upon you'—my law of love: 'for my yoke is easy, and my burden is light; and ye shall find rest unto your souls.'[1] What a comment upon the law as an inward force! Is not such a law entitled to all the miracles of the Bible, to re-establish it among men?

We are so prone to conceive of spiritual force as an axiom of reason, or as a thing to be defined and measured by outward rules, that we fail in our treatment of this subject of law. Can we define seeing to a blind man, or poetical inspiration to one who has no poetry in him? The family ties, true patriotism, and indeed the greatest forces acting in real life, are just as liable to be mistaken as the divine law, provided our knowledge of them were to depend upon a definition or an axiom of the reason. To love God with all the heart seems to the intellectual sceptic an utter impossibility. And it

[1] Isa. lvii. 20; Matt. xi. 30, 31.

would be so, if God had not provided the grace to fulfil the law in them who walk after the Spirit, or who have an inward fitness to understand and practise it in its true meaning and interest.[1] The infinite intelligence revealed to the human intelligence by reasoning from effect to cause, till we had reached the First Cause, is as far removed from the process by which we receive and walk in the light of God's law, as dealing with fox-fire is from basking in the sunbeams. No man can know the Father, but he to whom the Son shall reveal Him. We learn from Him to say, Abba, Father, as we first learned the lesson from our parents, by an affectional and not by an intellectual process.[2] The divine law is a power from God to order our lives by, on the one hand, as on the other we order them by the objects of sense.

The spiritual men in Israel of old give abundant evidence of accepting their law in a similar sense, as may be seen from their devotional language : 'Thy law is within my heart;' 'Grant me Thy law graciously,' or, Let me feel its power in my soul ; 'Thy law I love ;' 'Thy law is my delight;' 'His delight is in the law of the Lord ;' and many like passages, for which no outward rites can account, except as the representative of an inward power.[3] The prophets are equally explicit, speaking of 'the law as in the heart,' as 'in the inward parts, and written upon the heart.' 'Forsaking the law' with them meant more than a neglect of ceremonials ; for even 'the multitude of sacrifices' were alike complained of when not performed in a right spirit.[4] 'The fire of God's law' refers not so much to the lightning of

---

[1] Rom. viii. 1.   [2] Rom. viii. 15 ; John i. 18.
[3] Ps. i. 2, xl. 8, cxix. 29, 113, 174.
[4] Jer. xxxi. 33, ix. 13, xvi. 11 ; Isa. i. 11–15.

Sinai, as to the inward warmth of which the Psalmist speaks: 'My heart was hot within me; while I was musing, the fire burned.'[1] A law producing this divine heat in the soul is fitly called 'fiery.' If it was so in a dispensation of ceremonies, what must it have been when it became 'the law of the spirit of life in Christ Jesus?' Then it was accepted as a heart-force, and malice was murder, lust adultery; and 'the law' was felt to 'be spiritual,' and antagonistic to a life 'carnal, cold under sin.' Then the righteousness of the scribes and Pharisees, as merely outward, lost its value; and 'the righteousness of the law was fulfilled only in those who walked not after the flesh, but after the Spirit.'[2] Not that the divine code had itself changed, for it was the same to Adam, to Abraham, and to Moses as to us; but only that the human mind was in different states of receptivity or of spiritual discernment.

This idea of the law as a spiritual force proceeding from God, is contained in the Hebrew word by which it is expressed. That word is *torah*, of which *nomos* is the synonym in the New Testament; both words being used about five hundred times. The Greek word *nomos* has not with the apostles the same sense as in classical usage, but is determined by the meaning of *torah*, the general word for law in Hebrew. A word charged with so much of God's truth to man, should be prayerfully considered in 'comparing spiritual things with spiritual;' and in doing this, natural ideas or worldly modes of thought must be as far as possible excluded. It is true that, as a word of law or sovereign decree, *torah* is applied to specific enactments, such as burnt-offerings, jealousy, leprosy, uncleanness from contact with

---

[1] Deut. xxxii. 22; Ps. xxxix. 3.
[2] Matt. v. 22, 28; Rom. vii. 14, viii. 2, 4; Matt. v. 20.

the dead, and the like; and it is sometimes used for
civil laws or royal decrees, and once for the temper of
a good woman, 'upon whose tongue is the law of kind-
ness.'[1] But these various applications of a term do not
weaken or invalidate the stem thought or radical truth,
which in a great majority of cases it is used to express,
if indeed that thought is ever lost sight of. *Torah* is a
verbal noun formed from a verb which means to run
as a small stream, to trickle as water into a reservoir, to
flow, to inseminate, to lay a corner or foundation stone;
and Jonathan uses it for hurling a javelin.[2] The prevailing idea is action, as in running water, depositing
seed, laying a stone, hurling a javelin; and not only so,
but action from one point to another, or from one hand
to another. This seems to have suggested the idea of
mental action in imparting thought from one mind to
another; and hence, as in this process the teacher and
taught concur to a common result, the same word is
used to *teach*[3] and to *learn;* and *torah*, the derived
word, means doctrine, erudition, law, instruction, which
is an insemination of truth, or the shedding of thoughts
into the mind as rain upon the earth.[4] It includes also
the idea of casting the mind of the learner into the
mould of the teacher's by the interaction between them,
as a building takes form from the design in the architect's mind. This is the cardinal idea of inspired law.
It is an impartation from God to us, effected by concurrent action between Him and us, as it is said, 'Draw
me, we will run after Thee;' 'No man can come unto

[1] Lev. vii. 37, xiii. 59; Num. v. 30, xix. 14; Ezra vii. 26; Esth. i. 9, iii. 14; Dan. vi. 9, 13, 15.
[2] 1 Sam. xx. 20, 36.
[3] Judg. xiii. 8. Manoah entreated that the angel might 'teach' him, or impart his own ideal of training a deliverer for Israel.
[4] Deut. xxxii. 2; Isa. lv. 10, 11; 1 Cor. iii. 7-9; Ps. lxxii. 2.

me, except the Father who sent me draw him;' and many are the prayers in which God is desired to 'lead the soul in His righteousness,' 'in His truth,' 'in a plain path,' and to 'send out His light and truth to guide' and 'lead in the way everlasting.'[1] It is not providential drawing and leading which is chiefly contemplated in these passages, but a drawing to the true, the right, and the good, in obedience to the holy law.

Nor let it be supposed that this is too spiritual a law to be enforced by penalties. As in nature the greatest forces work the most silently, so in this case the greatest power acting upon man as a moral agent comes from his relation to God as a moral governor; and to violate the law of this relation entails a greater curse than to violate all the physical laws of our being. It is this that has reduced man from an angel to a devil, from a heavenly to a bestial life. It is this voluntary detachment from God that constitutes the pains of the second death. 'Depart, ye cursed, into everlasting fire, prepared for the devil and his angels,' is a sentence which simply affirms our own determination not to be ruled by God's law. If there is affinity between two trees growing near each other, their branches will interlace and intertwine into one globular top, and their duality can only be seen in their separate trunks. But if there is antipathy, as between a maple and a cedar, they will repel each other, and the maple will incline the other way, and will send out few and feeble branches on the side of its neighbour; and thus, though no contact ever takes place between them, its top will become mean and misshapen. If an unseen influence produces such effects among trees, what may

[1] Cant. i. 4; John vi. 44; Ps. v. 8, xxv. 5, xxxi. 3, xliii. 3, cxxxix. 24.

we expect from a soul in affinity with, or antipathy to, the Spirit of God? While the one developes beautifully, growing as it were into God, and becoming one spirit with Him, the other becomes deformed, leafless, twice dead, and plucked up by the roots. No contact, no overt act on the part of God, is necessary to ensure this damnatory result. The one 'is like a tree planted by the rivers of water, that bringeth forth his fruit in his season; his leaf shall not wither; and whatsoever he doeth shall prosper. The ungodly are not so; but are like the chaff which the wind driveth away.'[1] What but a silent, unseen force produces the agony of a convicted conscience? What gives a sense of repose in God, but feeling that in Christ we have accepted the holy law as our rule of life? Can a man have this repose while his heart rebels against any divine precept? Is not 'he that offends in one point guilty of all?'[2]

Not a little is done to kill the life of piety by mistaken views on this subject. They detach law from the nature on which it acts, or from the personal relation between God and the soul, and conceive of it as a separate power in God, or in the universe, or in a sort of universal conscience of how things ought to be, which demands to be satisfied, if not in one way, then in another. And they are more concerned to be assured that this universal conscience or this undefinable something is satisfied, than they are to be personally holy before God. This way of thinking comes from shaping our spiritual ideas to things as we see them in human governments. In our courts of adjudication, the judge, the jury, the prisoner, the witness, the advocate, and all who participate in the

[1] Ps. i. 3, 4.   [2] Jas. ii. 10.

proceedings, are held by the supreme power of law, as written in the statute books, to conduct the trial, to find a verdict, and to punish or acquit, according to prescribed principles, which the court has no more power to change than the criminal or any other person. They are, in a certain sense, tools which law uses to carry out its behests. Whatever their private sympathies for the poor man whom they doom to death, still the law and their oath compel them to execute the sentence. So, we conceive of God as alike bound by a law, or a principle, or an irresistible moral force of some sort, to punish without pity those who rise up against His government. If pity caused Him to waver in the least, the sceptre would fall from His hands, and the secret would be out that God countenanced sin, and trampled under foot His own law. By this view law is made a Moloch, to whose honour millions must burn in hell for ever, or somebody else must accept the entail of woe on their account.

The evil of this view comes not from establishing the certainty of a sinner's punishment,—for that is fixed in the irreversible laws of his own constitution, —but in foisting into a spiritual subject natural ideas, and judging of it by our human affairs. Dives in hell is separated by an impassable gulf from Lazarus in heaven, it is true; but what made it impassable? Was it that God's pity for the poor sufferer was overruled by law? Was it that the heart of Abraham and Lazarus was steeled towards him? Nothing of the sort is intimated. But he had lived and died an unpitying worldling and voluptuary, without one feeling qualifying him to share in the happiness of heaven. Indeed, heaven would have been worse to him than hell.[1] Moses and the law had been lost upon him in life, as they were likely to be upon his worldly brothers, failing to bring him to the divine law as his standard of character; and how could one from the dead do it? or how could the scenes of eternity make that law any more tolerable to him? No, the impassable gulf was in his own rebellion of heart against God—a rebellion just as stubborn, just as persistent, in hell as it had been in his marble palace and robes of purple and fine linen upon earth. It is in reference to this fixed and irrevocable nature of hostility to God in a worldly mind, this incapacity for any pleasure which is not remote from holy love and heavenly life, that the apostle calls it a law, a 'law of sin and death,' a 'law in the members,' and 'the body of the sins of the flesh,' which must be wholly 'put off' in order to that harmony with God which the holy law requires, but which it has no power to bring a worldling to accept. It was 'weak through the flesh,' or from the strength of the resisting force of worldliness; and it would be the most unpitying thing that could be done to Dives or any other man to take him to heaven, unless 'the law of the spirit of life in Christ Jesus had made him free from the law of sin and death.'[2] No idea ever betrayed greater ignorance of what is written in the Bible than this, of supposing that pity or benevolence would alleviate a worldly man who is only fitted for hell, 'made to be taken and destroyed,' by admitting him to heaven. So far from its being true that God is bound by this Moloch of law, of which some speak, to torture sinners up to the extent of their power of endurance, He allows them all the happiness of which their natures are capable. 'He maketh His

---

[1] Luke xvi. 31.   [2] Rom. viii. 2, 3, 7-23; Col. ii. 11.

sun to rise upon the evil, and sendeth rain upon the unjust,' 'doing them good, and filling their heart with food and gladness;' and He even commands us to do the same, if we would 'be perfect, as our Father in heaven is perfect.'[1] Such is the policy of God's government in dealing with sinners, so far as we see it; and how should we suppose that it is, or will be, anywhere or ever, different? Instead of being at the beck of an unpitying law, God is all love in His dealings with His enemies.

But it may be said, If law is so exclusively a matter between the soul and God, what guide does it furnish for the affairs of practical life? Is it not remote from any use to be made of it upon earth? I answer, Though the cardinal principle of God's law is thus a spiritual unit of love and devotion to God, yet it is reflected by many specific enactments, covering the whole outward life of man. Some of these were temporary and individual, and did not descend to the next generation; as the interdiction of a certain fruit to Adam considered as an outward fact, the duty enjoined upon Noah to build an ark, that upon Abraham to offer up his son, and many others. The outward duty imposed in such cases is based upon that of inward fealty to God; and apart from that, it would have no force. God's government has no outward police, and hence it cannot hold except _by binding the spirit. Indeed, in the case of Adam the outward law was a test of inward obedience, and that obedience had no means of being otherwise put to the proof to develope either guilt or innocence. 'Where there is no law, there is no transgression,' and no obedience, for the voluntary nature is without a moral regulator.'[2]

[1] Matt. v. 44, 45; Acts xiv. 17.   [2] Rom. iv. 15.

In the case of Abraham, faith, as an act of duty to God, was put to the proof. Some of the outward laws were for a particular race, as circumcision, the Sinai ritual, the entail of Canaan to Israel, and David's rights as a civil ruler. The object of all these, however, was to set forth in some of its relations the law as a spiritual force binding the soul to God.

The word *torah*—law—covers all these enactments, and indeed the whole word of God; though it is usually accompanied by more specifications, such as statutes, ordinances, commandments, judgments and testimonies. The word covenant is usually applied to the promises to Abraham, or to the tables of the covenant, the ten commandments, of which we propose to speak in our next chapter. All these subordinate provisions of law regulating the whole outward life of Israel, represent the spiritual law in some of its relations. They were addressed to men ruled by the flesh, and incapable of anything more spiritual, putting them under a rigid discipline as to their whole outward life, and making it death to swerve from any of the prescribed rules, except as purified by certain appointed ceremonies. This was to convict them of the sinfulness of their fleshly life, and how impossible it was for them to become right with God and His law without purification, or without becoming spiritual and holy. Men had lost all idea of a spiritual law; and how could they know what sin is in that state, any more than a dog can know what intellect is, or how degraded is his dog's life? The whole tendency of the enactments to Israel, and of God's dealing with them for fifteen hundred years, was to show them the difference between sin and holiness, clean and unclean, a life of fleshly and a life of spiritual ruling; and the extreme punctiliousness of the Pharisees in the time of Christ shows that they had outwardly grasped the idea, ignorant as they were of its spiritual and real import. The day of Pentecost, however, converted into power the letter of the law; and what sin and pollution really are as a fleshly and debased life of opposition to a spiritual law, flashed upon three thousand at once, extorting the agonized cry, 'Men and brethren, what shall we do?' These were perhaps as ceremonially pure as any men in the nation; but sin and holiness they found quite another thing from any idea derived from their misinterpreted law. Now was realized one of the last predictions of the last of their prophets: 'Then shall ye return, and discern between the righteous and the wicked, between him that serveth God and him that serveth Him not.'[1]

Thus the cardinal truth of law in the Bible bears like the atmosphere upon the whole outward life of man, by acting as a regulating force upon all that gives a moral character to that life. It purifies the fountain, and how should not its streams be pure? This is not done by the law and the prophets, not by the Abrahamic or Sinai covenant, except so far as they convinced of sin, and predicted a future Deliverer from its power; but it is effected by 'the precious blood of Christ' as applied by the quickening Spirit. The Holy Ghost is the sole power of killing the flesh that the spirit may live; which killing He effects not only by the law, but by the crucifixion of Christ, with whom we must be crucified, if we would have Christ, and law, and heaven live in us. Thus one idea of law obtains throughout the word of God—a law spiritual, holy, and heavenly.

[1] Acts ii. 37; Mal. iii. 18.

CHAPTER XIX.

THE NATURE AND USE OF THE LAW IN STONE.

IF all divine laws are based upon a relation to God and the spiritual world, to which our fleshly state renders us insensible, of what use are the ten commandments? What, in fact, is the use of any law founded in that relation? Is it not as unavailing as lessons in seeing to blind men? Certainly, they would be so in any other view than as a means of restoring the lost faculty. There is not a special enactment in the Bible that has not redemption in view, directly or indirectly, except that which prohibited a certain tree to the primeval man. All laws which God has enacted since the fall, are with a view to recovering men from the dominion of the flesh, and restoring them to the adoption of children in His spiritual family. Such legislation would be a farce of the gravest and most horrible kind among the hopelessly lost.

What makes redemptive legislation necessary is sin, —not specific sins, such as lying, theft, murder, and the like, but sin as a nature, a force or constitution which is just as susceptible of being propagated from generation to generation as any other characteristic of the *genus homo*. 'For when we were in the flesh, the motions of sin which were by the law did work in our members to bring forth fruit unto death.'[1] Being 'in the flesh' describes the corrupted nature as the seeding,

---

[1] Rom. vii. 5. See also Rom. v. 14-21, viii. 2, which clearly involves the idea of propagation.

of which all specific motions, passions, or tendencies to evil as developed in act, are the harvest. It is a harvest 'unto death,' as being devoid of all spiritual life in God. This idea of propagated evil enters as fully into the natural history of the race as the carnivorous appetite of a lion or a tiger, though it is only from the Bible we learn that it had its origin in sin as an *act*, becoming sin as a *nature*. As the normal condition of human nature involves sensibility to God and the realm of spirits as an all-controlling life-element, what but an abnormal and sinful condition could follow the loss of it? And such is the nature of the case, that the loss of it in the only two existing parents would ensure it in their children.

Now it is to break up this deep incrustation of carnality and materialism that the law is given, and especially the ten commandments. 'The motions of sin are by the law,' in the same sense that latent disease is by the potion which developed it, or as the convulsions of a drowned man are produced by the means used to restore him to life. The law does not create the sin, but brings it to the surface, reveals it to the man's consciousness, and awakens in him efforts to escape its dangerous power. 'I had not known sin but by the law; for I had not known lust, except the law had said, Thou shalt not covet;'[1] that is, I should not have known it *as* lust and a crime against God, and death to all my spiritual and immortal hopes. Sinai thunders are an assault upon the earthly enclosure in which the soul has encased itself, like some power that might be supposed to be brought to bear upon a savage race to convince it of its savagery, to show it in its most hateful light, and thus to act as a primary im-

[1] Rom. vii. 7.

pulse towards civilisation. 'The law was added because of transgressions,' just as medical science is added because of disease. 'It is a ministration of death, written and engraven in stone,' but ministering death with a view to a life not on the principle of law, but of grace. It is 'the strength of sin,' which without law could have no conscious existence and no power of conviction. 'What shall we say then? Is the law sin?' By no means. 'But sin, that it might appear sin, working death in me by that which is good; that sin by the commandment might become exceedingly sinful.'[1] Sin is not made exceedingly sinful by the law, for it is so in itself; but it is made to *appear* so in the soul's consciousness.

Having thus seen the use which inspired men ascribe to the ten commandments, the question arises as to what effect it can have upon men in a state of total indifference or deadness to spiritual truths? I have spoken of God's addressing us in our natural state in ways adapted to our apprehension, and thus of 'coming down' to us, and of 'knocking' at the outer gateway of the soul. This is especially true of the ten commandments as delivered from Sinai. It is an appeal to *fear*, the same as the cherubim at the gate of Eden, which we have already noticed. Fear of death, and of what is to ensue in another world, is one of the most active principles of human nature. What but this has given such force to Shakespeare's words, ascribing to it the consent to live under the world's irretrievable calamities?

'For who would bear the whips and scorns of time,
The oppressor's wrong, the proud man's contumely,

---

[1] Gal. iii. 19 ; 2 Cor. iii. 7 ; 1 Cor. xv. 56.

> The pangs of despised love, the law's delay,
> The insolence of office, and the spurns
> That patient merit of the unworthy takes,
> When he might his quietus make
> With a bare bodkin,
> But the dread of something after death ?"

What sacrifices, what self-inflictions, what outlays, to ensure the cover of a priesthood! what various devices of men to ease their burdened conscience, and assure themselves that all will be well with them when they meet their final doom! Though without right ideas on the subject, and with little regard to justice or truth, their selfish fears make them unwilling to die unshrived or unpardoned. Tribes sunk to the level of nature, and without even the idea of a God, if there be such, still cling to their amulets as a mysterious power to ward off evil and ensure them happiness. Intellectual men, who scout the idea of a hereafter, often find their courage failing as death approaches, and gladly seize on any semblance of faith as a support in entering the dark valley.

This is the principle to which the ten commandments make their appeal. They are thundered from Sinai, or uttered from the wilderness in the rough tones of John the Baptist, arousing men from their deep slumbers in sin to exercise repentance towards God. They give no power for the enforced duty, it is true; and yet, is it nothing that a race dead in sin should be made to stir in its sepulchre? Is it nothing to awaken in them the sense of needing something better than this fleshly life? It is a killing process; but how can they reach a resurrection till the sin in which they are dies, or till the nature from which they reap such a harvest of sins and woes is crucified with Christ? The law asserts God's righteousness in contrast to our own defilement, and thus is a schoolmaster to bring us to Christ.[1]

This killing work of law is as necessary as a preparation to salvation, as grace in effecting it. Those who have not learned enough of law to feel their helplessness, or who have not entered 'the inner chamber' of the soul's 'imagery, to see the abominations' that cover themselves there in darkness, need expect no signal victory over the world, the flesh, and the devil.[2] Their piety is a legalism of perpetual resolves to do better, in which failing, they are all the time miserable, and basing their hopes of salvation, perhaps, on the fact of this misery, as a sort of claim upon Christ's merits to make up the deficiency. If the law makes them cry out, 'O wretched man that I am!' it seems to suffice them, without their ever being able to say, 'I thank God, through Jesus Christ my Lord,' or to feel that they are 'free from condemnation' by being actually and consciously 'in Christ.'[3] I fear that the great majority of those who have named the name of Christ are in this dubious position between law and grace, living and dying without ever knowing the gospel, or the full freedom of the sons of God. I hope more fully, by God's grace, to enlarge upon these ideas in another place.

The fitness of the law in stone to do this killing work, may be seen from *the manner of its delivery*, from *the place and circumstances of its conservation*, from *the sense of guilt and helplessness which it awakens*, and from *the consenting response which it extorts from conscience.*

---

[1] Gal. iii. 24. The idea is that of a servant leading the children to and from school, and not of one to teach them. Christ is the schoolmaster or teacher.

[2] Ezek. viii. 6–18.   [3] Rom. vii. 24, 25, viii. 1.

The delivery or proclamation of an important enactment by European Governments is, by royal authority, by certain impressive ceremonies, and by threatened penalties, to awaken in the people the fear of transgressing it. But what ever equalled in this respect the proclamation of the ten commandments from Mount Sinai? They were first spoken by God Himself, from the smoking, lightning-riven summit of the holy mount, and reached the ears of the people in more than tones of earthly thunder. And as if spoken words, however impressive, and a visible scene so terrible that the people besought that it might not be repeated,[1] were not to be trusted with so great a delivery, they were engraven in two tablets of stone by God's own finger, to indicate a permanency attaching to no other part of the Sinai ceremonial.[2] They are a condensed view of how we are to work out in conduct our inward fealty to the Supreme Legislator; they enforce universal and eternal obligations; they have a basis in natural conscience as well as in revealed religion; and they assert the great principle, that no ceremonial in worship, no faith or professions of inward piety, and no claims upon God by pious parents or interceding priesthoods, can render us acceptable without good morals. Can we wonder that God should have surrounded Himself with the terrors of Sinai in delivering such a law, and that He should have added to its oral utterance its miraculous inscription in stone? And yet, such is human nature, that the event proved how impotent was the fear excited by the delivery of the law, since, a few days after, these same people who

[1] Ex. xx. 19.
[2] Ex. xxiv. 12, xxxii. 15, 16, xxxiv. 28, 29; Deut. iv. 13, v. 22; Ex. xx. 1.

heard and accepted it as their rule of life, violated its first and chief precept—not to have any God but Jehovah—and were shouting to a golden calf in their nakedness and revelry, 'These be thy gods, O Israel,' after the manner of the bestial worship in Egypt. And Moses, when he looked on the disgusting scene, was so indignant, that he broke, beneath the mount, the two tables on which God had written the law, to indicate the utter failure of all legal expedients to raise man from his earthliness to the spiritual and heavenly life for which he was created.[1] It was then proved that the law could only convince of sin.

The place and circumstances for conserving the law were as remarkable as its delivery. The two tablets, after being renewed by God Himself,[2] were deposited in a casket of shittim wood overlaid with gold, the lid of which was the earthly throne of Jehovah in administering the government over Israel. The law was the basis of this throne, called the mercy-seat, to show impressively how impossible it is for God to exercise mercy on any basis but law; or, in other words, that it would be no mercy to man to take him into favour with Himself, and raise him to heaven, in any way but that of restoring him to a holy and heavenly life. 'Make the tree good, and his fruit will be good.' Cleanse the fountain, and its streams will be pure. Dives in heaven, as before said, would be more miserable than in hell. The gulf is impassable. This ark was placed in the holy of holies—a large room from which light was excluded, to show that God dwells to us, as fleshly men, in thick darkness.[3] Over it, two

---

[1] Ex. xxxii. 1-19.   [2] Ex. xxxiv. 1, 28.
[3] Heb. x. 20. Christ has removed this darkness, by consecrating for us, 'through the veil of His flesh, a new and living way.'

cherubim, with expanded wings, stood face to face, the throne of God and His law being between them, upon which they kept watch and ward, to represent how intent all heavenly beings are to Him who sitteth upon the throne, and to His divine behests. This place where the law was deposited was separated by a veil from the holy place, and that again was surrounded by a circumvallation of courts and cloisters; and thus the two tables were excluded from all profane eyes, and could only be approached by the high priest once a year, after purification by blood, and while sacrifices and prayers were offered in his behalf on the part of the priests and people without. Can any outward device be imagined, to show more impressively that the precious blood of Christ must first flow, before the law can be fully restored to us, and that, when it is restored, it will be in the secret recesses of the soul, upon which no eye can look but our High Priest, 'who has passed into the heavens,' and 'who is set on the right hand of the throne of the Majesty on high?'[1] Unless the reader keeps in view the law of God as a unit of His ruling within our souls, from which He had been cast out by our coming under the ruling of natural ideas and fleshly lusts, and that this is the present condition of humanity, all this symbolism will be lost upon him; and what is worse, it will fill his mind with false ideas and corrupted theology. It is only by searching Scripture, and comparing spiritual things with spiritual, that the chaff can be eliminated from the wheat, or truth, as in the thought of holy seers, can detach itself from material symbols. You and I, reader, must accept the law as God's dominion in our souls by the Holy Ghost, or we can make no advance in salvation.

[1] Heb. iv. 14, viii. 1.

Another aspect in the working of the law written on stone is, that of the sense of guilt and helplessness which it produces in one who honestly endeavours to keep it. Who can by any effort of his own love God with all his heart? Who can repress concupiscence? How have millions, by their own confession, vainly struggled in the endeavour? Can we detach ourselves from our own nature, and take on one as foreign to ourselves as spirit is from matter, earthly from heavenly ideas? No; there must be a death of what we are, before we can have a resurrection to a state so exalted. And a dying process is always one of helplessness: the grave closes only upon those who were too weak to conquer disease and death; and a law that can only consign us to the sepulchre, or that can only say, 'Cursed is every one that continueth not in all things written in the book of the law, to do them,' comes infinitely short of the necessities of our condition.[1] To return to a former illustration: Suppose transmigration were possible, and you had a friend whose soul had gone into a dog, would it be enough to awake him to a sense of his condition? That would only torment him, unless it were a necessary measure of restoring him to his former state of manhood. This is all the law can do—convince us of the strength of our flesh, and of its own consequent impotence to raise us to a new life. 'The law entered that the offence might abound;' but we must look elsewhere for deliverance from its power.[2] By what we have before said, and are to say, in reference to the mode of reaching a resurrection life, the exact position of the ten commandments in the Bible, we trust, will become sufficiently clear. That after fifteen hundred years they

[1] Gal. iii. 10.   [2] Rom. v. 20.

had failed to give righteousness to any Jew, as the apostle states in Romans, or any independence of faith for justification more than a Gentile, shows how hopeless they are as a basis of salvation.[1]

The tables of stone were a covenant as well as a law, not being statutes imposed without the consent of the governed, but a contract between God and men. They were of a nature to obtain even from natural conscience a consenting response. Who can claim the right of turning from the God who has 'redeemed' him,—the reason assigned for having no God but Jehovah? Who is not forced to confess, that he ought not to steal? Such is the law, that it must *hold* upon moral natures like ours; and thus it cannot fail to awaken a sense of guilt in those to whom it is fairly brought home, however they may still continue joined to their idols of flesh. Hence we have not only God speaking the law from Sinai, but the people responding, 'All that the Lord hath spoken we will do; and Moses returned these words of the people unto the Lord.'[2] Though in one sense an absolute Sovereign in redemption, God rules only a consenting people. No being in the universe more clearly and decidedly respects the freedom of the human soul than He who endowed it with its prerogatives. Indeed, it would be reducing mind to a level with matter, to coerce it under any but a representative government, or a government depending upon the consent of the governed. If their consent is not obtained, they pass under another god and under another code, in hostility to Jehovah; but that cannot succeed in resisting the thunder of His power. They are free, but it is the freedom of hell.

[1] Rom. iii. 18, 19.
[2] Ex. xx. 5; Deut. v. 27; Ex. xxiv. 3, 7.

In reference to this agreement between God and the people, the tables of the law were called 'tables of testimony,' the ark 'the ark of the covenant,' and the tabernacle 'the tabernacle of witness,' because they were a sort of register-office to stand as a perpetual witness of the precise terms of the contract, and as a means of convicting delinquents of their violated pledges and dishonest dealings with God.[1] It is viewed in the light of a nuptial bond wedding the soul to God; and both Israel and the apostolic churches were charged with conjugal infidelity whenever they forsook their Head and Husband. Thus in the prophets;[2] and Dean Alford understands the adulterers and adulteresses whom James addresses among Christians in the same light, and he renders the succeeding passage accordingly: 'The Spirit He placed in us jealously desireth us.' He is 'grieved' by our wandering worldly desires, as a husband by the alienated affections of his wife.[3] The oneness of the parties in a marriage is spoken of as 'a great mystery,' because it pertains 'to Christ and His church,' or a 'joining of the soul in one spirit with the Lord.'[4] Who will say, that a law which represents sin not only as violating a solemn contract, but the heart's most sacred pledges, is not pre-eminent in its convicting power?

It is objected to the importance and perpetuity of the law in stone, that it tells us what *not* to do, but not what we *ought to do*. It is negative rather than

---

[1] Ex. xxxii. 15; Heb. ix. 4; Num. xvii. 7, x. 33; Deut. xxxi. 26.
[2] Jer. iii. 2, 9; Ezek. xxiii. 37, xvi. 38; Hos. iii. 1, iv. 12; Lev. xvii. 7; 2 Chron. xxi. 11; Ex. xxxiv. 15, and many others.
[3] Jas. iv. 4. 5; Eph. iv. 30.
[4] 1 Cor. vi. 17; Eph. v. 32.

positive. Eight of its precepts are negative; one of the other two has changed its form, and no such Sabbath as it enjoined upon the Jews now exists; while the other, enjoining duty to parents, is an instinct of nature, and therefore unnecessary.

It is sufficient to reply to this, that Moses, our Lord, and the Apostle Paul, condense the whole spirit of the law into love to God and man, showing that *they* at least conceived of it as expressing a principle that was not done away by the gospel, like the rest of the Sinai ceremonial, but is of perpetual obligation.[1] This is the principle considered in our last chapter, growing out of the soul's direct relationship to God as Spirit, involving the duty of coming under His ruling in all things, which is the meaning of loving God with all our hearts. Besides, each of the negative commandments involves positive duties; nor can it be observed without doing those duties. It guards a point at which the soul's affections and activities are liable to flow in a wrong direction; and if the crevasse is stopped, they will be confined to the true channel of love, duty, and obedience. It is as if a mighty river, now overflowing a wide extent of country, converting it into a vast quagmire, covering it with a deadly miasma, and causing it to breed crocodiles, serpents, and every noxious animal, were diked and confined to its proper channel, and this country was thus restored to green fields, blooming gardens, beautiful forests, and all the glories of cultivation. Thus, if the human affections and activities were confined at the points guarded by the law, they would flow in the direction of all that is virtuous, holy, and beneficent.

We have only to look at the terms of the first table

[1] Deut. vi. 5; Mark xii. 30; Rom. xiii. 10.

of the law, to see how fully it justifies making its fulfilment consist in supreme love and devotion to God. If we had no other God but Jehovah, what would ensue but the centring of all love, devotion, and obedience in Him? We are so constituted, that some passion and purpose will rule us. If it is not one thing, it will be another. By cutting off the stream in other directions, what can follow but its concentrated force in the only remaining channel? A man cut off from all other gods and all other ruling powers within or around him, cannot do otherwise, as he is constituted, but give Jehovah the supreme place in things, and thus fulfil the cardinal principle of all divine law,—that of having God rule us in all things. 'Thou shalt have no other gods before me' is a precept that admits of no construction but that of loving God with all our soul, and mind, and strength.[1] The wisdom of such a principle both in the individual and in society makes it worthy of God, and of a first place in His law. Who can be happy with divided and conflicting passions? Who does not need some such ruling force within him, in order to the harmonious action of the various impulses of his own being? 'Unite my heart to fear Thy name' is a prayer as necessary to one's peace as to his piety. And as to social order, how can we have it without a common and all-controlling centre, like the sun in the solar system? Never will the nations be secured against war till the principle of this divine enactment is adopted, and all are held by some supreme power of international law as a central force to regulate their intercourse among themselves. Philanthropy and statesmanship can never devise a better code than that

[1] Ex. xx. 2, 3.

which was enunciated nearly four thousand years ago from the broken summits of Peninsular Arabia.

The second commandment guards against the universal tendency of men to materialism in their theologies. As the flesh, the world, and natural ideas rule them to the exclusion of spirit, what could be expected of them but the worship of images in gold, silver, and precious stones; or that they should pay their adoration to animals, four-footed beasts, and creeping things? So wrapped up in these had the nations become, that they could conceive of only local divinities—nothing better, at least, than sun, moon, stars, and the forces of nature; and the idea of the one living and true God as an infinite intelligence had actually perished from the minds of men. Even Israel, for more than a thousand years of its national life, was ever backsliding into image-worship, and the other five hundred it gave to the idolatry of its ritual, which in the time of our Lord was little better than the heathenism of the surrounding nations. And even to this day, by far the greater portion of the world are idolaters,—a remark which may even apply to Christendom so called, since pictures, statuary, architecture, and a thousand ritual devices, enter so largely into its worship. The Catholics have even cancelled this second commandment, to save themselves from its maledictions in a practice which is as God-dishonouring as it is debasing to mankind. In all lands where this material theology obtains, an incubus rests upon civilisation and morals. 'Thou shalt not worship any graven image' is an interdiction that would preclude nine-tenths of the world's worship, and of its causes of depression and demoralization.[1] Considering the state of the nations,

[1] Ex. xx. 5, 6.

can we wonder that such a precept should be second in the tablets of stone written by God's finger, or that the Old Testament should be such a continual protest against idolatry? Not only material images are forbidden, but ideal ones, as consisting in false views of God and corrupt theologies, that all our thoughts of Him may be worthy of His adorable character, and that we may 'sanctify the Lord God in our hearts, and make Him our fear and our dread.'[1]

The third commandment touches a most active principle, that of introducing the name of God into speech. It does not forbid this; but only the 'taking of it in vain,' or with lightness, irreverence, and profanation: 'The Lord will not hold him guiltless that taketh His name in vain.'[2] Not only is cursing and swearing forbidden, but using God's name as an expletive to set off discourse or give power to affirmations. The idle repetition of it, as in heathen worship, where the name of the god is called over and over again, 'O Baal, O Baal,' as a Catholic counts his beads, or a savage his amulets, as if we were to 'be heard by our much speaking,' or by the charm of a name, is forbidden by our Lord; and our words are to be few and simple.[3] It forbids also the profanation of hypocrisy in worship, or of 'drawing nigh to God with our lips while our hearts are far from Him,'—thus imposing on ourselves and others, but not on the Searcher of all hearts.[4] This precept contemplates a purified speech, wherein the yea shall be yea, and the nay nay, to which truth and sincerity shall add force, and manifest integrity shall secure conviction.[5] Who can estimate the wide-reaching results

[1] Isa. viii. 13.
[2] Ex. xx. 7.
[3] Matt. vi. 7; 1 Kings xviii. 26.
[4] Isa. xxix. 13; Rev. ii. 23.
[5] Matt. v. 37.

Nature and Use of the Law in Stone. 231

of such a law? It would secure the house of God against mimicry and pantomime; it would purify and exalt social intercourse; it would put an end to the oaths which tremble on the lips of age, and are caught up and reverberated by the young; and it would ensure in discourse 'that which is good to the use of edifying, that it may minister grace to the hearers.'[1] Men will talk; men will employ the name of God; how else can they worship? And 'by their words they shall be justified, and by their words they shall be condemned,' because words are not only determinative of what is in them, but of what they are doing for the weal or woe of others.[2] Can we overestimate the law which gives God His due place in language?

The seed-thought of the fourth commandment is that of the divine holiness: 'Remember the Sabbath-day, to keep it *holy*.'[3] We are to '*hallow*' the Sabbath, not in the sense of making the time holy, but as a memorial of the divine holiness, and by cultivating in ourselves that holiness without which no man shall see the Lord.[4] The two ideas of *holiness* and *rest* are conjoined in the Bible, because they are inseparable in experience. Holiness is that harmony in God, or that due balance of His attributes, without which power would be tyranny, omniscience craft, justice revenge, and even the amiable attribute of mercy would degenerate into blind prodigality or undiscriminating fondness. And a mind in harmony within itself is in repose. No tempest of passion agitates it; no unsatisfied desires canker within. Hence our Lord assigns meekness and lowliness, that is, harmonized desires, as a reason why the weary and heavy laden would find

[1] Eph. iv. 29.   [2] Matt. xii. 37.   [3] Ex. xx. 9-11.
[4] Jer. xvii. 22; Ezek. xx. 20, xliv. 24; Heb. xii. 14.

rest in Him; and the perfect holiness of His nature ensured for Him, under all His pains and conflicts, the peace which He has bequeathed to His people.[1] The apostle also applies the term Sabbath to the rest into which believers enter, likening it to that into which God entered on the seventh day of creation; and He adds, 'There remaineth therefore a *sabbatizing*, or Sabbath of rest, to the people of God.' And they have already entered it by faith: 'for we which have believed do enter into rest.' To a like rest our Lord invites us, plainly showing that Sabbath stands for the holiest and happiest things of His church.[2]

God connected with His labours in creation, and with His care of this working-day world, the truth of infinite repose in Himself as the result of His perfectly balanced attributes, and not only entails the same to all of like character, but has institutionally held it forth from the beginning of time. With the loss of this truth, the Sabbath itself seems to have perished. Moses revived it in the wilderness with appendages in the civil government over Israel which have since ceased. But the institution in its primary and cardinal idea of the rest of holiness, as written in stone with the nine other commandments, is equally binding upon us to remember it as of unabated and undying obligation. In heaven it will be more to us, no doubt, than upon earth. It can no more perish than the divine holiness. The change of day and outward forms of observance, of which some make so much account, from failing to look at the scriptural truth of the institution, cannot abate its force. Even without this truth, and regarding it simply as a civil institution for

---

[1] Matt. xi. 29; John xiv. 27, xvi. 33.
[2] Heb. iv. 1-9.

natural men, how beneficent its effects upon man, the labouring animals, and the whole social system!

That I do not err and am not fanciful in this view of the fourth commandment, any one may see by looking at the two words applied to the institution in Hebrew, and their use in other connections. They are שֶׁבַע, shebah, seven; and שַׁבָּת, shabbath, rest. Seven was a sacred number among the Hebrews, and is used for an oath; and the verb from which it is made expressed the most hallowed idea of which they had a conception.[1] It was also used for completeness or fulness in the times of worship;[2] for the utmost extent of calamity;[3] and for punishment in full measure.[4] Thus the idea of completeness, fulness, perfection, inheres in the term; and, as applied to God, it refers to the infinite perfection of His nature, as illustriously displayed when the first Sabbath dawned upon His completed work of creation: 'the morning stars sang together, and the sons of God shouted for joy.' It denotes, not that God ceased to energize through all nature, but the eternal harmony of His attributes as brought out in His works, leading heavenly beings to single out this attribute before all others in their cry of 'Holy, holy, holy.' This cry comprehends all God's attributes, and all His works in their harmonious adjustment, as beauty all the features in their united result. Neither love, justice, nor truth, in its separate capacity, can come up to an angel's conception of God, more than a single feature in our idea of a beautiful face. Holiness is beauty.[5]

This attribute of harmony is marvellously reflected

[1] Gen. xxi. 28; Ex. xxxvii. 23; Lev. iv. 16, 17.
[2] Ps. cxix. 164.   [3] Prov. xxiv. 16.
[4] Lev. xxvi. 18, 21.   [5] Ps. cx. 3.

even in material nature, adding force to the saying, that 'the undevout astronomer is mad.' For millions of years, so far as we know, the spheres have maintained their mystic dance without jostling or colliding. What has in it more of the sublime than the rest or quietude with which the solar orbs perform their cycles through the ethereal expanse, traversing infinite spaces, and, in doing so, giving birth and being to innumerable forms of life, all noiseless, quiet, harmonious? Who can imagine a more glorious showing in material things of the infinite harmony in which they had their origin, than the Sabbath of God's completed works had to offer?

Thus we have, in the first table of the law, the one Jehovah as the central fact of creation and of redeeming power; we have true ideas of His adorable character enjoined; we have His name as an inspiration of truth, reverence, and sincerity in His worship; and we have the rest of holiness as the complement of the first table of the law, including love to God with all our heart, mind, and strength,—the sum of all piety and of all happiness.

> 'And those who stand upon the sea of glass,
> And those who stand upon the battlements
> And lofty towers of New Jerusalem,
> And those who circling stand, bowing afar,
> Exalted on the everlasting hills,
> Thousands of thousands, thousands infinite,
> With voice of boundless love, answered, Amen;
> And Father, Son, and Holy Ghost,
> The one Eternal, smiled superior bliss;
> And every eye and every face in heaven,
> Reflected and reflecting, beams with love.'

CHAPTER XX.

THE DIVINE INDWELLING IN OUR SOCIAL RELATIONS.

GOD, in the adytum of man's nature, on the basis of law, works Himself out in all our external relations, symbolized in Israel by an orderly people and a fruitful land; and doctrinally stated in the gospel as glorifying God in body and spirit, showing forth His praise, and adorning the doctrine of God our Saviour in all things.[1] And it is in reference to the sanctity which the character of all believers is supposed to acquire from their new interior life, that they are called saints, holy brethren, partakers of the heavenly calling; and they are exhorted by the mercies of God, thus inwardly manifested, to present their bodies a living sacrifice, holy and acceptable unto God, which is their reasonable sacrifice.[2] That these terms have gone into disuse in expressing discipleship, indicates a falling off in sanctity; insomuch that the circles are comparatively few to which saint, holy brethren, would not be felt to be a misnomer. But as we write to develope seed-truths in the word itself, and not their supposed germination in existing character, we are compelled to keep to what is written of God's enthronement within on the basis of law, and its out-working in the life.

[1] 1 Cor. vi. 20, x. 31.
[2] Heb. iii. 1 ; Rom. xii. 1 ; 1 Cor. i. 2, *et al.*

No imagery is more glowing than the representative outworking of enthroned divinity in the exterior life of His ancient people. Sons were as olive-plants around their board; daughters as polished stones cut in the similitude of a palace; garners full of all manner of stores; sheep bringing forth ten thousands, and oxen strong to labour; no breaking in, going out, nor complaining in the streets: thus happy is that people whose God is the Lord.[1] The early and latter rain causing the springing of the pastures, the fruitfulness of vine and fig-tree; barns full of wheat; vats overflowing with wine and oil; plenty and satisfaction on every hand, betokened God's presence in the midst of His people.[2] The Lord caused them to ride on the high places of the earth, even in passing through the deserts of Arabia Petrea, to eat the increase of the fields; to suck honey out of the rock, and oil from the flinty rock; butter of kine, and milk of sheep, with fat of lambs, and rams of the breed of Bashan, and goats, with the fat of the kidneys of wheat: they were fed, and drank of the pure blood of the grape.[3] Such are the glowing images which represented to a sensuous age the outworking of divine truth and love, overspreading the whole external scene with bloom and beauty; thus foreshadowing the blessedness of an indwelling Saviour to a regenerated people.

It is often asked wherein the Mosaic law in stone is superior to the institutes of other legislators? Do not even heathen and savages honour parents, condemn murder, adultery, thieving, lying, and infringements upon other's rights? And the codes of Solon, Lycurgus, Numa, and others, are urged with a leer of triumph, as more than offsetting the words claimed to be spoken

---

[1] Ps. cxliv. 12-15.   [2] Hos. ii. 21-23.   [3] Deut. xxxii. 13, 14.

and written by Jehovah on Mount Sinai. But these codes were political rather than personal, distributing men into classes, and prescribing the functions of each as members of the state, and not with a view of regulating the interior life. Solon made property instead of birth the basis of citizenship; Lycurgus divided the state into three orders, made a distribution of the lands, provided a common table, prescribed a rigorous system of gymnastics, and required the state to own and train the children, chiefly with a view to power in war. Numa enacted a politico-religious system, classifying the people, determining the duties of pontiffs and the rites of religion; but giving no hint, not even by symbol, of a new condition of the inner nature, fitting it for consociation with a personal God, or as a dwelling-place of the Infinite Spirit. Their institutes are as remote from the animus and intent of the Sinai covenant, as the tactics of the Prussian army, or the legislation of Parliament or Congress.

Moses' law hinges upon a right condition of the soul towards God, in obedience to the first table, regulating the spiritual relations as a prerequisite to social and civil life. It is fundamental to revealed religion, and a basis for universal duty, in heaven as well as on earth, and is as pervading and enduring as the power of moral obligation. It includes all the elements of a spiritual and holy life, as our Lord's interpretation and illustration of it in His teaching and life, thus magnifying it and making it honourable, clearly prove. The Episcopal Church is to be honoured for its weekly repetition of the ten commandments; but among other denominations how rarely do we hear them, and how much more rarely still do we hear expositions of their several precepts, that contain anything like an exhaustive view of their underlying spiritual truths! God's law is viewed too much as an abstraction, a transcript of the divine nature, which nobody knows anything about—'the ethical nature of God,' the public sentiment of the universe, which as a Moloch calls for blood, blood, and cannot be appeased towards sinners till they or their surety suffers a sanguinary death. Such is the law of the pulpit—a mighty antagonistic force to the gospel, an enemy to be eschewed by him who would seek salvation; whereas the law of the Old Testament and of the New is a unit in being fulfilled alike and only by love, but weak in bringing us to love, from the strength of our hatred and our sin: this object being accomplished only by the blood of Christ as inflowing life from God, shed on Calvary, to convert it into power for this express purpose, that the law may be fulfilled in us, that is, the law of love; and that it may be put into our minds, written in our hearts, and imprinted upon our inward parts.[1] So little are the ten commandments understood, that I have heard earnest Christian men speak of them as done away in Christ, mistaking the law itself for the mode of its administration. The law in stone is now the law in the heart.

I do not propose an exposition of the second table in detail, but chiefly as showing that each precept, like a sign-post, guards a point where we are liable to go wrong, and that it is alike adapted to bodied and disembodied life. These two points, bearing directly on our main purpose, will fully appear as we consider the commandments of the second table *seriatim*.

The duty of honouring parents, and its reward, are among the clearest things to natural conscience and observation.[2] It is a general law of subordination in

---

[1] Heb. viii. 10; Jer. xxxi. 33.   [2] Ex. xx. 12.

the social state. 'Some are, and must be, greater than the rest.' This subordination, which is an instinct of childhood, extends to those who divide with parents their prerogatives, and prescribes a like duty to rulers, teachers, employers, masters, and superiors. And that this obligation is a point of danger, or of temptation and trial to character, all experience fully shows. Are not children prone to have their own way? Are not nations restive under authority? Are not pupils often in open rebellion against their teachers,—apprentices against their masters,—employees, as individuals or trade-unions, against their employers? Instead of rising up before the hoary head, are not the young often impertinent to venerable years?

The law is fixed as a guide-post at the corner of these divergent ways, crying out for subordination, promising a great ensuing good—for it is the first commandment with promise [1]—and forewarning us, that he who curses father or mother shall die the death.[2] Who can imagine the train of evils to ensue without subordination, or the good to accrue from duly observing it in all our relations? If the required honour is rendered, and the enjoined social subordination maintained, order and happiness ensue; but if superiors are oppressive in their exactions, and subordinates are rebellious, anarchy succeeds. The reward and penalty inhere in the conditions of the relation, and are not created by enactment any more than the duty itself.

This is the law of all social relations, in the higher world as well as in this, as there are degrees in glory, and both greatest and least in the kingdom of God.[3]

---

[1] Eph. vi. 2. [2] Ex. xxi. 17.
[3] 1 Cor. xv. 40-42; Matt. v. 19, xi. 11, xxv. 40.

Pre-eminence in that kingdom is real, and not fictitious, as it often is in this, depending on the power to serve or to impart to others the greatest good.[1] Differences in the principle of precedence and subordination do not unsettle the fact or the accruing duty; but they show the universal adjustment of the law to all social relation in the universe, to 'principalities and powers in the heavenly places,' as well as to those on earth.[2] Might and dominion are not only of this world, but of that which is to come. It is a law that bears alike on the parties concerned; and parents are required not to provoke their children to wrath, and rulers are to exercise their functions in the fear of the Lord.[3]

In the family, this is the first duty of which we are cognizant, as in entering the spiritual kingdom submission to God is the first lesson we learn. To obey is better than sacrifice. Can we wonder that a precept so wide-reaching, so necessary to authority in family, church, and state, so elementary to all duty, should have the first place in the second table? Honouring parents includes sustaining them by moneyed contributions in the helplessness of old age, as our Lord teaches; and a man must not think to escape this duty by consecrating his wealth to religion or to charity.[4]

The sixth commandment is, like the others, positive, as well as negative, requiring us not only not to kill, but to preserve life, by sanitary laws, by caring for the sick and infirm, and by promoting general health, security, and contentment.[5] These duties pertain not only to natural, but to spiritual life; and it forbids us to corrupt men's souls, thus exposing them to the death

---

[1] Mark x. 42; Luke xxii. 25, 26.   [2] Eph. i. 21, iii. 10.
[3] Eph. vi. 4; 2 Sam. xxiii. 3.   [4] Mark vii. 10-13.
[5] Ex. xx. 13.

that never dies, as well as to refrain from whatever is prejudicial to animal life. Cain was a murderer in the latter sense; but Satan was a murderer from the beginning, by swerving from the truth, and seducing others, thus bringing 'death into the world, and all our woe.'[1] Men who rejected the gospel incurred blood-guiltiness, by destroying their own souls and endangering others; and the reason assigned why 'he that sheddeth man's blood, by man shall his blood be shed,' is, that 'man was made in the image of God,' as if defacing that image was the head and front of a murderer's act.[2]

This law, therefore, seemingly altogether a thing of the flesh, runs up into the infinite and eternal, and applies with greater force to pure spirits, as embodying in themselves more of existence than we do. In any world where God has transferred His image to a creature, the law thunders its maledictions against the killing, which consists in defiling and defacing that image. It is the great safeguard of life, natural and spiritual, and is commensurate in its claims with the moral government of God.

Nor does it merely prohibit the act, but the state of mind from which it took its rise; and 'whoso hateth his brother is a murderer.'[3] All settled malignity is murder. To *intend* the crime, as did the conspirators against Paul's life,[4] but fail from the impossibility of executing it, is entered as murder in His account who searcheth our hearts. So careful is our Father in heaven of the life of His children, that He required in the building of houses, that they should be surrounded by a battlement, to prevent a fall from the roof; and if

---

[1] John viii. 44.
[2] Acts xviii. 6; Gen. ix. 6.
[3] 1 John iii. 15; Matt. v. 21, 22.
[4] Acts xxiii. 13-15.

a man kept an ox known to be dangerous, and the ox should kill a man, both the owner and the ox should die. If a person was found slain near a city, its elders should be held responsible for his death till they had cleared themselves from the imputation. 'For blood it defileth the land: and the land cannot be cleansed of the blood that is shed therein, but by the blood of him that shed it.'[1]

How necessary, in the present state of the world, is it to reduce mines, railway management, navigation by steam, and the whole range of our activity, to a sanatory police, to ensure security to limb and life! It is amazing that a precept expressed by four short words should cover interests so vast, so universal, so enduring.

It is one of the anomalies of human nature, that there should be two ways in a case like this—to create temptation, and to require a guide-post to point out the one in which we ought to walk. How can one entertain a hostile intent against another's life? Impossible as it may seem, murder has its charms to growing multitudes, even under the light of our civilisation, to provoke from a distinguished essayist a treatise on 'Murder as a fine art.' Few periods have evinced more hellish skill in the practice of it than our own. To say nothing of the multitude of private murders, what an amount of slaughter in wars of revenge, of ambition, of conquest, and from the lust of territorial extension! Six millions are said to have perished in the Bonapartean wars of a past age; and this is but an item of the sacrifices made to that Moloch of the balance of power in Europe; while in America hundreds of thousands have fallen in the endeavour to perpetuate the slavery of four

[1] Deut. xxii. 8; Ex. xxi. 21; Deut. xxi. 1-9; Num. xxxv. 33.

millions of people. Who will say that Infinite Wisdom uttered an unnecessary interdict in proclaiming, in a voice of thunder, from the rugged peaks of Sinai, 'Thou shalt not kill?'

The seventh commandment, 'Thou shalt not commit adultery,'[1] reflects also a spiritual as well as a natural truth. As it bears extensively on the interests of this life, so of our relations to a higher world, where 'the bride, the Lamb's wife,' enjoys high and holy communion with Him by whom she has been redeemed and presented without spot to God.[2]

Sex itself, out of which marriage takes its rise, involves the radical truth of one thing complemented by another,—love by truth—will by understanding—body by soul—soul by spirit—Christ by His church, His body, the complement or fulness of Him who filleth all in all.[3] As it is through the church that Christ acts upon this world to restore it to God, how is He complete as a Saviour without it? On this mysterious law,—seen in the sunbeams, where light is complemented by heat,—seen in the meanest plants, seen in everything, and most of all in the spiritual coalescence of the soul with God,—on this all-pervading principle the apostle bases his doctrine of marriage. This is a great mystery, that two should be one; but I am speaking of Christ and His church.[4] Marriage, in our earthly views of it, never comes fully up to its prototype in the spiritual universe.

The interdict of the seventh commandment bears alike upon our mortal and immortal relations. It prohibits idolatry; it condemns wandering affections; it enjoins purity of heart, that thus we may see God.

[1] Ex. xx. 14.
[2] Rev. xix. 7, xxi. 9; Eph. v. 27.
[3] Eph. i. 23.
[4] Eph. v. 32.

Our union with God is not institutional, not the result of ceremonial vows, though vows may be an expression of it; but the tie of supreme devotion of heart, as affection must precede marriage to render it valid. Our marriages expire at death, but our union with God is eternal.

As we said in our last chapter, the seventh commandment does not forbid, it sanctifies the union of the sexes, by imposing the restraints which ensure the happiness of the parties, the training of children, and beneficent results to general society. Hence arise the parental and filial affections; thence brotherly and sisterly love; thence the endearments of home; and thence the care of the sick and aged in the bosom of affection, to smooth their pathway to the grave. With singular accuracy of inspired discernment, the opposite of marriage in the intercourse of the sexes is spoken of as a state of estrangement; 'the stranger,' 'strange woman,' or 'women,' denoting separation from family, home, children, and domestic ties,—those cast off from the social system amid the loathing of kindred, and becoming the bane of virtue and order.[1] States derive their stability from the exclusiveness of the family ties —one man with one woman, till death parts them, as our Lord teaches;[2] and they cannot long survive the unsettling of this relation. Rome laid the foundation of her power while her matrons were in honour; she lost it when concubinage succeeded to their place.

The seventh commandment is interpreted by our Lord to prohibit the unchaste desires in which the violations of it originate; which is a further evidence that the second table, like the first, is primarily an

---

[1] Prov. ii. 16; 1 Kings xi. 1; Prov. xxii. 14, xxiii. 27.
[2] Matt. xix. 6.

interior force, and not a regulator of conduct imposed from without. The apostle also takes a like view of lasciviousness, as a power within dominating the man, and precipitating him upon 'uncleanness with all greediness.'[1] That this is a point of temptation, and needing such a law to warn us against the house 'where the dead are, and her guests are in the depths of hell,' who will doubt?

Property rights are inseparable from personality. In whatever state or world a being exists as a personal entity—a responsible individuality—his intellect, his power to give or receive happiness, to serve or be served, and all within the range of his voluntary agency, are his to use or refuse, as much as any material possession. If another uses what is his, it must be by his consent, or it is stealing. May not gifts of mind be appropriated without the consent of the owner, as well as of money? Is not many a slave, without money, robbed of his ingenuity by having it coerced into another's service, and many a man of intellect compelled to use his gifts to enrich others rather than himself? Locks and keys may be unknown in heaven, but not so of property rights.

The eighth commandment—'Thou shalt not steal'[2] —is therefore equally comprehensive with the others. Stealing is depriving another of his property without his consent, and becomes robbery when it is done by violence or fraud, when the consent is obtained on false pretences. When it is the result of political power, it is despotism. It is coercing subordinates into subserviency, to build up privilege on their blood, bones, and sinews. This is the worst of all stealing, because it robs a man of himself, under various institu-

[1] Matt. v. 28; Eph. iv. 19, 29.   [2] Ex. xx. 15.

tional powers and pretexts; by education and habits conducted and formed under a social incubus,—depriving millions of their right by taking away their sense of it or power to assert it,—dooming the many to a poverty that wrecks their manhood, to ruin the few by luxury and idleness. Alas for the founders of empire, that they did their work with so little regard to the voice of God speaking from Sinai!

Cicero reasons on the morals of trade in a way that might prove edifying to our times. He supposes the case of a ship from Alexandria, loaded with wheat, arriving at Rhodes in a time of famine, with the knowledge that other ships would soon come in with like cargoes to glut the market; and the question is, Would her crew be bound to make known this fact, or could they with impunity accept famine prices for their own cargo? He quotes an old Greek moralist as denying their right to do it. Would we in our times deny that right? Says an old catechism: 'The eighth commandment requires the lawful procuring and furthering the wealth and outward estate of ourselves and others.' Another still says: 'It commandeth us to beguile no man, to occupy no unlawful wares, to envy no man his wealth, and to think nothing profitable that either is not just, or differeth from right or honesty.'

This law is also violated, by depriving of their just expectations those who are dependent upon us, through idleness, prodigality, gaming, or self-indulgence. Parents who thus beggar their children, husbands or wives who thus abuse their power over each other, bringing ruin by extravagance, are violators of God's law of property. A wife has no right to live beyond her husband's means, nor a husband and father to dispose of his income in disregard of the claims of his family. In all these relations we have a mutual property in each other; and in the sense of God's law, it is stealing to disregard each other's claims. We condemn stealing in the ordinary sense, and yet we perhaps practise it in subtler and more fatal methods. By idleness and prodigality, how many paupers are thrown upon the public charge! How many are robbed of education and position! How many wrecked by gambling! How much fraud is committed by the falsification of weights and measures, by misrepresentations in buying and selling, by monopolizing the market to raise the price of articles on which the masses subsist, and other ways of doing by others just as we would not have them do by us![1]

This law involves the positive as well as the negative, binding us to promote the wealth of others, to seek not our own good exclusively, but that of our neighbour,[2] and to refrain from all occupations which do not afford to society an equivalent for what we take. That we need the admonition of such a precept always before us, as a guide to justice, truth, and right in every transaction of life, is clear from all the experiences of the commercial world. Does not the word from Sinai—'Thou shalt not steal'—meet a great necessity, and cover infinite and eternal interests?

Nor is the duty of truth-speaking less pervading or significant. It covers the whole extent of our powers of communication, by speech, by gesture, by deeds, or even of our not speaking or doing with intent to deceive. In character, what is more beautiful than truth and sincerity?—than lying, what more odious? What insult is sooner avenged than the given lie? Men most false in themselves still honour truth, as Balaam

[1] Matt. vii. 12.   [2] 1 Cor. x. 24.

with criminal intent could exclaim, 'Must I not take heed, and speak that which the Lord hath put in my mouth?'[1]

Truth is of God and heaven, and the basis of all true happiness. He that came from God brought with Him 'grace and truth.'[2] 'Thou shalt not bear false witness against thy neighbour,'[3] is a precept which aims at bringing us up to a heavenly standard, that God's will may be done here as there. Every departure from truth is an assault upon the God of truth, and upon a chief constituent of social happiness. Lying is false witness *to, about,* or *against* a neighbour, because it is a communication or impression for somebody to receive, and from its nature is social, not solitary. When it is *about* a neighbour, it is slander —the most cruel of all personal assaults.

> 'Good name, in man and woman, dear my lord,
> Is the immediate jewel of their souls.
> Who steals my purse, steals trash; 'tis something—nothing;
> 'Twas mine, 'tis his, and has been slave to thousands;
> But he that filches from me my good name,
> Robs me of that which not enriches him,
> And makes me poor indeed.'[4]

How often have the roses of health faded from the cheek of a victim of scandal, when the cause was not suspected! The poison is more dangerous and deadly, for the stealthy manner in which it is infused. How often have nations been convulsed and deluged in blood by lying diplomacy!

Detraction in its mildest form; telling what is true of another, with intent to injure him; keeping back the truth, to avoid doing him a service; disparaging innuendoes; dubious hints to excite suspicion; retailing

---

[1] Num. xxiii. 12. [2] John i. 17.
[3] Ex. xx. 16. [4] *Othello,* Act iii. Sc. 3.

another's scandal, under the disclaimer of not believing it; interlarding conversation with what will draw from others words of detraction, and thus virtually saying, 'Report, and we will report it;'[1]—these are some of the innumerable practices in our complicated civilisation against which Sinai levels its thunders—'Thou shalt not bear false witness against thy neighbour.' 'Better be a deaf man who heard not, and in whose mouth are no reproofs,' than deal uncharitably with another's good name.[2]

Teaching false doctrines is wholesale lying, like poison in the conduits that supply a city with water, unsettling the faith of thousands, and perhaps corrupting their morals. Those who built up Paganism, Mohammedanism, and the Papacy, may be too numerous, and spread over too many ages, to be charged personally with the wrong—as a general malaria can be traced to no particular source—but is the bane less deadly? Is it not the sad entail of a thousand generations? Does it not take within its fell swoop thousands of millions of human beings?

A restored law, that should render truth the basis of personal character and of social life, would preclude infinite evils from the human family, both in this and the world to come. It would establish confidence between man and man, give security to trade, make friendships secure and happy, and inspire the truly poetical song, 'Surely His salvation is nigh them that fear Him, that glory may dwell in our land. Mercy and truth are met together; righteousness and peace have kissed each other. Truth shall spring out of the earth, and righteousness shall drop down from heaven. Yea, the Lord will give that which is good, and our

[1] Jer. xx. 10. [2] Ps. xxxviii. 13, 14.

land shall yield her increase. Righteousness shall go before Him, and shall set us in the way of His steps.'[1] When the point of temptation comes, let us look up and read what God has written, and avoid all incentives to violate the ninth commandment.

The law from Sinai is the first code to aim at disciplined desires. All other legislation contents itself with external acts. But when the full force of the current remains, what avails to dam it at one point, merely to have it break out in another? The current itself must be absorbed or turned in the direction of beneficence and truth, or nothing is gained, except the semblance of security. Disciplined desires, contentment with what we have in hand or in prospect—this is the end of the last of the commandments: 'Thou shalt not covet.'[2]

It bears upon every other precept in the decalogue, by promoting the state of mind which ensures obedience. The others may be merely externally obeyed, but this one never. It takes effect directly on the internal man; and there is no obedience which does not put that in a state of moderated and truthful desire. It anticipates in law what is taught in the Gospel, 'Ye must be born again.'[3] No man can have a subdued and chastened spiritual life without God's restored dominion in his soul, or Christ dwelling in him by faith.[4] By this we learn, in whatever situation we are, therewith to be content.[5] This new life in God is the only fulfilment of the last commandment.

Men may exercise over themselves a philosophical restraint, may study quietude from selfish motives, may stoically accept pain as coolly as pleasure, may

---

[1] Ps. lxxxv. 9-13. [2] Ex. xx. 17. [3] John iii. 3.
[4] Eph. iii. 17. [5] Phil. iv. 11; 2 Cor. vii. 4.

restrain exorbitant desires which they cannot gratify because they are annoying, may repress the emotions of anxiety and fear, may have a constitutional hardihood that carries them through trying scenes with much equanimity, and in many ways simulate the condition contemplated by the tenth commandment. But the soul is a fountain of desires, the jets of which gush up; and there is no way of dealing with them, but to find a direction in which they may be allowed full scope. This is God's way of curing covetousness, changing the bent of desire towards all that is pure, and good, and holy. And a soul in that state is in no danger of coveting his neighbour's house, his neighbour's wife, his neighbour's man-servant or maid-servant, nor his ox or ass, nor anything that is his neighbour's. How should he, when his resources of happiness are already complete?

It is on the basis of this spiritual fulness that many of the exhortations of the gospel are rendered possible, and escape being positively ridiculous, such as, 'Rejoice evermore,' 'Be careful for nothing,' 'Take no thought for the morrow,' and the like, which, on any other ground, would be like telling a man not to feel under the surgeon's knife.[1] The idea of Renan, that such teaching is a mere reflection of the simplicity and carelessness of Galilean life, is contradicted by all experience of shepherds and shepherdesses, or men in a rural state, whose discontent is often quite equal to that of men in cities or in more refined circles. It is not in the outer life that the exhortation against carefulness takes effect, but in such an absorption in divine love, and such a hold on heaven, as neutralizes our carking worldly cares, and gives us infinite repose in

[1] Phil. iv. 4–7; Matt. vi. 25.

God. It is in a faith overcoming the world, not in a philosophy that silences the clamours of sense; and hence it is, that the greatest delectation is sometimes seen in the midst of painful disease and inevitable death.

This cursory view of the commandments is sufficient to show us how remote their proper seat is from all other codes, — the *sanctum sanctorum* of human nature, thence throwing out their influence over the whole life; how central their spirit is to the gospel, as their letter was to the Mosaic institutes; how applicable to all worlds of accountable agency; how admonitory against all the ways of evil towards which we are tempted; and how complete a summary they contain of all piety and virtue.

CHAPTER XXI.

THE THEOCRATIC AS A TYPE OF THE SPIRITUAL MAN.

BEFORE dismissing the subject of law, we will consider the character of the man who outwardly lived up to its requirements. He stood as an effigy of what 'grace, reigning through righteousness unto eternal life by Jesus Christ our Lord,' now accomplishes upon a truly believing soul.[1] Such an one is in *spirit* all that the theocratic man was in *form*. God rules in his soul; the kingdom of heaven there has its seat;[2] and in him is realized the original plan of human nature as actuated by the inbreathed divinity.[3] This is redemption, this is seeking and saving that which was lost.[4]

As the lost state consists in being ruled by fleshly impulses and natural ideas to the extent of incapacitating men for conceiving what it is to be ruled by the Spirit of God, it pleased the Lord to present the idea to them in the theocratic man, who stood related to the spiritual reality as the mould to the implement to which it gives form. The mould, though of base material, and unfit for use except as a mould, is carefully polished, clear in outline, and perhaps a more perfect ideal than the implement which it shapes. So the theocratic Israelite, though a mere thing of form and ceremony, may furnish a more perfect type of what we ought to be as spiritual men, than doctrine, or than any other example except Christ Himself. Christ alone

[1] Rom. v. 21.   [2] Luke xvii. 21.   [3] Gen. ii. 7.   [4] Matt. xviii. 11.

fulfilled the law-ideal, in His perfect subordination in all things to the will of the Father who sent Him.[1] The theocratic man was all outline, and could easily be defined; but believers are often a rough casting, though of the genuine stuff. 'Art thou a master in Israel, and knowest not these things?'[2] said Jesus to one of the best characters formed by the law; showing how totally ignorant he was of the true spirit and intent of his own ceremonial observances. He was a good model, but useless as an organ of spiritual power. The Jews who were most exact in observing their law, were the greatest enemies of Him who was the sole exemplar of its spirit and power.

The theocratic man acknowledged God's absolute property in his person and inheritance, by paying yearly his half-shekel of ransom money, and a tenth of his proceeds.[3] This was done with the significant formulary, 'A Syrian ready to perish was my father,' and 'he went down into Egypt, where he endured hard bondage;' and 'the Lord brought us forth with a mighty hand.' 'And, behold, I have brought the first-fruits of the land which Thou, O Lord, hast given me.'[4] Thus his Syrian forefathers and their descendants were conceded as owing their preservation to God; his half-shekel was the ransom money of a forfeited life; and his very possessions were not his own, but the property of Jehovah, to whom the annual rental was due, and served as a perpetual bond for his allegiance. And the captivity of Israel was ascribed to their unfaithfulness to the terms on which they held their land, in not allowing it the rest of its Sabbath; and thus, by cruel

---

[1] John iv. 34, vi. 38, xvii. 4; Isa. xlii. 21; Matt. v. 17.
[2] John iii. 10.   [3] Ex. xxx. 12, 15.
[4] Deut. xxvi. 5–11, xxvii. 30.

bondage for seventy years in Babylon, they were brought to a sense of God's absolute right to them and their inheritance.[1] This was a great literal truth to that people; but how much greater in its spiritual significance to us, who have been redeemed from hell by the precious blood of Christ!

The theocratic man abstained from all intercourse in eating, drinking, or social communion with a Gentile;[2] would not buy meat in a heathen market, lest it should be unclean, or had been offered to an idol; and thus he kept himself from all ceremonial pollution.[3] If by any means he had become polluted, he instantly resorted to the required sacrifices to set himself right with his law.[4] He was a constant and earnest student of the Old Testament Scriptures; and a man every way actuated by his religion in the minutest affairs of life. No nation on earth could know a true Jew without knowing him *as* a Jew, because he carried with him the mark of his religion wherever he went, and made it conspicuous in all his active life. The Roman historians[5] speak of him as distinguishable in the imperial city for his religion, as the negro for his sable skin or woolly head. Is this no lesson to us to come out of the world and be separate, and touch not the unclean thing? Must there not be always, in every place, and among all people, a difference, obvious and unmistakeable, between a man ruled by heaven and those who are ruled by earth?[6] The Jewish mode of

[1] Lev. xxvi. 34; 2 Chron. xxxvi. 21.
[2] 'They eat and lodge with one another only.'—Tacitus, Book v. ch. v.
[3] 1 Cor. x. 25-28; Rom. xiv. 2, 3, 15.
[4] Lev. v. 1-10.
[5] 'Whatever is held sacred by the Romans, with the Jews is profane.'—Tacitus, Book v. ch. iv.
[6] 2 Cor. vi. '7; Rev. xviii. 4.

showing devotion to Jehovah was the outward mould into which our spirit is to be cast, not with perishable, but imperishable materials. Our heart devotion to the divine love which is the fulfilling of the law must ever be in the ascendant, to make our religion the ruling power; and so far as we fail therein, our sacrifice of repentance and our faith in atoning blood must be resorted to, to set us right with God. That we draw our life from Him, must be so clear a fact, that the world shall 'take knowledge of us, that we have been with Jesus.'[1]

Our religious terms are chiefly derived from what pertained to this theocratic man. We are 'pardoned,' not simply in the sense of being exempted from punishment, but of being restored to true holiness, as he was by sacrifice to ceremonial purity. A sacrifice that did not restore him thus was unavailing; as also is the death of Christ, if it does not result in the setting up of the kingdom of heaven in our souls. As our holiness was the object of His death, how is it to succeed so far as we live under the dominion of the flesh? There remaineth no more sacrifice for sins to those who know the truth, but will not live under its ruling.[2] Sin and punishment being inseparable, God's pardon in cancelling the one destroys the other, and never, like ours, releases a man from prison to send him out a criminal the same as at first. It removes the punishment by taking away the love of sinning. Herein is seen the efficacy of Christ's death, and not otherwise. Ceremonial and human pardons leave the criminal as he was before; God's restores him to the obedience of faith.[3]

[1] Jer. vi. 27; 1 Pet. i. 7-9; Acts iv. 13.
[2] Heb. x. 26.   [3] Rom. i. 5.

So of justification: it is to become just and right with God, by faith working with love as a power to make us what we are declared to be, or what we actually ought to be, through the imparted life from Christ. God never accepts as just one who does not fulfil the righteousness of the law by walking, not after the flesh, but after the Spirit. No sacrifice can avail to his justification which does not make him a spiritual man. 'The just shall live by *faith*,' as a power doing all for him that sight did for Adam in his innocency, so far at least as the ruling power in his soul is concerned.[1] The actual dominion over us to which Christ succeeds when we receive Him by faith, is the substance of which all other justification is shadow. It is 'the righteousness of God by faith,' or that we take hold of, enjoy, and practise, when we truly 'believe to the saving of our souls.' As the sacrifice under the law could not avail to justify a delinquent Israelite, unless he brought it to the priest, and was a party in offering it, no more can that of Christ to one who does not accept the Holy Spirit's ruling in his soul.[2] The work of making sinners just and right with God is no abstraction of law; but a concrete and experimental fact of the life, lifting the soul to all that is good, and pure, and holy. The motions of sin in the members are not indeed dead, nor are we beyond Satan's fiery darts; but our security is in continuing practically in Christ, 'walking not after the flesh, but after the Spirit,' and then we shall have 'no condemnation.'[3] Justification stands related to sanctification, as the child to the man; being complete in all his members, but not yet grown to 'the measure of the stature of the fulness of Christ.'[4]

---

[1] Heb. ii. 4; Rom. i. 17; Gal. iii. 11; Heb. x. 38.
[2] Rom. iii. 22; Heb. x. 39.   [3] Rom. viii. 1.   [4] Eph. iv. 13.

The law of Moses, as we have seen, legislates in reference to thoughts, feelings, and motives—ground unapproached by any civil code—but without the power of doing more than convince us how wrong we are to the very core of our being; but the gospel comes to realize the end and purpose of this stringent legislation. It is a power to cleanse the sanctuary of the soul, 'that Christ may dwell in our hearts by faith,' and that we 'may be filled with all the fulness of God.'[1] The theocracy was contrived with reference to restoring this lost truth of an indwelling God, doing it at first in effigy, to prepare for the substance in them that believe in Jesus. It was a vast polity controlling every minutia of a man's life; and yet having no head or sovereign, except the Invisible God, ruling from the hidden recesses of the temple. No other government is like it. We have governments ruling by that ideal thing called a constitution, which, as the supreme law of the land, distributes its powers among those who are sworn to carry out its provisions. Thus in England, from the Queen to the constable, all rule by an idea; all exercise prerogatives not personal to themselves, but in virtue of the constitution or the nation. Not so in Israel; all power there centred in a personal God ruling from the mercy-seat. It was a divine autocracy, and yet administered according to the covenant entered into between God and the people. There was no sharer in the throne—no successor; but His prerogatives were eternal: no cabinet of ministers; no counsellors of state; all authority inhering in the personal God. His behests had no other reason but ' I am the Lord.'[2] His moral code is grounded in His

[1] Eph. iii. 17–19.
[2] Lev. xviii. 5, xix. 2; Ex. xx. 2;-Isa. xli. 4, xlix. 7.

The Theocratic as a Type of Spiritual Man. 259

right to rule us. So far as prophets, priests, or kings were called into His service, it was by His appointment, and to exercise only such prerogatives as He assigned them.

Our Christian theology derives thence its doctrine of the kingdom of heaven among men, as consisting in 'righteousness, peace, and joy in the Holy Ghost.'[1] Thence comes one 'citizenship of the saints and of the household of God;' the co-heirship of Jews and Gentiles as children of Abraham by faith; our general assembly and church of the first-born which are registered in heaven; our New Jerusalem coming down from God to rule in the souls of men; and, in fact, all the main features of the Christian scheme are cast in this theocratic mould.[2] Following Christ in all things, and being ruled by Him; going forth without the camp, bearing His reproach; being crucified with Him; reigning with Him; regarding ourselves as not our own, but bought with a price; redeemed from the earth by His blood, and all similar ideas, may be distinctly traced to this old dispensation.[3]

Things were indeed tolerated under the theocracy in themselves evil, as we wink at the foibles of children, not as sanctioning them, but in accommodation to the weakness of the people or 'the hardness of their hearts.' On this principle polygamy was tolerated, though a violation of the original marriage law.[4] The right of parents to take the life of their children, which prevailed at Rome many ages after Moses, was

[1] Rom. xiv. 17.
[2] Eph. ii. 19, iii. 9 ; Rom. iii. 30 ; Heb. xii. 22.
[3] Matt. xvi. 24; Heb. xiii. 11-13; Rom. v. 20, 21, viii. 17; Matt. xix. 28 ; 1 Cor. vi. 20.
[4] Matt. xix. 7-9 ; Gen. ii. 22, 23.

not absolutely repealed in the Levitical law, but only fenced around by restraints to render it innocuous. The avenger of blood was not regarded as criminal in taking life for life; but the cities of refuge provided a means of escape to the manslayer, with a view to a trial of his case before impartial judges.[1] Thus the theocracy, though based upon the authority of a personal God, was one of adjustment to human infirmity, and not a Utopia of heavenly life. It assimilated into itself, no doubt, customs borrowed from Egypt, from the nomadic tribes of Arabia, as well as those descending from the patriarchs, to fit itself to the ideas of the age and the state of human progress. The tribal division of the nation and the authority of heads of families were recognised, though deprived of their former sacerdotal and kingly prerogatives. The priesthood was confined to the tribe of Levi; and civil authority was exercised by judges and kings, whose authority was limited by the priestly and prophetic offices, which were always a restraint upon royal authority. The king could hold office only by divine appointment, and was restricted in the costliness and splendour of court pageantry, and was required to govern by law,—a provision never departed from without entailing calamity.[2] The kingly throne was deemed an anomaly, and conceded to the demand of the people; though Samuel recorded his protest against it, and God deemed it a rejection of Himself as the nation's sovereign.[3] This principle of accommodation to human infirmity is as conspicuous under the reign of grace as that of law; and the Holy Spirit bestows His gifts upon persons that come far short of

---

[1] Deut. xxi. 18-21; Num. xxxv. 9-34.
[2] Deut. xvii. 14-20, xviii. 15-22; 1 Sam. xv. 10-31.
[3] 1 Sam. viii. 4-22.

the highest standard of Christian character, and upon organizations that neither in a social, civil, nor ecclesiastical point of view can be accepted as the kingdom of heaven among men.

Indeed, 'they that are whole need not a physician, but they that are sick;' and as God's mission to men is to heal and restore them, His reign is a perpetual contest with individual and organic evil.[1] Where else is the place of the physician, but among the sick? The theocracy was the ruling of a personal God, not over angelic beings, but over a lost race, centring all power in Himself, whether in tolerating evils or enjoining good, and extending His requisitions over the whole life of man.[2] This is the original idea: God ruling us; the spirit-world in the ascendant over the natural; reason and conscience regulating the appetites and passions; and the whole man, in his individual and social condition, in his inward and outward life, subject to heavenly laws. If the theocratic man was not perfect, he was an heir of promise, and his hope took hold upon a brilliant future.[3] He derived his blood from one born out of the order of nature, and he carried in his flesh the seal of his covenant with God.[4] His law was the efflorescence and fruitage of the divine seeding in the life of Abraham, constituting a sure basis for his great anticipations. How should not the promises which had rendered his past illustrious, be destined to a still greater consummation in the future? What other nation was ever founded upon hope, and for four thousand years

---

[1] Matt. ix. 12.
[2] Acts xiv. 16, xvii. 30. God is here represented as acting on a like policy of 'winking' at evils in dealing with all nations.
[3] Gen. xii. 3, xviii. 18; Ps. lxxii. 17; Acts iii. 25; Gal. iii. 8.
[4] Gen. xviii. 9-15, xvii. 10.

kept distinct from all others, awaiting the fulfilment? Is it not a miracle of providence? What an exact type have we here of the Christian life, which is one of hope rather than realization! 'We are saved by hope;' and the Holy Spirit dwells with us as a 'Spirit of *promise,* and the *earnest* of our inheritance, until the redemption of the purchased possession, unto the praise of His glory.'[1]

The theocratic man was 'cut off from his people,' if he did not 'afflict his soul' on the great day of atonement, if he acknowledged a strange god, if he practised magic, if he was guilty of blasphemy, if he cursed his parents, if he profaned the Sabbath, if he was guilty of adultery, the same as if he kidnapped or murdered.[2] Death was the penalty in all these cases, not as an example for us in our civil legislation, but to set forth the terrible sin and punishment of him who sacrifices his duty to God, and his life in God, to gratify his selfish desires; to conform to his natural ideas, instead of those of the Spirit that dwelleth in us; or to achieve any worldly end at the expense of glory, honour, and immortality. The spiritual man is taught by the theocracy that God is with him and in him, everywhere and at all times; and not to eat, and drink, and do everything to His glory, is treason against His government. Would a subject in the very audience-chamber of his sovereign dare to be thus unmindful of him? The Jew was under a government that appealed to him oftener, and in more ways than any

---

[1] Rom. viii. 24; Eph. i. 13, 14.
[2] Ex. xxii. 20; Lev. xx. 5, 6; Deut. xvii. 2-5; Ex. xxii. 18; Deut. xviii. 9-22; Lev. xix. 31, xxiv. 15, 16; Num. xv. 32-36; Ex. xxi. 15, 16; Lev. xx. 9; Deut. xxi. 18-21; Ex. xxi. 12-14; Deut. xxii. 13-27, xxiv. 17.

other on earth. It pressed upon him at all points like the ambient air. Stamp-duties and income-taxes are no such reminders of the civil authorities as were offered of God's right by every foot of land from Dan to Beersheba. The people could not go out or come in without meeting passages of the law inscribed upon their door-posts. In putting on or taking off their garments, they found them fringed with reminders of God. If in the house as families, or walking abroad as friends, the one topic, God and His law, was the subject of conversation. In eating, washing, sleeping, in labour and in rest, they were still to think of God. And if all else failed, the Sabbath of days, of weeks, and of years, with the jubilee trumpet resounding through the land to arrest the course of labour, to cancel debts, to free the enslaved, and to produce a general overturning of business and social relations, could not fail of bringing home to every house and heart a sense of the mighty force of law holding all alike in its grasp.

'Ye are bought with a price; therefore glorify God in your body, and in your spirit, which are God's,' are words enforced by two thousand years' previous history, beginning with Abraham and culminating in Christ's glorification and the Spirit's baptism.[1] 'What manner of persons ought we to be, in all holy conversation and godliness,' since in us as Christians centres all this legislation! We are the chosen generation, the royal priesthood, the holy nation, the peculiar people, to show forth the praises of Him who hath called us out of darkness into His marvellous light.[2]

[1] 1 Cor. vi. 20.   [2] 2 Pet. iii. 11; 1 Pet. ii. 9.

CHAPTER XXII.

GOD BORN OF MAN, THAT MAN MAY BE BORN OF GOD.

AS all divine laws centring in the theocratic man failed to raise him from a fleshly to a spiritual life, the question is, How is this indispensable thing to be done? How is God to enter through the closed gates of the soul, and resume His rightful dominion? How is the kingdom of heaven to come among men? What must God do, and what must we do, that we may be saved? The law raised the question, but failed to answer it, or to impart the required holiness, 'through the weakness of the flesh,' or because we were 'without strength' to keep its precepts.[1] The answer given by infinite love and wisdom we are now to consider, especially in those points of view which bear upon our general subject.

Those aspects of the question which pertain to law as a transcript of the Divine Mind, the ethical nature of God, or the public sentiment of the moral universe, that God is bound to respect in dealing with sinners, we leave to those who understand them—we do not. Of the laws governing the Infinite and the Incomprehensible, the writer claims to know nothing. 'I am the Lord' is the only reason He deigns to give of His conduct. And it is as unscriptural as it is unphilosophical to speak of law in any other sense than as

[1] Rom. v. 6, viii. 3.

arising from the nature and relation of creatures. The laws of the vegetable and animal kingdoms are not things to be reasoned about or known in the abstract, but only as acting through plants and animals. And moral laws, except as seen in the nature and relations of moral agents, are to us a nonentity; and I fully agree with an able and orthodox divine in England, that to speak of them as a transcript of God's nature is an absurdity. As they cannot exist without God, so they cannot without creatures to feel the weight of the imposed obligation.[1] What the soul needs to give it 'peace with God' is 'faith in our Lord Jesus Christ' as the restored Divinity, doing for him all and more than open vision for a sinless Adam or for angels, justifying him in the sense of making him just, and redeeming him by sanctifying him through the truth, and giving him the adoption and the spirit of a child in God's family.[2] This is the direction which the whole New Testament record takes in dealing with the incarnation; and we would humbly follow its leading.

Can we wonder that seed-truths of inspired men centre in the Divine Incarnation? Does the universe know a greater fact? God's tally of the ages is different from ours. Kingdoms, conquering armies, diplomatic agencies, and material progress, elicit no pæans in heaven; but over one repentant sinner the angels rejoice.[3] God marks off the cycles of time by

---

[1] Since writing these sentiments, the following passage from Dr. Wardlaw's *Christian Ethics* has come to the notice of the writer: 'Of the abstract subsistence of principles [that is, of law] independent of all being whatever, we are incapable of forming any conception; nay, the very attempt to form it involves an immediate contradiction. There can be no principles without mind; and to annihilate mind is to annihilate principles' (p. 240).

[2] Rom. v. 1, 2, viii. 15.   [3] Luke xv. 7.

spiritual progress. The patriarchal worship had its use, but failed to extend God's rule over a lost race. It had no doctrine, no organization, no separation; and therefore succumbed first to lust and the flood, and then to idolatry and demonism.[1] Abraham pledged his race to Jehovah alone, on the principle of a rigid separation from all other nations, and thus began a cycle of covenant, to which the law, 'because of transgressions,' or as a guilt-revealer, was 'added four hundred years afterwards,' to prepare the way for Him who came as 'the end of the law for righteousness to every one that believeth.' He effects the death of the natural man upon which the law took hold, and thus cancels its claims—as the law of marriage by the death of one of the parties is cancelled—that by this process a resurrection-life might ensue, the divine ruling in the soul,—a result which the previous dispensations had failed to effect.[2]

Under all these ages of ceremony the world became darker and darker, more and more fleshly and material; and from Malachi to the birth of John the Baptist, a period of five hundred years, we have no record of either miracle or inspiration.[3] Even heathenism had

[1] Gen. vi. 11, 12, xi. 1-9.
[2] Gal. iii. 17-20; Rom. vii. 6, x. 4.
[3] The Old Testament describes the Jews as 'stiff-necked' and material in their general type of thought, and the same character of them is given in the New. The Roman poets, a little later, speak of them in like manner. 'The Jews,' Juvenal says, 'will sell you any dreams you please for the minutest coin' (*Satire* vi.).

> 'Now the once hallowed fountain, grove, and fane,
> Are let to Jews, a wretched, wandering train,
> Whose wealth is but a basket stuffed with hay.'
> JUVENAL, *Satire* iii. 13.

To this day they are the most material of all the races. Such was the nature that Christ took upon Himself to redeem it to holiness and

lost much of its conservative influence, and been succeeded by vice, levity, and atheism. The first chapter of Romans gives a doleful picture of its condition.[1] Little vigour remained in anything but Roman law, magnificence and its iron-clad legions uniting the world in a one-man power. That old serpent the Devil and Satan exulted in the completeness and finality of his dominion over man, and his imps, as 'unclean spirits,' ran riot with the people.[2].

Such was the period of the Divine Incarnation. In Heaven's account this is the central fact of human history, and is so represented by prophets and apostles, being spoken of by the one as 'the last days,' 'the latter days,' and as 'the days of these kings,' alluding to the Roman rule, 'the end of sins,' in the sense of cancelling its power to them that believe;[3] and by the others, that is, the apostles, it is spoken of as 'the fulness of times, when God sent forth His Son,' who 'was manifested in these last times,' 'now once in the end of the world,' 'the ends of the world are come,' 'the fulness of times,'—all centring upon the incarnation and apostolic ministry.[4] Thus, both in anticipation and retrospection, among the inhabitants of heaven first, and through them afterwards revealed to human thought and experience, God's union to man in flesh, in order to unite man to God in spirit, is the central luminary, irradiating all of human history deemed worthy of the notice of inspiration. The world without it would be worse than a polar winter. The

heaven, as if success there must give Him success everywhere in recovering a people to Himself out of all nations.

[1] Rom. i. 18-32.
[2] Matt. iv. 24; Mark ix. 38; Luke iv. 41, ix. 1.
[3] Gen. xlix. 1, 10; Num. xxiv. 14-19; Dan. ii. 28, 44, ix. 24, et al.
[4] Gal. iv. 4; 1 Pet. i. 20; Heb. ix. 26; 1 Cor. x. 11; Eph. i. 10.

heading of this chapter is one of the pithy and comprehensive sayings of Augustine, that 'God was born of man, that man might be born of God.'

God in human flesh leading the way in which every soul must follow to reach eternal life, is another form of the same thought. The oft-repeated words of Christ, 'Follow me,'[1] have a deeper significance than simple imitation of His virtues. What makes our modern pulpit so weak is, that it is occupied by so many men who are incapable of more than an outside view of following Christ, or who have no idea of it as a death of sinful flesh in order to a resurrection-life in spirit. 'Taking up the cross to follow Christ' does not mean, as too many suppose, doing public duties or making public professions from which we shrink; but it means the crucifixion of sin as our nature or as ourselves, that Christ may live in us in place of self, and 'that the life we live in the flesh may be by the faith of the Son of God, who loved us and gave Himself for us.'[2] Our Lord speaks of those who had 'followed Him in the regeneration,' plainly intimating that the process of death to His flesh, through which He was passing to reach His resurrection and glorification, was an example of what all flesh, as a ruling power in the soul, must pass through in order to our reaching a spiritual and heavenly life.[3] 'For the suffering of death He was crowned with glory and honour;' and to join Him in His glory, 'sitting on thrones judging the twelve tribes of Israel,' we must have that sort of 'fellowship in His sufferings' which only the crucifixion of the sin of our flesh can give us.[4] The death of flesh as to its ruling

---

[1] Matt. iv. 19, ix. 9; Mark ii. 14; Luke v. 27, et al.
[2] Matt. xvi. 24, x. 34; Luke xiv. 27; Gal. ii. 20.
[3] Matt. xix. 28. [4] Heb. ii. 9; Phil. iii. 10.

is purification from sin; and they who are in this sense dead and buried with Christ in a spiritual baptism, are freed from sin.[1] Hence following Christ in the regeneration is, in the gospel view, sharing with Him in His spiritual life and resurrection glory. He calls us to nothing in which He does not lead the way.

'The Word was made flesh.'[2] The term 'Word' in this passage is God, and the term 'flesh' is man. The Word, as a designation of God, is applied to Him as ruling in the temple, His presence on the mercy-seat in the holy of holies giving name to it as 'the Word,' or 'oracle;'[3] and the Jewish rabbis in Chaldea rendered 'Jehovah' by 'Word' in Greek, in the passage, 'The Word created the world,' and so throughout.[4] John, in like manner, begins his Gospel, 'In the beginning was the Word, and the Word was with God, and the Word was God. The same was in the beginning with God. All things were made by Him; and without Him was not anything made that was made.'[5] He was the source of being and of life, and the life in the incarnation became the light of men, to illuminate their pathway out of the darkness of fleshly dominion into spiritual and heavenly light. John elsewhere speaks of Him as 'the Word of life' and 'the Word of God.'[6]

The relation of the Word both to God and to man is poetically set forth in Proverbs:

'When He prepared the heavens, I was there;
When He set a compass on the face of the deep:
When He gave the sea His decree,
That the waters should not pass His commandment;

---

[1] Rom. vi. 3-9. [2] John i. 14.
[3] 2 Sam. xvi. 23; 1 Kings vi. 16, viii. 6; 2 Chron. iv. 20.
[4] Gen. i. 1. [5] John i. 1-3.
[6] 1 John i. 1; Rev. xix. 13.

> When He appointed the foundations of the earth ;
> Then I was by Him, as one brought up with Him.'

Then the passage closes with His human proclivities, thus :

> 'Rejoicing in the habitable parts of the earth ;
> And my delights were with the sons of men.'[1]

Identity with God and affinity with man are included in the name JEHOVAH; and it was He who became 'the Seed of woman.' 'Great is the mystery of godliness. God was manifest in the flesh.' It is in view of this connection of Christ with the Jehovah of the Old Testament, that the apostles so uniformly refer the salvation of believers to causes beginning in eternity, but revealed in time. They accepted their Redeemer as one who had come to effectuate the work of love on which He had been engaged from the foundation of the world; and what He was doing in their own souls, and in others through their ministry, was a basis of conscious connection with Him who made the world, and who is the dwelling-place of His people in all generations. This connection makes believers the elect of God, the bride, the Lamb's wife.[2]

There is genuine elevation of soul in one who has the spirit of Christ. He is a king and a priest unto God. His name is written in heaven. Everlasting purposes of love centre in him. He is honoured with angelic ministrations. Who can separate him from the love of Christ? His anticipations are as great as his retrospections. He looks for a far more exceeding and eternal weight of glory. His election of God is not a theory, but a faith. How should not a child feel himself an heir of all his father's past and prospective

---

[1] Prov. viii. 27-31.   [2] Rev. xxi. 9.

riches and honours? This election is a thing of which no one can conceive without an inward gracious experience.

But what was the flesh that the Word was made? What a world of reasoning has this question from first to last elicited! And yet how could language or fact make it plainer than inspired pens have left it? Flesh is man as a creature of this earth, or as produced out of the dust of the ground. Thought, intellect, natural conscience, æsthetical taste, the social sentiments, and the power of civil organization, all enter as fully into our conception of man in acting among the elements of this world, as flesh, blood, or bones, or as instinct in animals in fitting them for self-preservation. Man became spiritual, heavenly, and immortal by the inbreathed divinity, which was an act separate and distinct from that which fitted him for a merely earthly life. This was ruled out when he came under the dominion of the flesh, and he became thenceforth animal and worldly in all his proclivities, except so far as his fitness for spiritual life gave place to magic, idolatry, and demonism. His religion was from hell rather than from heaven.

The question is often agitated, whether Christ took flesh in its lapsed state, or in its primeval innocency? The Westminster Confession pertinently answers, that 'the Son of God did take upon Him man's nature, with all the essential properties and *common infirmities* thereof, yet without sin.' Leo, an early writer, says: 'The properties of each substance being all preserved and kept safe, there became by majesty, humility; by strength, infirmity; and by eternity, mortality.' Cyril says: 'Flesh is not the flesh of God, but still continues flesh, although it be the flesh of God.' The apostle says, that 'in all things it behoved Him to be made like unto His brethren,' and that 'He was in all points tempted as we are, yet without sin.'[1] And our Lord says to His disciples, 'Ye are they who have continued with me in my temptations.'[2] The devil tempted Him to a selfish exertion of His miraculous powers, in commanding the stones to become bread for His appetite; to ambition, by showing Him all the kingdoms of the world as within His reach; and to presumption, by casting Himself down from the pinnacle of the temple.[3] Each of these impulses perfectly coincides with the natural feelings which Christ inherited with His flesh, without which He could no more have felt the suggestions of the tempter as a temptation than a brute or a stone. The external temptation must find in the tempted a coincident impulse, a nature suited to take the impression, or there could be no approach to all 'the points' wherein we are tempted.

One thing is perfectly conclusive: that whatever may have been the source of our Lord's temptations, they left Him 'holy, harmless, undefiled, and separate from sinners.' 'He offered Himself without spot to God.' 'He did no evil, neither was guile found in His mouth.'[4] This character of our great Sin-offering was essential to all the types and prophecies of the previous ages. One sin, one stain upon His holy soul, would have unfitted it to be an offering for sin.[5] While this is fully conceded on all hands, is there no danger of robbing Christ of His glory as a conqueror 'travelling in the greatness of His strength,' by withdrawing His nature and condition in flesh from the

---

[1] Heb. ii. 17, iv. 15. [2] Luke xxii. 28.
[3] Matt. iv. 1-12. [4] Heb. vii. 26, ix. 14; 1 Pet. i. 19.
[5] Isa. liii. 9, 10.

ordinary category of humanity, to make sure that He should be immaculate? The Catholics make Him angelic rather than human, representing not only that His own flesh was unlike that of all other men, but that His virgin-mother was equally so, and was transported bodily to heaven. Many Protestants sympathize in these unscriptural views so far as to make Christ's human nature like that of Adam, or at least of a very different type from that of His brethren, which the apostle says it was like. The apostle is very explicit, first denying that He took the nature of angels, and then affirming that He did take the seed of Abraham, which in the Old Testament is charged with greater proclivities to sin than any other race of human kind.[1]

Indeed, the flesh that Christ took upon Him, as being that of man, over whom it had dominated from the beginning of time, had come to be another name for sin. Hence it is called 'the body of the sins of the flesh;' a sinful indulgence is a 'garment spotted by the flesh;' it is spoken of as 'lusting against the spirit;' and our Lord, in taking such a nature, is said to have been 'made sin for us.' This last passage is generally amended by those who quote it, into sin-offering, thus taking from the passage the very gist of its meaning. The idea the apostle expresses is, that as Christ was made sin for us by being born into a nature which is sin in all others, so we, by being born of His Spirit, become in Him the righteousness of God. This exchange of natures, by a mutual birth of Him into us and we unto Him, loses all its force by making

---

[1] Heb. ii. 16; Ex. xxxii. 9, xxxiii. 3-5, xxxiv. 9; Deut. ix. 6, 13, xxxi. 27; 2 Chron. xxx. 8; Isa. xlviii. 4.

[2] Col. ii. 11; Jude 23; Gal. v. 17; 2 Cor. v. 21.

Him simply a sin-offering. The birth of the Word into the 'likeness' and 'fashion of man' as a sinner, was symbolized by Moses in making the brazen serpent in the likeness of the reptile which had infused the bane it was to heal; and our Lord was lifted up in the similitude of the sinful nature which He died to redeem.[1] If there is any truth in language, therefore, or any reliance to be placed upon symbols, the flesh which our Lord took upon Himself was like that of His brethren whom He died to redeem, and not the flesh of Adam in his pristine purity, any more than it was the nature of angels who have never sinned. 'For both He that sanctifieth and they who are sanctified are all of one,' that is, one in blood, one in condition, though infinitely different in character; one in the process of glorification by means of death to flesh; and therefore 'He is not ashamed to call them brethren.'[2] 'And through death He delivers them who through the fear of death were all their lifetime subject to bondage;' and this He does by the crucifixion of their flesh, and their resurrection life in Him, giving them the inward assurance, that 'whether living or dying, they are the Lord's.' As the death and life of Christ were not of Himself as a man, but under the ruling of the Father, whom He obeyed in all things; so the believer's death of sinful flesh and his resurrection to a new life are not of himself, but by the power of the Holy Ghost, and in that sense they are God's. This is evidently the meaning of the saying, 'Whether we live, we live unto the Lord; and whether we die, we die unto the Lord: whether we live therefore, or die, we are the Lord's. For to this end,' or to effect this death and life in us, 'Christ both died, and rose,

[1] Phil. ii. 7, 8; Num. xxi. 9; John iii. 14. [2] Heb. ii. 11.

and revived, that He might be Lord both of the dead and living,' or the presiding power both in the dying and living process.[1]

Now, whatever the condition of the nature which our Lord inherited from the Virgin, the absolute ruling of divinity over all its impulses, even to that of its voluntary sacrifice upon the cross in obedience to the Father's commandment, sanctified it, and made it an expiatory offering for our sins. As the Captain of our salvation, He was thus 'made perfect through suffering;' and this became Him, or was necessary to Him, in bringing many sons unto glory, or in leading us through a like crucifixion of the flesh to spiritual and heavenly life.[2] The apprehension of imputing fleshly pollution to Christ, by admitting that He took human nature in its effete, decayed, and materialized state after four thousand years of pravity, comes from failing to consider that pollution does not arise from the nature, except so far as it is a ruling power. To all others it was sin, because it was the dominant power of their lives, and they were without strength to make it anything else. But in Him it was conquered; it was ruled by the Spirit, which He had without measure; it was from first to last, in the temptations of life and in the suffering of death, so absolutely dominated and subdued by the divinity in Him, as to be as holy as God. Hence, though He was made sin, or what was so to all others, yet it was not so to Him: though He had the serpent-form, He had not its venom, but, on the contrary, a life-giving spiritual energy to counteract and scotch the serpent, to bruise his head and destroy

---

[1] Heb. ii. 15, Rom. xiv. 8, 9; with which compare John x. 18, xv. 10, Acts ii. 23, 34, John iv. 34, v. 30, vi. 39.
[2] Heb. ii. 10.

his power over believing souls; in reference to which He says exultingly, 'I beheld Satan as lightning fall from heaven;' and again, 'Now is the judgment of this world: now shall the prince of this world be cast out; and I, if I be lifted up from the earth, will draw all men unto me.'[1] He had entered Satan's den of fleshly pollution; He had taken the nature dominated by Satan in its effete and decayed condition; and He through the Eternal Spirit had held it uncorrupt, and was ready to offer it upon the cross without spot to God, bruised as to His heel, but crushing the serpent's head.[2] This was our Lord's victory; in this we see Him travelling in the greatness of His strength,—a victory and a strength of which the mistaken zeal of some Christians would deprive Him, by denying that His heel ever touched the serpent's head, or that He conquered in the actual likeness of sinful flesh.

Man, in his very constitution, is a being of specific impulses, whose guilt or innocence is determined by the ruling power to which he submits himself, acting in freedom; nor was it possible for our Lord to take it upon Himself without the temptations thereto incident, any more than a civilised man, with all the views and feelings of his training, can take upon himself a savage nature, and its savage and brutalized associations, without a struggle between himself and his assumed life, in the same proportion more intense than that of savages themselves, as the resisting force within him is greater. We may be allowed this comparison, though infinitely removed from the case in hand. Civilisation and savagery are relative conditions of the same state of sin; and spiritually, one may be as far from the life of God as the other. If such a

[1] Luke x. 18; John xii. 31, 32.   [2] Gen. iii. 15; Heb. ix. 14.

transition might be supposed agonizing, and the civilised man might feel death preferable to a life so abhorrent to all his proclivities, what shall we say of One from the centre and seat of infinite holiness, One from the bosom of God, One from eternity inheriting the Father's full glory, One to whom all angelic praises had been offered, One with the fulness of the Godhead bodily dwelling in Him,—what shall we say of such a One in a nature four thousand years dominated by the flesh, and in a state whose confirmation in sin had grown with the ages, till it had reached the culminating point of earthliness and depravity? The agony of Messiah, under such circumstances, was beyond all our powers of illustration or conception. Can we wonder to hear Him say, 'My soul is troubled,' ' My soul is exceedingly sorrowful, even unto death;' that ' His sweat should be, as it were, great drops of blood falling down to the ground;' or that He should pray on the cross, 'My God, my God, why hast Thou forsaken me?' Or can we wonder that psalmists and prophets, foreseeing His great conflict here in the flesh, should give words to His agony thus: 'Thou hast laid me in the lowest pit, in darkness, in the deeps. Thy wrath lieth hard upon me, and Thou hast afflicted me with all Thy waves. . . . Thou hast put far from me lover and friend, and mine acquaintance into darkness.' 'He was oppressed, and He was afflicted, yet He opened not His mouth: He is brought as a lamb to the slaughter, and as a sheep before her shearers is dumb, so He openeth not His mouth?'[1] Such words, in describing a suffering Messiah, are too numerous for quotation.

[1] John xii. 27 ; Matt. xxvi. 38 ; Luke xxii. 44 ; Ps. xxii. 1 ; Matt. xxvii. 46 ; Ps. lxxxviii. 6–18 ; Isa. liii. 7.

By excluding the divine nature of Christ from all participation in His sufferings, and making them merely human, do we not misrepresent the Gospels, and reduce His sacrifice infinitely below the place assigned it in the law and the prophets? We start with the postulate that God cannot suffer; that our Lord's agony was merely that of a man—no greater than many a martyr has endured; and to make up the deficiency of it as a substitute for our punishment in hell for ever, we add the dignity of His character. This is the philosophical view to formulate the subject to our reason. But, 'without controversy, great is the mystery of godliness: God was manifest in the flesh, justified in the Spirit, seen of angels, preached unto the Gentiles, believed on in the world, and received up into glory;' nor can our reason lift the veil of this mystery.[1] I do not know a passage in the Bible to justify this theory; but, on the contrary, He is affirmed to have given HIMSELF for us, and made His SOUL an offering,—terms which can include nothing short of His whole personality.[2]

The nature of Christ was a unit, though of a duplicate parentage—the one divine, the other human; the result of which is an individual consciousness; and what is of both parents is as completely one in that consciousness as if they had been of the same race. 'His two natures have knit themselves the one to the other,' says Cyril, 'and are in that nearness as incapable of confusion or distinction.' All that Christ felt and thought, whether arising from His oneness with His Divine Father or with His human mother, was as much a unit in His conscious selfhood as that which comes from our bodily or from our spiritual relations

---

[1] 1 Tim. iii. 16.   [2] Tit. ii. 14; Isa. liii. 10, 12.

is a unit in us. This qualified Him to suffer as God as well as man, and is the uncontroverted mystery of the incarnation of which the apostle speaks. He had not only infinite powers of thought and action, but of endurance in suffering; and was as truly God in the one as in the others. How much more can a man endure than a beast! 'The spirit of a man will sustain his infirmity; but a wounded spirit who can bear?'[1] He has not only greater wounds than a beast, but greater power to sustain them. If this is so with us in comparison with inferior creatures, how much more with the infinite Son of God as compared with us!

True, Jesus had no remorse; but still 'the iniquity of us all was laid upon Him,' and 'He suffered the just for the unjust, that He might bring us nigh to God, being put to death in the flesh, but quickened by the Spirit.'[2] And if He suffered His death-struggles, beginning with the manger and ending only with the cross, in leading us forth to a spiritual and heavenly life, then He suffered not as a man merely, but infinitely more—as God. No case of sweating blood from purely mental agony, in a constitution untouched by disease and uninjured by excess in any form, has ever been authenticated, except in Him who in Gethsemane bore up under a burden of woe which no human power could support, and to which an angel lent a helping hand.[3] Everywhere in Scripture the sufferings of the Messiah are represented as equal to the infinitude of His character; and so they were regarded by Christians, till a pretentious philosophy stepped in to remove from them the veil of mystery, by dividing His powers of endurance, and assigning His

[1] Prov. xviii. 14.   [2] Isa. liii. 6; 1 Pet. ii. 24.   [3] Luke xxii. 43.

sufferings only to the human part of His nature. But the Holy Spirit, in making His blood a power to salvation, works upon those who are too much absorbed by a sense of their sins to think of dividing their Saviour's character; and the cross is to them the organ of an infinite woe endured for their redemption.

> 'Alas! and did my Saviour bleed?
> And did my Sovereign die?
> Would He devote that sacred head
> For such a worm as I?'

The universality of these words, in spiritual worship, shows their fitness to every converted man's experience. All this He endured, not for the sake of any remote principle or abstract element of the moral government of God, but 'that we, being dead to sins, should live unto righteousness, by whose stripes we are healed.'[1] His travail of soul in flesh was with a view to its glorification in Himself, that by a like travail in His elect they may attain to a spiritual and heavenly life. How this latter result is achieved will be considered in what follows.

[1] 1 Pet. ii. 24.

CHAPTER XXIII.

DYING TO LIVE.

WHAT most of all confirms our view of inspired teaching as to the nature, condition, and necessities of our race, and what shows, at the same time, how extraordinary is the work of its restoration to virtue and happiness, is the change contemplated in it, and the means of effecting that change. Owing to an objective or philosophical treatment of the subject, instead of one purely biblical,—a treatment dating back to the early centuries, when atoning efficacy, from being a subjective experience, as with the apostles, became a matter of reasoning and speculation after the manner of Platonists and Gnostics, and which is continued to this day,—owing to these causes, I say, the real nature of what the gospel proposes to do for our souls is ignored, or held more as a theory than as a present power working death to flesh, that the spirit may live. The crucifixion which Paul speaks of as wrought on him, that Christ might live in him,[1] is not now deemed integral to the atoning process, but merely a consequence of its prior existence. The atonement, in this view, spent its force on some great principle of the divine government, quite apart from any direct effect upon those for whom it was made, as if the congregation of Israel had been atoned for without any partici-

[1] Gal. ii. 20.

pation of their own. They had brought no sacrifice; had not assembled at the door of the sanctuary; had not afflicted their souls, nor abstained from labour, nor shown any interest in the matter; and yet their high priest had effected for them a perfect reconciliation to God on the mercy-seat.[1] Under like circumstances of abstraction of us from Christ, and Christ from us, it is supposed our reconciliation was complete, though it remained to bring it home to us by effectual vocation.

Thus, by disjoining things that the apostles unite in one, many are encouraged to hope for salvation who give no signs of effectual vocation, and who have only an atoning process in which they have never participated to rest upon. I fear the greater portion of those who expect heaven at last have no better basis than this; not having approached the vestibule of that spiritual sanctuary in which now God on the mercy-seat awaits the approach of a people showing the effect upon their souls of what the blood of His Son represents. They are, to all intents and purposes, merely natural men, and know nothing of being crucified and raised with Christ; but conceive of His atonement as a makeweight thrown into the scale to supply the defects of their carnal lives. They have no thought of blood as a spiritual purification, lifting their souls to the holiness of heaven. Power to assert themselves sons of God, living or dying, which is the essential thing in one to whom Christ's blood is effective, is utterly beyond their experience. 'They are poor sinners, but have a great Saviour,' is the confession of many who have no faith to stretch out their withered members to Christ for instant healing. Never can Christianity enter upon its final triumph till such theo-

[1] Lev. xxiii. 26–32.

logy and such ways of living give place to the faith which is our victory over sin through the blood of the Lamb![1]

It is remarkable that this professed reliance upon the atonement to make up deficiencies should be connected with the legal spirit of doing to live, rather than living to do. How many pass their lives in the vain endeavour to amend to-day what they did yesterday, to pacify their uneasy consciences, and render themselves acceptable to God, instead of walking by faith! In this they know and confess their failures; but Christ died for them, and that fact produces a fictitious quietude in reference to their final prospects. They are neither cold nor hot, not indifferent; and yet not believing to the present saving of their souls. No, they have the notion of a grace to cancel their defects when they die; but not to reign in them while they live, as their power to walk with God. That power they conceive of as in themselves; and thus practically they are under the law, and not under grace, in spite of all they say of depending upon the atonement for salvation. In fact, their view of the atonement is one of the great errors of their life; because they accept it as the offset to a fleshly ruling, and not as introducing the reign of heaven into their souls. Death with Christ as to the natural man, that Christ may live in them as a controlling power—which the apostles everywhere make essential to atoning efficacy—is no part either of their experience or their acceptation of Christianity. Such a faith in the atonement, however it may conduce to a life of legal struggles and failures, does not reflect the gospel view, nor give peace with God through our Lord Jesus Christ. Its throes and contortions are

[1] John i. 12; 1 John v. 4; Rev. xii. 11.

of the natural man, growing out of fear, a regard to character, nervous disease, or a sensibility of conscience disproportioned to their power of obeying its dictates. It is not apostolic Christianity.

This state of things among Christians may perhaps, in many cases, be set to the account of the resisting force of the natural man in those with whom God has begun a good work; as among the Corinthians carnality rendered them babes when they ought to have been men.[1] But more usually, I fear, it arises from defective theological teaching in the pulpits, in creeds, in books, in tracts, in newspapers, Sunday schools, prayer-meetings, and through all the channels for shaping public and private religious conviction. Another standard than that of Christ actually living and reigning in the soul to trample under foot its enemies of flesh and devil is adopted,—a standard which accepts the makeweight view of the atonement to cover the defects of those whose names are enrolled in the church; who pay to support its institutions; who are not immoral; who admit that they are poor sinners, and wish they were better, although not one sign of grace appears in them, and they are even more worldly and selfish than their unbelieving neighbours. The policy of building up sects, and increasing their wealth and power by admitting into them such materials, prevails on all hands to a sufficient extent to account for the limited victories of our present Israel. Hence it is that so many earnest men, as Wickliffe, Huss, Luther, Calvin, Knox, Wesley, and Whitfield, felt themselves compelled to act a revolutionary part in the organizations which gave them their training, as our Lord did in reference to Judaism.

[1] 1 Cor. iii. 1-3.

Who ever heard of such a party leader as Jesus of Nazareth? When the amiable young man who had great possessions kneeled to Him, though Jesus loved and might desire him as an associate and helper in His incipient cause, still He made the terms of discipleship so rigorous as to drive him away for ever.[1] One predominant worldly passion—as the love of money, for instance—any uncrucified lust, would make the richest and most powerful convert in the world a source of weakness rather than of strength in such a cause. Jesus did not come among men to build up a party, but to hunt out the prodigals and restore them, by a death to what they once were, and a new life to what they were henceforth to be. His was an errand of salvation from carnal ruling to the kingdom of heaven in the soul; and He had no party that could be benefited by those who would not submit to this radical process. His was a kingdom that suffered violence, and that only the violent in dealing with all the obstructions of their fleshly nature could enter.[2] He had no atonement to offer for sin that did not crucify the sinning nature, and establish in its place a spiritual life. This doctrine must be revived from the rubbish of fifteen hundred years of objective and philosophical reasoning on the subject of atoning efficacy, before the sacramental host can be led to victory and the millennium.

Under the former dispensations, this idea of death on the one hand, in order to life on the other, a fleshly crucifixion and a spiritual resurrection, was kept before the world by the blood of sacrificial animals. From the predicted bruising of Christ's heel in crushing the serpent's head, to this day, blood is the great expedient in redemption; four thousand years of this time being

[1] Mark x. 17-21. [2] Matt. xi. 12.

used as a symbol, and more than eighteen hundred as spiritual power. 'Redeemed by the precious blood of Christ:'[1] this is the doctrine of doctrines, the only sun among ten thousand luminaries; and it behoves every one to see to it that he does not darken its beams by perverted views, nor rob his soul of its efficacy by looking elsewhere for its fruits than in the death of flesh and life in spirit. May the Holy Spirit help us faithfully to represent and truly to use so great a doctrine!

This doctrine of salvation by blood is without precedent in profane history, or in other religions. Herodotus does indeed mention blood as a pacificator between the contending tribes of Western Asia; the chiefs wounding their arms and absorbing each other's blood, in sealing their compacts of amity.[2] And blood in religious ceremonies is not unknown among the heathen. In these cases, however, nothing is found approaching the Christian doctrine of atonement. And those philosophical Christians of our age who make blood the representative of a martyr influence; or of the potency accruing from an example of self-sacrifice; or a sympathetic expedient to move men to virtue, as a mother uses her tears with refractory children; or of arguments to convince the reason of moral truth; or of an appeal to natural conscience to give it an impulse towards reform: whoever, I say, resorts to such means of explaining the position assigned to blood in the Bible as an expedient for reclaiming a lost race, is as false to the sacred text as to the facts and necessities of the human condition. Is it to be supposed that inspired men would make so much account of so small a matter? Or is reform among men so easy a thing as these reasoners would represent? As to the Catholic view

[1] 1 Pet. i. 19.   [2] *History*, Book i. sec. 75.

of material blood, as having an inherent efficacy to take away sin, or that the loaf blessed by a priest or the wine from sacerdotal hands becomes the veritable flesh and blood of Christ, it is too absurd to be dealt with by truth or argument.

It is simply as the representative of *spiritual* efficacy to take away sin, that blood is used in Scripture. As we said in our first chapter, spiritual truths must have a seeding in words and symbols, in order to be apprehended by men; and there are obvious reasons, as we shall see, why Infinite Wisdom should assign to blood the mission of representing to us the power that cancels sin. Blood, as the life-current, represents life; as it is said, 'The life of the flesh is in the blood; and I have given it to you upon the altar to make atonement for your soul: for it is the blood that maketh atonement. No soul of you shall eat blood, neither shall any stranger that sojourneth among you eat blood.'[1] It was death to transgress this law. Not only is blood the life, but it is a term also for death, and blood-guiltiness was murder.[2] Life and death, or death and life, is the stem-thought or germinal idea in this symbol. It represents the process by which the Son of God wrought out redemption, 'dying for our sins, and being raised for our justification;' 'delivered by the eternal counsel and foreknowledge of God to be crucified and slain;' 'whom God raised up, having loosed the pains of death.' With such an expedient in view from the beginning of time, can we wonder that blood was used to represent it?[3]

But the death and resurrection of Christ derive their potency in human history from being a representative

---
[1] Lev. xvii. 11, 12.
[2] Gen. xxxvii. 26; Lev. xvii. 4; Ps. li. 14.
[3] Rom. iv. 25; Acts ii. 23, 24.

and forerunner to a like process in all that believe, of dying to live. If there had been no Holy Spirit to reproduce the death and resurrection of Christ in the experience of men, and they had stood as isolated facts of history, would they have occupied the place they do? Does not redemption give them their value to us? Even the precious blood that fell in Gethsemane, and trickled down the rugged wood of the cross, had only a representative force. It is not in clotted corruption nor among dead men's bones that we are to look for atoning efficacy. 'He is not here, for He has risen,' is the direction of the angel where to look for the living power in redemption.[1] Our atoning High Priest has passed into the heavens, there to appear on the right hand of God for us; and thence alone proceeds the saving power represented by blood.[2]

Dying to live was the maxim which ruled throughout our Lord's earthly experience. It began in the stable at Bethlehem; was carried on in His retired life at Nazareth, in a state so unlike the heavenly choirs from which He came; was exemplified in His forty days' conflict in the wilderness; in His subsequent career of labour and poverty, not having where to lay His head; in bearing our sicknesses and infirmities; in nightly vigils and prayers; in the calumny of His enemies, over whom He wept bitter tears; in the agonies of the garden; in the taunts and insults of the closing scene, and finally in His death upon the cross. What was this, from beginning to end, but a process of crucifixion to all His feelings as a man? As human nature was the same in Him as in us, it could not have been otherwise. No worldly good accrued to Himself or family from His extraordinary powers, which to them

[1] Matt. xxviii. 6.   [2] Col. iii. 1; Heb. ix. 14, 15.

was a cause of complaint; and they demanded that He 'should show Himself to the world' as a wonder-worker, and thus raise Himself and them to worldly pre-eminence.[1] The impulse ruling Him from above admitted no such display, but urged Him to the perfection that suffering only could give. The Eternal Spirit energizing in Him bore Him forward in this career of woe, till His manhood succumbed, not to sin, but to pain and death, His heel bruised in bruising the serpent's head, and He fell a victim to that world for which He came to die. Thus it was that He provided to conduct us to spiritual life by crucifying in us the body of the sins of the flesh, achieving the only victory and glory which He sought or could receive—the victory and glory of infinite love.

There is nothing in the New Testament answering to the universal use of blood in the ceremonies of the Old, but this process of dying to live, first in Christ and then in us; and no other possible exhibition could reduce in human nature the dominant flesh to the subordination necessary to the coming of the kingdom of heaven. The words ἱλάσκομαι, ἱλασμὸς, and ἱλαστήριον—*hilaskomai, hilasmos,* and *hilasterion*—rendered in our common version, to reconcile, propitiation, and mercy-seat, are but a few times used by the apostles, and cannot be designed to fill the place of *kapporeth*, atonement, which, with the verb from which it is derived, is a hundred and forty times repeated in the Old Testament.[2] The root of the word *kapporeth* means literally to cover, probably to express the idea that though sin may be hid from view, and no longer operate to our condemnation, the fact of its exist-

[1] John vii. 4.
[2] Heb. ii. 17; Rom. iii. 25; Heb. ix. 5; 1 John ii. 2, iv. 10.

ence can never be annihilated. The idea of hiding sin, casting it behind the back, and remembering it no more, is no doubt derived from this primary meaning of the word used for atonement or expiation.[1] The stem-thought of *kapporeth* is that of removing from persons and things whatever renders them unfit for the service of God.

As the New Testament has no synonym for atonement in Hebrew, the idea is expressed by facts rather than by particular epithets. We are at enmity with God, and alienated from Him by wicked works. God is angry with the wicked every day;[2] and the atonement is that which reconciles the parties. Our enmity may be chronic rather than acute, and only a serious effort to detach us from our idols of concupiscence or from our worldly ideas could perhaps fully bring it to light. So God's anger may be simply the settled antagonism of His holiness to our unholiness, His spiritual law to our fleshly nature. But whatever His anger or our enmity, an irreconcilable difference exists between the parties; and how are they to be reconciled? One or the other of them must recede from his ground, or both must undergo a change and meet half-way; and which is it—God or we, or both? 'God in Christ, reconciling the *world* to Himself,'[3] is the way the apostle states the case, and not *Himself* to the world. He has nothing to recede from, being infinitely right in all things, and the change must be wholly in us. We have everything to give up, because we are wholly wrong; and our only inability to be at peace with God is, that we are in the

---

[1] Ps. li. 9, ciii. 12, xxv. 7, lxxix. 8; Isa. xxxviii. 17. The scapegoat expressed a like idea. See Lev. xvi. 10, 26.

[2] Rom. viii. 7; Eph. iv. 18; Ps. vii. 11.

[3] 2 Cor. v. 19.

flesh and under its ruling, and we cannot please God.[1] Imputation of another's righteousness to cover our defects is unworthy of God; and besides, it would effect nothing till the body of our sins was destroyed, that we should not serve sin. A mind under the ruling of the flesh cannot be made happy by imputation, nor by any expedient short of a fleshly crucifixion in order to a spiritual resurrection with Christ. This, therefore, is the substance of which the blood of beasts under the law was a shadow. It is only in this view that we can enter into apostolic teaching on this subject. If sin were anything but the rule of a nature in opposition to God, or divine anger anything but the antagonism of infinite holiness to such a nature, then we might talk of expedients to pacify that anger, or of taking away sin by something short of a crucifixion of the opposing nature; but as the case stands, and as it is represented from Genesis to Revelation, we have only to look into the facts to see how utterly unavailing is any atonement which is not a dying to live. This is the way that Christ leads, and we must follow. This is the cross to be taken up, and not that of doing public duties to which we are reluctant, as many suppose. The atonement is a history, not a theory; it is a concrete fact of our inward and outward relations to God, and not an abstraction of justice, of law, or of government.

The Holy Spirit is the positive energy in conducting the process in all that believe. 'He takes of the things of Christ, and shows them to us,' and 'does not speak of Himself.'[2] Much more is meant by this passage than suggesting to us Christ's words, or opening to us the doctrines which He taught. His words and doctrines, great as they are, do not equal His

[1] Rom. viii. 8.   [2] John xvi. 13, 15.

deeds. 'Laying down His life, and taking it again,'[1] by His own voluntary act, and in obedience to His Father's commandment, or through the Eternal Spirit, by whom He offered Himself to God, in order to lead the way for a like experience in us, is the greatest of all His achievements. He thus *acted* what had been taught from the beginning of time: that spirit is greater than nature; that nature must perish before spirit can reach its full development; that the forces entitled to rule us are not the fleshly ideas and feelings by which we are so insanely impelled, but those which come from the unseen and the eternal; and that we need not fear to trust to the wreck of all our earthly fortunes, if only everlasting life is an abiding energy in our souls. These are the truths that Christ enacted, and that must by the Eternal Spirit be re-enacted in us, or the first step towards reconciliation has not yet been taken. Christ went through the process as a man, and in sympathy with humanity, for whose infirmities He is 'touched' with tender compassion;[2] but He did it not for Himself, but 'for us,' or to commute His own power into a permanent energy for the reproduction of a like process in all that believe. This energy is the Holy Ghost, who has nothing of His own to offer, but only this great record in Him whom He represents. Dying to live was the culminating point of types and prophecies, and it was that which the apostles determined only to know in preaching nothing but Christ and Him crucified.[3]

In things the unfitness for God's service which atoning blood removed, was not inherent, but representative. It arose from the corrupt use to which everything pertaining to man's life had been devoted, and

[1] John x. 18.   [2] Heb. iv. 15.   [3] 1 Cor. ii. 2.

the consequent vicious associations with which it had been connected in his mind. To reclaim a voluptuary, his vicious haunts must be broken up or forsaken; and he must be surrounded only by things fitted to inspire him with pure and honourable sentiments. So our language, our literature, our institutions, our usages, our associations, our possessions, and our whole outward life, must feel the atoning influence operating in ourselves, to give them a new aspect and direction, and altogether higher and more beneficent uses. 'If any man be in Christ, he is a new creation; old things are passed away; behold, all things are become new.' That the apostle refers this change to the atoning process, is evident from the words immediately following: 'And all things are of God, who hath reconciled,' or atoned, 'us to Himself by Jesus Christ.'[1]

This new attitude towards all that concerned us in our former state could only come of our dying to what we once were, and being raised with Christ to a new and heavenly life. Our Lord alludes to the same when He says, 'He that hateth his life in this world, shall keep it unto life eternal.' And this hatred He extends, in another place, to father, mother, wife, children, brethren, sisters, yea, and his own life, as necessary to discipleship: that is, hate and crucify our whole outward condition, so far as it interferes between our souls and God. This is having the world crucified unto us, and we unto the world.[2] Can we wonder that, in shadowing forth such an idea, blood should be required to make priest, people, altar, tabernacle, and all its implements of divine service, acceptable to God?

[1] 2 Cor. v. 17, 18.   [2] John xii. 25; Luke xiv. 26; Gal. vi. 14.

CHAPTER XXIV.

THE KINGDOM OF GOD WITH POWER.

OUR subject, it will be seen, is a historical rather than a theoretic view of human nature. It pertains to redemption in its present working among the elements of the world, and not in its millennial or heavenly consummation. True, it is never complete in the present life, but always in conflict with insurrectionary foes in the new man himself which must be kept in subjection,[1] and with assailing powers from without. Still it is the kingdom of heaven of which all the regenerated are subjects; and it is with power, because under the reign of the Holy Spirit, which our Lord speaks of as power from on high.[2] Power supposes resistance to be overcome; and the idea is nowhere associated, I believe, with God's rule of holy beings. No force coerced the angels to render their homage to the Infant of Bethlehem, inferior as He seemed to themselves; but gladly they obeyed the call to worship Him.[3] Only in this process of crucifixion to the dominant flesh and resurrection to a new life in God do we see 'the exceeding greatness of that power which wrought first in Christ in raising Him from the dead,' and then in rendering the preaching of the cross the power of God to our salvation.[4] The

---

[1] 1 Cor. ix. 27.
[2] Luke xxiv. 49.
[3] Heb. i. 6; Luke ii. 9-14.
[4] Eph. i. 19; 1 Cor. i. 18.

cross, as representative of our Lord's regeneration of blood, becomes, in the hands of the Holy Spirit, the efficiency to a like regeneration in all that believe. This is the kingdom of God with power.

Owing to partial views of the subject, we are prone to underestimate the greatness of this achievement. Many who think themselves Christians are conscious of no such wonderful transition in themselves, and they doubt its existence in others. Perhaps they are right in estimating their own condition; for the natural man is liable to various changes of thought and purpose,— changes, too, that seem improving to moral character, and are mistaken for the spiritual life, though remote as possible from dying to live. Others, in whom the good work has really been wrought, are so overwhelmed with a sense of the evils in themselves yet to be overcome, as to underestimate the work done in their hearts. They are so far from ' apprehending that for which they have been apprehended of Christ Jesus,'[1] that they seem to themselves almost without a standing as spiritual men. But with all these abatements and misgivings in estimating what the Spirit has really done for us, is it not true that war has been inaugurated against the dominant flesh-and-devil power? Is there not a powerful phalanx prosecuting this war under the leadership of the Holy Spirit? Did not our Lord exult in the fact that such a war had begun when He sent out the seventy disciples?[2] The spiritual David stood face to face with the giant foe, defying him in the name of Jehovah of Israel.[3] The inauguration of such a war, in the person of Jesus and in every believer, is contesting the right of the flesh to rule, and embodies elements of certain victory.

[1] Phil. iii. 12. [2] Luke x. 18-22; Matt. xi. 27. [3] 1 Sam. xvii. 45.

'Resist the devil, and he will flee from you; draw nigh to God, and He will draw nigh to you.'[1]

This failure of dying to live, on the part of so many Christians so called, and this weakness of faith in so many others, have had the injurious effect in our theologies of magnifying Christ's death towards God and His government, to make up for the apparent deficiency of its influence among men. Though nobody were really saved, still Christ would be a great Saviour, because He has offered to divine law and justice an equivalent for the salvation of many. And if they are not saved under the ruling of the Holy Ghost in the present life, if elected they will be, under death's dominion dissolving their mortal bodies; so that however selfish, however carnal, however worldly, however miserly and malignant up to the last pulsation of their congealed blood, they will step into eternity quavering with their attuned voices the song of Moses and the Lamb. With this vast background of law appeased and justice satisfied, can we not sufficiently magnify atoning efficacy, and set it off gloriously, even with the failure of a veritable death of the sin of flesh, in order to a spiritual resurrection with Christ?

This process of lowering down the requirements of God's kingdom on earth by magnifying them in heaven began early to work as a 'mystery of iniquity,'[2] or as a deep stratagem of the adversary to content Christians with an atonement infinite and glorious in everything but that for which it was designed—a power in them to kill their sin, and make them victorious in faith and holiness. What does the great deceiver care for the greatness of the atonement, if he can only use it to

[1] Jas. iv. 7.   [2] 2 Thess. ii. 7; 1 John ii. 18.

fasten our fleshly chains? This mystery of iniquity began to wax strong when Christianity, from being a spiritual life, with all its glowing sympathies, became a science of the schools side by side with speculative philosophy. Among the first questions, it was asked, To whom did Christ pay the price of our redemption? Origen, of the third century, thought He paid it to the devil, to whom the redeemed had before belonged. Others disputed the position; and after a few ages of debating, by pen, pulpit, and council, the question was resolved into our present theory, that Christ's death was a sacrifice to law and justice. It was, as others express it, to appease the indignant ethical nature of God in letting the guilty go free. Divine anger and the outraged moral sentiment of the universe demanded a victim for man's sin, and that victim must be the sinner himself, or his substitute; and as the Son of God consented to take the sinner's place, the Father poured on Him the full vials of His wrath.

It comes therefore to this, as stated by an advocate of the theory, that God was angry with Himself, punished Himself, and became a self-immolated victim in the person of His Son, to pave the way to pardoning the guilty. What simple-minded person under conviction for sin could take in such a concatenation of ideas as the basis of his hope? It is the feeling that Christ died for him, and he must relinquish his sins for such a Saviour, and lead a holy life by His grace, that gives him hope. And yet this death to sin and life to righteousness is deemed by many no adequate exposition of atoning efficacy. The exacting flesh demands something less taxing to self, under the idea of doing greater honour to Christ. Some become Antinomians under the subtle influence; others spend their days in a doubtful position between nature and grace; and not a few die in hope, because their life has been one of torture, not of triumph, and they think Christ's blood will make up for their deficiencies. There are many honourable exceptions to this painful picture; but not enough to restore professing Christians as a body to the energy of a faith that it is a real dying to live, or of a piety that can conceive of no atonement or reconciliation with God on any principle but that of a baptism and regeneration of blood. No wonder that a piety so killing to flesh and so quickening to spirit should be a power when it is really exercised.

Look at what ensued to Christ's followers fifty days after His death. They were a simple-hearted unchivalrous company; from the most virtuous circles of their age, no doubt; but from stations and callings quite out of the line of heroic achievement. Their life, after leaving their cottage homes, had been a wandering one, and without motive, except to hear the words and witness the deeds of the young man whose person and influence had such a charm to their feelings. A mysterious attraction drew them after Him, leading them to call Him Master and Lord even in His poverty. Why they did so admitted of scarcely a logical conclusion; and to a mind severe in its worldly calculations, they would have been deemed vagabondish and unavailing. Those who had an eye to the loaves and fishes were better understood, and soon fell off as from uncongenial affinities, neither wanting nor being wanted, neither helping nor helped in their main purposes. They found themselves with a Master who had no leisure but for prayer, no powers or resources that brought a worldly requital, no position or intellectual culture, and who practised none of the arts of kingly command among men; and those who were looking out for the main chance soon found that they had nothing to hope from such a leader. Still a mysterious influence invested Him, winning harlots to purity, and publicans to justice and liberality. All felt the magic of it, stirring them to love or malignity.[1]

While He lived, there was no transfer to others of His power, excepting the healing of diseases and casting out devils in His name.[2] Not a man of His followers rose above a worldly estimate of things; and hence the question, in the very hour of His ascension, 'Wilt Thou now restore the kingdom unto Israel?'[3] He could not speak fully of the end of His mission, because they could not 'bear' it, nor comprehend its import.[4] They had glimpses of a higher life; but, like their successors in after ages, they were looking to a temporal kingdom, or to some mysterious effect upon the government of God, or to vast and unknown changes in somebody or something besides themselves. How little do we realize that things are great in their simplicity; and that to set on foot a power to make the carnal spiritual, the earthly heavenly, the selfish benevolent, the sinful holy, is an enterprise that needs no adventitious aids to make it great and glorious! The touch of the surgeon's lancet, simple as it is, becomes great to him whose life is saved by its means. Can we wonder that the patriarchal and Mosaic ages accomplished so little, when these disciples were so slow in learning what they really needed, and under such a Teacher too, and when so few retain the significance of what Pentecost taught them? 'Fellowship with Christ in His sufferings,' or actual communion with

[1] Matt. xxi. 32; Luke iv. 22, v. 27, xix. 2; John vii. 46.
[2] Luke ix. 1, x. 17.   [3] Acts i. 6.   [4] John xvi. 12.

Him in them, in order to conformity to His death; alas, how few have acquired such an experience in them as to attain to His resurrection!¹

Aware of the ruling of natural ideas in His disciples, our Lord directed them to tarry at Jerusalem till they should be endued with power from on high. And they did wait in prayer and supplication for ten days after His ascension, Mary His mother being of the company, who is not afterwards mentioned, because, when her Divine Son ceased to be known after the flesh, and was known only in His glorified state, His earthly relations were lost sight of.² The tabernacle was now completed, and only awaited its occupant; the victim was upon the altar, and needed only fire from heaven to exhale it into heavenly odours. Intense were the longings of these simple-hearted men for a good hoped for, but dimly outlined, when the accordant note of faith and prayer was at length reached, as when the priests of the temple made one voice to be heard on high, and 'there came a sound from heaven, as of a rushing mighty wind, and it filled all the house where they were sitting,' investing them with a heavenly element, and filling them with the Holy Ghost.³ 'Arise, O Lord God, unto Thy resting-place, Thou and the ark of Thy strength; let Thy priests, O Lord God, be clothed with salvation, and let Thy saints rejoice in Thy goodness.'⁴ Thus the death of earthly hopes and ideas, and the concentration of hope and prayer upon heavenly things, proved the birth to a new life, new powers, and the realization of the original conception of manhood, as uniting in itself the power of two worlds.

This was the coming of God's kingdom in power.

---

[1] Phil. iii. 9-11. [2] Acts i. 13, 14.
[3] Acts ii. 1-4; 2 Chron. v. 13, 14. [4] 2 Chron. vi. 41.

The Divinity now absorbed in Himself the ideas and energies of human nature, and reigned within, single and alone. The tongues of flame, denoting a propagating power, made it a kingdom for all of every nation who render the obedience of faith. It demanded expansion, and could not be restrained by a thick-ribbed Judaism. Who can estimate the efficiency which speech thus acquired for man's regeneration? Where shall we find a full record of the results of a spiritual power thus obtained? Church history is, like painting, a mere surface-view of Christianity. Its soul is unlimned and unseen. Reasoning on the subject, as upon worldly connections of cause and effect, to reduce it to the level of our natural plain of thought, is far more absurd than to attempt an explanation of the mysteries of gravitation or of central forces. The results of speaking the word in demonstration of the Spirit have more than realized the sword of flame at the gate of Eden, and the tongues of fire on the day of Pentecost.

> 'When one who holds communion with the skies
> Has filled his urn where these pure waters rise,
> And once more mingles with us meaner things,
> 'Tis e'en as if an angel shook his wings:
> Immortal fragrance fills the circuit wide,
> And tells us whence their treasures are supplied.'

The first sermon delivered under the new impulse is remarkable for its pointed charge of guilt 'in killing the Prince of life, whom God hath raised from the dead,' and in identifying the person of Jesus with the Jehovah of Abraham and of Moses, whom David always saw before his face, and thus in concentrating all previous type and prediction upon a church crucified with Christ, and raised by the Spirit's baptism. The fishermen and their associates no longer lived their natural lives.

The Holy Spirit was the ruling power within them, to realize the primeval inbreathing of man's creation. It commuted their weakness into strength, their folly into wisdom, their timidity into courage, their low, confined ideas into thoughts high as heaven, vast as eternity, and their death into life. It opened to them visions of the glorified, to cancel their fear of mobs and martyrdoms. And like effects appeared in their converts, who 'daily attended with one accord in the temple, and breaking bread from house to house, partook their food with gladness of heart, praising God, and having favour with all the people.'[1]

It will be seen that we take our example of God's restored kingdom with power, from what may be thought an extreme case, and nowise answering to the general examples of Christianity which we see around us. But, which is our rule of judging in the case,—What God has done, or what man has done? Besides, in all cases where the power for a holy life really exists, is there not an approximation to apostolic experience? Was it not so with Luther and many of his associate reformers? Was it not so with Whitfield and Wesley? Was it not so with Edwards and Brainerd? And has it not been so in all our great revivals of religion? Millions of Christians realize in themselves a death and resurrection with Christ, whose sex, whose circumstances, whose poverty, sickness, and necessary seclusion, compel them to an undemonstrative life, so far as this world is concerned, but who have that infinitely greater cause of joy than the power of casting out devils, that their names are written in heaven.[2]

But how about miracles? Were they not an in-

[1] Acts ii. 46.   [2] Luke x. 20.

tegral part of the apostolic kingdom of God? Yes; and so was that of having their property in common, —a state of things not now possible, but towards which people always converge the more they are ruled by the Holy Spirit. Whenever there is a large amount of spiritual influence among the churches, untold amounts of wealth become a fund for charity, for missions, for education, and for all the purposes of doing good, although a like necessity for living from a common treasury nowhere exists as with the first church in Jerusalem. That was a church, to a large extent, of strangers on a religious mission to the Holy City[1]— 'devout men, out of every nation under heaven;' and how could they subsist except on the common-stock principle? As to miracles, though they convert no man, they were a necessity to an age whose materialism was proof against all the ordinary modes of appeal, and whose attention to the new visitation could not be otherwise arrested. But is there not in all cases of remarkable spiritual manifestations much that borders on miracle? What will be said of the extraordinary things in the lives of such men as Bunyan, Wesley, and of even Muller of Bristol, in our own times? Do they not record events and experiences quite out of the ordinary connection of cause and effect?

Besides, the power of God in regeneration is supernatural, if not miraculous. As Augustine quaintly sets it forth, 'more easily did my body obey the weakest willing of my soul, in moving its limbs at its nod, than the soul obeyed itself to accomplish in the will alone this its momentous will. Whence this monstrousness, and to what end? Let Thy mercy

[1] Acts ii. 5–11.

gleam, that I may ask; if so be that the secret penalties of men, and those darkest pangs of the sons of Adam, may perhaps answer me. Whence is this monstrousness? and to what end? The mind commands the body, and it obeys instantly; the mind commands itself, and is resisted. The mind commands the hand to be moved; and such readiness is there, that command is not distinct from obedience. Yet the mind is mind, the hand is body. The mind commands the mind—its own soul—to will, and yet it doth not. Whence this monstrousness? and to what end? It commands itself, I say, to will, and would not command unless it willed; and what it commands is not done. *But it willeth not entirely.* For so far forth it commandeth as it willeth; and so far forth the commanded thing is not done, as it willeth not. For the will commandeth that there be a will,—not another, but itself. But doth not command entirely; therefore what it commanded is not. For, were the will entire, it would not even command it to be, because it would already be. It is therefore no monstrousness partly to will, and partly not to will; but a disease of the mind, that it doth not wholly rise, being by truth upborne, by custom down-borne.'[1]

Out of this dilemma no power but that of the cross can raise a man. It is a miracle of grace to concentrate our wills upon being and doing what is utterly repugnant to all our currents of desire. 'To will is present with me; but how to perform that which is good I find not.'[2] When deliverance comes, it is always with a burst of gratitude that it comes 'through Jesus Christ our Lord;' and that we are relieved from condemnation by being 'in Christ,' in the sense of

[1] *Memoirs*, pp. 156, 157, 158.   [2] Rom. vii. 18.

being crucified and raised with Him. Hence every such transition is by a power above nature, and is really more effective for building up the kingdom of God than any number of material miracles.[1] Whenever it is genuine, or a real death of the body of sin and a real resurrection to a new life, it becomes the starting-point of a new series of psychological facts, called 'the fruit of the Spirit, love, joy, peace, long-suffering, gentleness, goodness, faith, meekness, temperance,'[2]—graces existing in a form and with modifications utterly unattainable to the natural man. 'Against such there is no law,' because the new life is accepted as a fulfilment of the design and purpose of all legal requisitions. The law is fulfilled in those who walk after the Spirit; and thus the atoning process is complete.

In the use of the word rendered atonement in the Old Testament, it is applied to the going forth from the offending party of what is accepted by the offended party as a token of reconciliation. It was so applied, first to the offering of beasts by which Jacob conciliated his brother Esau.[3] It is next applied to the half shekel required of each Israelite that was numbered after the exode, it being called atonement money. It was not applied to the paschal lamb. The blood of that sprinkled on the door-post was a token to the destroying angel that he should pass on and destroy Egypt, who held the people in bondage, but leave unharmed the inmates of all the blood-stained houses. As a sign of redemption, it denoted the relaxing of the power of sin holding the soul in bondage, and of life and freedom to the escaping emancipated spirit,—death to flesh, and life in God.

[1] Rom. vii. 25, viii. 1.   [2] Gal. v. 22, 23.   [3] Gen. xxxii. 21.

But the money to which the term atonement or covering of sin is applied paid for the flour, incense, wine, oil, fuel, salt, priests' garments, and whatever was used in the daily service of Jehovah. It furnished the fuel of the consecrated flame ascending from the altar, burning there night and day, and from age to age, as a symbol of those prayers, praises, and devout affections which believers unceasingly offer to God. It comes up before God as a new psychological development in humanity produced by His Holy Spirit, and as such is a 'memorial for our souls,' or a reminder that we are subjects of His restored kingdom among men.[1] These affections in us which are symbolized by the daily offerings in the tabernacle are spoken of as 'the sacrifices of praise continually, that is, the fruit of our lips, giving thanks to His name,'[2] and are the living evidence that the blood of the cross is more to us than an abstraction of law; that it is indeed a positive force, killing our Egypt of sin and giving life and freedom to our souls, of which our holy aspirations and praises are a standing memorial. They are the life-blood of Christ our Paschal Lamb, as seen on 'the two side-posts and upper door-posts,' to indicate that the soul within is to go free.[3]

If we would have our sins covered and cancelled, therefore, we must be sure of a reigning Christ within us by His viceregal Spirit, clothing us in a robe of such beautiful graces, virtues, and gifts, that we 'may be presented to Him a glorious church, not having spot, or wrinkle, or any such thing; but that we

---

[1] Compare Ex. xii. with Ex. xxx. 11-16.
[2] Heb. xiii. 15, 16; Rom. xii. 1; Ps. li. 17, l. 13-15; Hos. vi. 6; Mic. vi. 7, 8.
[3] Ex. xii. 7.

should be holy and without blemish.'[1] But let us not delude ourselves with a covering of satisfied legal penalties in which we have no participation. Let us not think to appear in a robe of righteousness which somebody else wore, but which we show no signs of having put on. Let us not trust our hopes of heaven on the death and resurrection of Christ's body, as absorbing in itself all the vengeance due to us, when we show no signs of fellowship in His sufferings, or of conformity either to His death or resurrection. Alas for the piety of millions! Whatever covering for sin it trusts to, it is certainly not that of being influenced by the mercies of God in giving His Son to die for us, which shows itself in 'presenting the body a living sacrifice, holy, acceptable unto God, as a most reasonable, as a most righteous service.'[2]

It is in a state of endeavour that God meets with us as a resurrection power. And is not the true doctrine of the cross full of inspiration to a higher and still higher spiritual life? Did Christ die and rise again that we may die and rise with Him, and shall we spend our days in this sepulchre of fleshliness and partial sanctification? Oh that there were one universal movement among Christians to realize in themselves the full effects of atoning blood! All discovery, all advance even in natural things, comes to us in an attitude of endeavouring it; and can we hope for it otherwise in the divine life? This chilling unbelief as to the possibilities of our holy vocation represses endeavour, and renders thousands children when they ought to be men. They are not even 'feeling after God, if haply they may find Him,' and how can they hope that the kingdom will come with power to their souls?

[1] Eph. v. 27.   [2] Rom. xii. 1.

CHAPTER XXV.

SUFFERING AS THE INITIATIVE OF POWER.

THE use of suffering in redemption, as seen first in our Lord's passion, and then in the experience of His followers, is a subject that requires careful consideration. Who does not shrink from passing under the rod? Yet it is God's chosen means of disciplining and saving us. True, suffering in itself is no cure of sin, tending rather to exasperate the guilty one into hatred and malignity against God and His government. We read of those who 'gnawed their tongues for pain, and blasphemed the God of heaven, because of their pains, and because of their sores, and repented not of their deeds.'[1] This is the uniform effect of suffering, in itself considered. It is the prison to the thief, the gallows to the assassin, an object of detestation and a cause of exasperation against the government that inflicts it.

But suffering as a throe of agony in casting off sin, out of regard to the holiness of God, becomes a point of coincidence between the soul and the grace that saves it; an initial moment in passing from fleshly to spiritual and heavenly ruling. This is what the apostle calls κατὰ Θεὸν λύπη, *sorrow out of regard to God*, as distinguished from τοῦ κόσμου λύπη, *sorrow of the world;* the one working repentance to salvation,

[1] Rev. xvi. 10, 11.

the other the death of increased guilt and misery.[1] The one is a sense of sin, and an effort to throw it off; the other unsatisfied desire, disappointed hope, and intensified malignity. Sorrow for the sin of nature, out of a regard to God, is the soul's moulting period, so to speak, wherein it is reduced to the last point of weakness in a struggle to disburden itself of guilt of the past, and take on a renewed and infantile life. This is being converted and becoming little children.[2]

Our Lord reached this extreme point of weakness, in disrobing Himself of mortality, and assuming His crown of glory, when He cried, 'My God, my God, why hast Thou forsaken me?'[3] This cry was at the moment—which always comes in such cases—when the cup of agony is exhausted to its dregs, when the baptism of blood, at its point of lowest submergence, exhausts the last resource of earthly life. Our Lord's human nature wrought in Him as powerfully as in us, when He felt Himself thus dropped, as it were, into a bottomless sea of agony, detaching Him from all He held most dear on earth; and no exclamation can be conceived more fitting to the occasion. It was truth and nature putting into words as much of an infinite woe as could be expressed.

In the garden His body was spared, except as it sympathized with His agonized mind; and besides, an angel lent a helping hand. But now body and soul accepted the destiny which both He and His Divine Father had chosen for Him; and no angelic intermediation could longer delay the crisis of suffering, in commuting mortal into immortality, or in converting *himself*, His WHOLE SELF, into spiritual power working

[1] 2 Cor. vii. 10.   [2] Mark x. 15; Luke xviii. 17.
[3] Matt. xxvii. 46.

in human nature as leaven in meal, that 'He might redeem us from all iniquity, and purify unto Himself a peculiar people, zealous of good works.'[1] How could the Father, how could angels, how could the Son Himself, stave off the crisis, when all were a unit in 'the predetermined counsel and foreknowledge,' that He must thus 'by wicked hands be crucified and slain,' and that the ruling flesh in man could not otherwise be subdued to the kingdom of God?[2] And yet, because neither the Father, nor angels, nor the Son Himself could afford relief, consistently with the Scriptures or with the demands of the occasion, was pain therefore the less painful to the sufferer Himself, or the breaking up of one mode of existence in order to enter upon another less dreadful to every sensibility? These were the throes of His human birth to a higher life, and 'the twelve legions of angels' that He might have commanded to His deliverance would only have defeated the purpose of His mission; and of course the Father's interference was equally impossible. Suffering has a mission in redemption; and well said our Lord, 'How am I straitened till it be accomplished!' This cry of agony, 'My God, my God, why hast Thou forsaken me?' has infinite appropriateness to the occasion and the Sufferer.

Is it not strange that so plain a case should be put into the unnatural shape of an indignant Father pouring His wrath upon His Son; that outraged law should wreak its vengeance on His holy soul; or that the public conscience of the universe, demanding a spectacular scene of blood, should have made His death an equivalent for hell-torments? Alas for theory and philosophy! How remote the apostolic account from anything of the kind!—everywhere representing Christ

[1] Tit. ii. 14.   [2] Acts ii. 23.

as 'the Well-beloved,' 'the only begotten Son,' 'in the bosom of the Father,' always an object of His 'delight,' and never more so than in this tragic act of His life.[1] 'Therefore doth my Father *love* me, *because* I lay down my life.' '*For* the suffering of death, He was crowned with glory and honour.'[2] And Jesus in the next breath, to His complaint of being forsaken, says, 'Father, into Thy hands I commend my spirit.' Does this look like one labouring under a sense of divine anger? With such a feeling of delight in each other at bottom, can we imagine the pantomime of an acted scene of wrath?

Still, our Lord's sufferings were consequent upon sin, as the pain inflicted by the surgeon's knife is a consequence of the disease of which it is the cure. He owed His sufferings to His human relationship, or the lost condition of the nature which He had assumed,—a nature in which He had done no sin; and therefore His immortality was ensured without dying, much more than was that of Enoch and Elijah by anything they had done. He died, therefore, as He Himself says, that His death might become a power of regeneration to others. 'I tell you the truth: it is expedient that I depart [die]; for if I depart not, the Comforter will not come to you; but if I go [die], I will send Him to you.'[3] His death did not detach Him from humanity; so far otherwise, it was converting Himself into a permanent and all-pervading power, acting upon and in them that believe, to raise them from a carnal to a spiritual, from an earthly to a

---

[1] Matt. iii. 17; John xii. 28; Ps. ii. 7; Isa. xlii. 1; Matt. xii. 18, xvii. 5; Mark i. 11; Luke ix. 35; Eph. i. 6; Col. i. 13; 2 Pet. i. 17; John i. 18.
[2] John x. 17; Heb. ii. 9.   [3] John xiv 2, 3, xvi. 7, 8.

heavenly life. In this sense, on Him was 'laid the iniquity of us all;' in this sense, 'He was wounded for our transgressions, He was bruised for our iniquities: the chastisement of our peace was upon Him; and with His stripes we are healed.'[1]

It is in the light of this initial process to a like experience in us, of suffering as a means of freedom from sin, that the subject has so great an interest to a lost race. The apostle so uses the event when he says: 'Forasmuch, then, as Christ has suffered for us in the flesh, arm yourselves likewise with the same mind: for he that hath suffered in the flesh hath ceased from sin; that he should no longer live the rest of the time in the flesh to the lusts of men, but to the will of God.'[2] Let us therefore consider a few of the cases in which persons have been 'armed with the same mind,' or in whom suffering has conduced to a like result; and note also the intellectual validity of such experiences in evincing the cross to be, not merely a symbol, but a living power among men.

Paul's account of this process in himself includes his pharisaical life; his malignity as a persecutor of the church; his journey to Damascus, and the mid-day splendour shining upon him, eclipsing the sun; the voice calling to him from heaven, and assigning his mission; the blindness, the fasting, the baptism, the renewed Paul in place of a dead Saul the legalist; and, we may add, his subsequent career in 'filling up that which is behind of the afflictions of Christ in his flesh, for His body's sake, which is the church.'[3] Paul on many occasions adduces the evidence of such an experience in confirmation of the gospel he preached,

---

[1] Isa. liii. 5, 6.   [2] 1 Pet. iv. 1, 2.
[3] Acts ix. 1-23, xxii. 1-21, xxvi. 4-23; 1 Tim. i. 13.

or to show its power in his own case. Before mobs and kingly courts he stood forth as an example of resurrection power, and of the efficacy of atoning blood. His heart glowed with his theme, and evinced the power of experimental preaching above all other modes of address.

Examples of like character, though less signal, dot the ages from Paul to this day; and it is hard to select where so much is offered to our choice. Bunyan was a tinker, an ignorant, brutal sort of man; but the new life has made his name a household word to the civilised world. After a death-struggle of some continuance, 'he came up with the cross, when his burden loosed from his shoulders, and fell from his back, and began to tumble, and so continued to do, till it came to the mouth of the sepulchre, where it fell in, and I saw it no more. Then was he glad and lightsome, and said with a merry heart, "He hath given me rest by His sorrow, and life by His death." Then he stood still awhile to look and wonder, for it was very surprising to him that the sight of the cross should thus ease him of his burden.' Here the cross and sepulchre are cause operating to the believing soul in producing death to sin and life to righteousness: Christ's experience is cause, the soul's experience is effect; the two corresponding to each other as light to the eye in producing seeing. Andrew Fuller, not as the great theologian, but as an untaught farmer boy, says of his experience, then and there: 'I was like a man drowning, looking every way for help, or rather catching for something by which he might save his life.' It is hard for flesh to give up to die. After floundering among false doctrines about a Christ only for the elect, he adds: 'I felt something attractive in the Saviour. I must—I will—yes,

I will trust my sinful soul in His hands. And as the eye of the mind was more and more fixed upon Him, my guilt and fears were gradually but insensibly removed. I now found rest for my soul; and I reckon that I should have found it sooner, if I had not entertained the notion of having no warrant to come to Christ without some previous qualification.' The incarnation annihilates the distance between us and God; and the blood of the cross is a positive efficiency to bring the consenting, believing soul nigh, however far off he may have been before. The atoning efficacy and the will to trust are both parts of the same perfect whole.

The general character of this class of inward experiences is thus beautifully expressed by Cowper:

> 'I was a stricken deer that left the herd
> Long since. With many an arrow deep infix'd
> My panting side was charged, when I withdrew
> To seek a tranquil death in distant shades.
> There was I found by one who had Himself
> Been hurt by the archers. In His side he bore,
> And in His hands and feet, the cruel scars.
> With gentle force soliciting the darts,
> He drew them forth, and healed, and bade me live.'

It must be obvious to an impartial observer, that such psychological facts, of which the record is illimitable, do not occur except in connection with the cross; showing that Jesus, in consenting to die, is not disappointed in His purpose of commuting His life into a permanent spiritual power, acting as leaven in meal among our human elements. The Holy Spirit is this power proceeding from Him; and by working in us mightily, He exerts over the whole area of our earthly affairs a directing and a sanctifying influence. Our bodies thus become a living sacrifice, holy and acceptable, being quickened to something better than a merely carnal life by His indwelling Spirit; and our eating, and drinking, and lowest activities, reflect the divine glory shining in and through us.[1] That Christ's death has thus proved the emanating source of a power working outwardly as well as inwardly, shaping the currents of human thought, moulding institutions, directing the outlay of enterprise and wealth, supplying material for art, science, and literature, and producing an extensive impression upon human affairs, who can deny? And who can deny that it has done this by means that in their inception were, humanly speaking, wholly inadequate to such results? The words, 'I am Jesus, whom thou persecutest,' thrilling upon the soul of Paul, and 'the just shall live by faith,' vibrating upon every chord of thought and feeling in Luther, laid a foundation, the first for changing the religion of Rome from Paganism to Christianity, and the other for detaching a third part of the nations from a dominant apostasy, arousing thought and enterprise in all departments, and leading on to a train of consequences infinite and eternal. What a potency in single seed-truths falling from the tree of life as represented by the cross!

It is no abstraction of penal law, no intellectual conviction, no spectacular scene of punishment to pacify a universal conscience demanding a victim as an offset to hell-torments; no, it is power as really as gravitation is power, though, as pertaining to God, the soul, and eternity, it is of infinitely greater significance. The divinity becomes identified with humanity in a far higher sense than the inbreathing into man at his creation, giving him power to become a redeemed son of God. There is nothing in a peasant's daughter to

[1] Rom. viii. 11, xii. 1; 1 Cor. x. 31.

suggest the impossible hope that she may be married to a prince; but if she were to see the prince coming down from his throne and his palace to woo her, sacrificing his royalty for her menial condition, exchanging his robes for her rags, and his dainties for her crumbs, then a new-born hope within her might aspire to being his wife. And when married to him in his rags, she might then aspire to a throne and a diadem, as he should resume these prerogatives of his birth. Such is the incarnation and the cross in human history. 'If so be that we suffer with Him, that we may be also glorified together.' Having followed Him in His regeneration of blood, and in His spiritual baptism, how can we doubt that we shall reign with Him?[1]

In all cases wherein such a hope takes its rise, it is from a like crisis of abandonment to pain and woe with that which extorted the cry, 'My God, my God, why hast Thou forsaken me?' The baritone song of a dying flesh has in this cry its keynote. In the three thousand pentecostal converts it was, 'Men and brethren, what shall we do?' In the Philippian jailor, 'Sirs, what must I do to be saved?' In Saul of Tarsus, 'O wretched man that I am, who shall deliver me from the body of this death?' It is the cry of a sense of total abandonment to pain and woe, in Christ working out salvation for us; but of sinking to hell in us, as we feel we richly deserve. It is like the throes of the convict ending in the stillness of death under the executioner's axe: with this difference, that the blow is stayed, as Abraham's was in beheading his son; and we fall into the arms of infinite love, 'forgiving all our iniquities, healing all our diseases, redeeming our life from destruction, crowning us with loving-kindness and

[1] Rom. viii. 17.

tender mercies, satisfying our mouth with good things, so that our youth is renewed like the eagle's.' Thus Christ, our forerunner, sunk into death and the grave, but was caught in the arms of a resurrection and glorification power, to be henceforth the cause of a like transition in us. His experience is reflected in ours, as the central figure of a grand saloon repeats itself in the mirrors by which it is surrounded.

This law of suffering as cause may be traced to everything of value among men. Is not our very earthly being itself a product of suffering? Did not that quiet man Newton work out his problems of the universe by many a throe of agony? Was not the steamboat set adrift, and the locomotive launched upon its iron track, by a generation or two of agonized endeavour? This is the law in everything. Who looks for offshoots of beneficence from dilettante, pleasure-loving minds? Suffering in the inauguration of spiritual power is no isolated fact of human experience.

But the question is, What value is to be attached to Christian experience, so called, as evidence of anything divine or extraordinary in the doctrine of the cross? What is it worth, as tried by the ordinary tests of evidence and of truth? I am aware that there is much talk of fanaticism, mental disease, and of dreamy fancies, as accounting for all this class of psychological development. Even the religion of Sir Isaac Newton was sneered at by Voltaire as the offshoot of a diseased mind. But there are certain principles on this subject that cannot be well disputed.

First, the agreement of such an experience with our moral nature is worthy to be thought of. If a man had been confined all his life from the approach of light, and should suddenly be introduced to the opening expanse of the dawning morning, could he doubt the validity of his sensations and experiences in becoming familiarized to the new element? Its agreement with his eyes leaves not a doubt in his mind of their being made for each other. No evidence beyond his own sensations would be needed to complete the demonstration, nor would the sneers of the blind at his fanaticism unsettle his convictions. He knows that, whereas he was once blind, now he sees.[1]

So we are, by reason of sin, in the darkness of a natural material sort of life, and the truths and beatitudes of our relation to God and a spirit-realm are hid from us. Still our instinctive longings after immortality, our undefined and unsatisfied feeling of connection with something higher than this earthly world, remain, like the tendency to seeing in eyes excluded from light, or like the craving of infant appetite for untasted food. Conscience spurs us up to a virtue to which we have not yet attained, and after which we grasp, without being able to reach it. Like men in total darkness, we feel that we are made for something better, and are burdened and heavy laden from a sense of incapacity to assume our proper position. This condition of human nature is the necessary result of being cut off from its higher relations; just as plants without sunlight have only a feeble, diseased, and unproductive life. Did the old heathen symbolize this state by the vultures gnawing at the vitals of Prometheus?.

But in a genuine Christian experience the needed light is admitted; the inward torture is relaxed; the lacking power of reaching one conscience-ideal is supplied in the righteousness of the law fulfilled in us; and an undefined sense of satisfaction diffuses itself,

[1] John ix. 25.

like a gentle heat or a sweet soft radiance, through our whole being. We feel that all is right with us, and we are as sure that our hearts do not deceive us, as the blind of the verity of their sensations on first seeing. Peace and joy reign within, and, if withdrawn, duty remains; God remains; love remains in its practical working, if not in its sensational delights; and our energies are taxed in a perpetual race of glory to God in the highest, and good-will to men, and in the unceasing battle of overcoming evil with good. Nothing short of this comes up to the Bible ideal of a new man in Christ.

Second, Christian experience, so far as it is genuine and effective, leads to right living. It makes the contentious peaceable, the intemperate temperate, the profane devout, the dishonest honest, the licentious chaste, and the riotous useful and orderly citizens. Such is its tendency, however counteracted, or however defective in the spurious examples of it sometimes brought to our notice. Peter's love of his Master, though undying, had its intermissions, costing him tears and poignant regrets. As animal life is still life, though in conflict with disease and its causes, so the restored divinity of our souls is beleaguered, and victory may sometimes waver all along the line of battle. To estimate what grace actually achieves, we must take into account what its subjects would have been without its restraining influence. Is it nothing that the soul, even in its failures, is held to a divine, a superhuman ideal of moral excellence?

The general as well as the specific results must also be considered in estimating Christian experience. Think of its martyr-subjects, whose blood is the seeding of Christianity in the earth. Think of the Puritan stock, hardy, resolute, freedom-loving, unwisely mixing piety and politics, ready always for a tilt with the enemies of God, and quite unlovely in many of their features; but still baptized in

> 'Siloa's brook, that flowed
> Fast by the oracle of God,'

and wielding spiritual truths and the temporal sword in a way beneficent to British institutions and to general liberty. We do not claim to estimate the good or ill of Puritanism in Europe; but we are certain that the Pilgrim Fathers, despite their faults, have done a great work in America. It was their new life in God that embarked them in the enterprise of planting their religion amid nature's wilds and among savage men; that founded their churches and free schools, now the pride and glory of forty million people; and laid the foundation of an empire so far in advance of the older Catholic colonies of Mexico and South America. They had to do with the infinite and the eternal directly and in their own persons, and not through priestly intermediation; and this of itself was a power fitting them to distance their more servile neighbours. This Puritan seeding in the New World is, what the Roman stock was among the tribes of ancient Italy, the assimilating force which is melting the country so largely into its own type of politics and religion, and imparting its own energy into all the departments of business. The use of the word *Yankee*, once applied as a term of reproach to a limited section, but now as a designation for two-thirds of the nation, shows clearly the progressive character of the stock to whom it properly belongs. That religion as a heart-work was the leading idea with the Puritans is conceded; and whatever may be thought of their influence as a whole, no one can look at English history, or witness their achievements in America, without confessing that they have been a power in the earth. With far less advantages for action and demonstration than other classes of religionists, they have really achieved more than any of them.

How can we doubt the validity of the new life in God, to which at least much of this history is owing? A restored Bible; a revived literature; universal education; communion with God, as the privilege of our daily conscious life; the power of prayer; a state without a king, and a church without a bishop; the laws supreme over palace and cottage;—these are some of the doings and designings of this Puritan contact of earth with heaven. Even in the Papal Church, the Pascals, the Fénélons, the Bossuets, the Bourdaloues, and men most in sympathy with piety as an inner life, have shed around them the most genial influence, and have done most to bless the world. If a tree is to be judged by its fruit, what better one can be found than this? Call it a dream, a vision, fanaticism, bigotry, or by any other hard name; still neither the power nor the beneficence of Christian experience can thus be scorned out of existence.

Third, another fact to be considered in evidence of the genuineness of Christian experience, is the power it gives over the conscience. Men may be deceived in their reasoning, but they are not likely to be as to what is adapted to move their instinctive feelings. Does not a mother know what is suited to move her maternal sympathies? Does not stage acting assume that the passions have their appropriate language and gestures, and that when these are used they are sure of a response from a listening audience? The picture of a Roman daughter who for six weeks sustained the life of her father, condemned to die of starvation, by stealing into his prison and feeding him with the food that nature provided for her infant, will make its impression even upon disobedient children,—so sure is an action of the kind to meet a response from the inner chords of our being.

But what has proved a greater power, as before hinted, than experimental preaching? When an apostle's life hung upon his speech, as before the mob at Jerusalem and the court of Agrippa at Cæsarea, he did not trust to the elaborations of his intellect, but to the simple rehearsal of what God had done for his soul. And Gibbon concedes the mighty influence which the Christian pulpit had upon the destinies of the Roman world. Fervid men giving utterance in ten thousand pulpits, once, twice, or thrice a week, of their own vital experiences on subjects most momentous, could not fail to affect the currents of thought and feeling in a great empire. How prodigious the effect of Whitfield's ministrations on a London mob, and upon all classes, not from the strength of his reasoning, in which he never excelled, but from the tide of genuine feeling which he poured over his audiences! Speech in such cases gives vent to infinite and eternal realities, swaying minds as the tempest the reeds that grow in its track. An argumentative, unsentimental discourse has no such effect, because it appeals to very different principles of human nature. The one is an assault upon the reason, the other upon the conscience.

Is there not genuine nature and reality, therefore, in an influence which has proved itself such a power to conscience for so many ages, and to men so diversified in condition and culture? The brutalized savages of an American forest felt the burning words of Brainerd, and were quite as demonstrative under his appeals as Peter's audience on Pentecost, as Whitfield's in London or Bristol, or as Massillon's and Bourdaloue's among the *élite* of Paris. A soul kindled at God's altars has always been, and always will be, a power in the earth. The chords of the harp give no surer response to the touch, than the soul of man to the divine word spoken in power by one who comes to testify what he has seen with his eyes, what he has heard, what he has looked upon, and what his hands have handled of the Word of Life.[1] No sham can succeed in such a work, no mimicry of another's acting, no intonations assumed for the sake of effect, no attitudinizing to impress the senses: nothing but genuine Christian experience, not of a former date or as a past memory, but as a living, glowing reality, to modulate the voice and infuse sincerity into every gesture at the moment of speaking, can ever meet the demands of the ministerial calling. Where this is, silence is power, and a look eloquence. 'It is not ye that speak, but the Spirit of my Father that speaketh in you.'[2]

[1] 1 John i. 1.   [2] Matt. x. 20.

Biblical Commentary on the New Testament. By Dr. HERMANN OLSHAUSEN. Continued after his death by Ebrard and Wiesinger. Carefully revised, after the last German Edition, by A. C. KENDRICK, D.D., Greek Professor in the University of Rochester. Six vols., large octavo. Price, cloth, $18.00.

> "I regard the Commentary as the most valuable of those on the New Testament in the English language, happily combining the religious spirit of the English expositors with the critical learning of the German. The American editor has evidently performed his task well, as might be expected from his eminent qualifications."—*President Sears, of Brown University.*

The Annotated Paragraph Bible. According to the authorized version, arranged in Paragraphs and Parallelisms, with Explanatory Notes, Prefaces to the several Books, and an entirely new Selection of References to Parallel and Illustrative Passages. An issue of the London Religious Tract Society,—republished. Complete in one royal octavo volume, with Maps, &c. Price, library sheep, $8.00.

The Annotated Paragraph New Testament. In one octavo volume, uniform style. Price, muslin, $2.50.

> "I have carefully examined a considerable portion of the work, and consider it eminently adapted to increase and diffuse a knowledge of the Word of God. I heartily recommend it to Christians of every denomination, and especially to teachers of Bible Classes and Sabbath Schools, to whom it will prove an invaluable aid."—*Rev. Dr. Wayland.*

Tholuck on the Gospel of John. Translated by CHARLES J. KRAUTH, D.D. One vol., octavo. Price, $3.00.

> "We hail with much pleasure the appearance of Krauth's translation of 'Tholuck on the Gospel of John.' We trust the work, in this its English dress, will find a wide circulation."—*Bibliotheca Sacra.*

STANDARD AND MISCELLANEOUS BOOKS.

Baird's Classical Manual. By JAMES S. S. BAIRD, F.C.D. One vol., 16mo. Price, cloth, 90 cts.

> It is an epitome of Ancient Geography, Greek and Roman Mythology, Antiquities, and Chronology.

Croquet as played by "The Newport Croquet Club." By ONE OF THE MEMBERS. 16mo. Price, paper, 25 cts.; cloth, 50 cts.

> "This manual is the only one which really grapples with a difficult case, and deals with it as if heaven and earth depended on the adjudication."—*Atlantic Monthly.*

Helps to the Pulpit. Sketches and Skeletons of Sermons. One vol., large 12mo. Price, $2.00.

> "Here is a work that may be a help by its proper use, or a hindrance by its abuse."—*Christian Messenger.*

Pulpit Themes and Preacher's Assistant. By the author of "Helps to the Pulpit." One vol., large 12mo. Price, $2.00.

> "We have no doubt but that it will be a welcome book to every candidate for the ministry, and also to pastors in almost every congregation."—*Lutheran Herald.*

A Text-Book of the History of Christian Doctrines. By K. R. HAGENBACH, Professor of Theology in the University of Basle. The Edinburgh translation of C. W. Buch, revised, with large Additions from the fourth German Edition, and other sources, by HENRY B. SMITH, D.D., Professor in the Union Theological Seminary of the City of New York. Two vols., octavo. Price, cloth, $6.00.

> "It exceeds, in point of completeness, every other treatise, English as well as German, and we have, therefore, no hesitation in calling it the most perfect manual of the History of Christian Doctrines which Protestant literature has as yet produced."—*Methodist, N. Y.*

STANDARD AND MISCELLANEOUS BOOKS.

The Life and Labors of Francis Wayland, D.D., L.L.D. Late President of Brown University; by his sons, Hon. FRANCIS WAYLAND, and Rev. H. L. WAYLAND. Two vols., 12mo., illustrated by two steel-plate Likenesses of Dr. Wayland Price $4.00.

This is a most interesting memoir of one of those noble specimens of a man, who now and then appear and direct, and give tone to the thoughts of their generation. The volumes are enriched by Dr. Wayland's correspondence with most of the leading men of his day.

DR. WAYLAND'S WORKS.

Principles and Practices of Baptists. By FRANCIS WAYLAND, D.D. 1 vol., 12mo., cloth. Price, $1.50.

"We hope the book will find its way into every family in every Baptist church in the land, and should be glad to know it was generally circulated in the families of other churches."
Christian Chronicle.

A Memoir of the Life and Labors of the Rev. Adoniram Judson, D.D. By FRANCIS WAYLAND, D.D. Illustrated with a fine Portrait of Dr. Judson. Two vols. in one, 12mo. Price, $2.50.

The Elements of Intellectual Philosophy. By FRANCIS WAYLAND, D.D. One vol., 12mo. Price, $1.75.

Sermons to the Churches. By FRANCIS WAYLAND, D.D. One vol., 12mo. Price, $1.00.

"Dr. Wayland is a clear thinker, and a strong and elegant writer. His Sermons are models worthy of study."—*Christian Intelligencer.*

Waiting for the Verdict. By Mrs. REBECCA HARDING DAVIS, author of "Margaret Howth," "Life Among the Iron Mills," &c., &c. One vol., octavo, illustrated, bound in cloth. Price, $2.00.

> This is a story of unusual power and thrilling interest.
> "It is not only the most elaborate work of its author, but it is one of the most powerful works of fiction by any American writer."—*New York Times.*

The Life and Letters of Rev. Geo. W. Bethune, D.D. By Rev. ABRAHAM R. VAN NEST, D.D. One vol., large 12mo., illustrated by an elegant steel-plate Likeness of Dr. Bethune. Price, $2.00.

> This is one of the most charming biographies ever written. As a genial and jovial friend, as an enthusiastic sportsman, as a thorough theologian, as one of the most eloquent and gifted divines of his day, Dr. Bethune took a firm hold of the hearts of all with whom he came in contact.

Dr. Bethune's Theology, or EXPOSITORY LECTURES ON THE HEIDELBERG CATECHISM. By GEO. W. BETHUNE, D.D. Two vols., crown octavo (Riverside edition), on tinted paper. Price, cloth, $4.50; half calf, or morocco, extra, $8.50.

> This was the great life work of the late Dr. Bethune, and will remain a monument of his thorough scholarship, the classical purity and beauty of his style, and above all, his deep and abiding piety.
>
> "When the Rev. Dr. Bethune, whose memory is yet green and fragrant in the Church, was about to leave this country, he committed his manuscripts to a few friends, giving them discretionary power with regard to their publication. Among them was the great work of his life; in his opinion *the* work, and that from which he hoped the most usefulness while he lived, and after he was dead, if it should then be given to the press. This work was his course of lectures on the Catechism of the Church in which he was a burning and shining light.—*New York Observer.*

STANDARD AND MISCELLANEOUS BOOKS.

Neander's Planting and Training of the Christian Church by the Apostles. Translated from the German by J. E. RYLAND. Translation revised and corrected according to the fourth German edition. By E. G. ROBINSON, D.D., Professor in the Rochester Theological Seminary. One vol., octavo, cloth. Price, $4.00.

"The patient scholarship, the critical sagacity, and the simple and unaffected piety of the author, are manifest throughout. Such a history should find a place in the library of every one who seeks a familiar knowledge of the early shaping of the Christian Churches. An excellent index adds to its value."—*Evangelist.*

Bible Illustrations. Being a Store-house of Similies, Allegories, and Anecdotes—with an introduction by RICHARD NEWTON, D.D. One vol., 12mo. Price, $1.50. Every Sabbath School teacher should have this book.

"It is impossible not to commend a book like this."—*Editor of Encyc. of Religious Knowledge.*

"We think that Sabbath School teachers especially would be profited by reading it; and many of the anecdotes will help to point the arrow of the preacher."—*Christian Herald.*

SPURGEON'S WORKS.

Sermons of the Rev. C. H. Spurgeon, of London, in uniform styles of binding.

First Series. With an Introduction and Sketch of his Life, by the Rev. E. L. MAGOON, D.D. With a fine steel-plate Portrait. One vol., 12mo., pp. 400. Price, $1.50.

Second Series. Revised by the Author, and published with his sanction. Containing a new steel-plate Portrait, engraved expressly for the volume. Price, $1.50.

Third Series. Revised by the Author, and published with his sanction. Containing a steel-plate view of Surrey Music Hall, London, engraved expressly for the volume. Price, $1.50.

The Life and Letters of Mrs. Emily C. Judson (Fanny Forrester), third wife of the Rev. Adoniram Judson, D.D., Missionary to Burmah. By A. C. KENDRICK, Professor of Greek in the University of Rochester. With a steel-plate Portrait of Mrs. Judson. One vol., 12mo. Price, $1.75.

The Sexton's Tale, and other Poems. By THEODORE TILTON, Editor of the New York Independent. Illustrated by an ornamental title-page and elegant tail-pieces for each Poem, printed on tinted paper, and bound with beveled boards and fancy cloth. One vol., 16mo. Price, $1.50.

This is the first collected edition of Mr. Tilton's poems, many of them as sweet as any thing in our language.

The Autobiography of Elder Jacob Knapp, the great Revivalist. One vol., large 12mo., with steel-plate Likeness of the Author. Price, $2.00

In this book the author gives an account of the many wonderful scenes through which he has passed, more interesting and remarkable than any tales of fiction.

A new Enlarged Edition of Mrs. Putnam's Receipt Book, AND YOUNG HOUSEKEEPER'S ASSISTANT. A chapter on Carving has been added, and a very large number of new receipts, with special reference to economy in cooking. One vol., 12mo. Price, $1.50.

A Complete Manual of English Literature. By THOMAS B. SHAW, Author of "Shaw's Outlines of English Literature." Edited, with Notes and Illustrations, by WILLIAM SMITH, LL.D., author of "Smith's Bible and Classical Dictionaries," with a Sketch of American Literature, by HENRY T. TUCKERMAN. One vol., large 12mo. Price, $2.00.

STANDARD AND MISCELLANEOUS BOOKS.

Life of George Washington. By EDWARD EVERETT, LL.D. With a steel-plate Likeness of Mr. Everett, from the celebrated bust by Hiram Powers. One vol., 12mo., pp. 348. Price, cloth, $1.50.

> "The biography is a model of condensation, and, by its rapid narrative and attractive style, must commend itself to the mass of readers as the standard popular Life of Washington."—*Correspondence of the Boston Post.*

The Science of Government, in connection with American Institutions. By JOSEPH ALDEN, D.D., LL.D., President of State Normal School, Albany. One vol., 12mo. Price, $1.50. Adapted to the wants of High Schools and Colleges.

Alden's Citizen's Manual. A Text-Book on Government in connection with American Institutions, adapted to the wants of Common Schools. It is in the form of questions and answers. By JOSEPH ALDEN, D.D., LL.D., President of State Normal School, Albany. In one vol., 16mo. Price, 50 cts.

> "There is no more important secular study than the study of the institutions of our own country; and there is no book on the subject so clear, comprehensive, and complete in itself as the volume before us."—*New York Independent.*

Macaulay's Essays. The Critical, Historical, and Miscellaneous Essays of the Right Hon. THOMAS BABINGTON MACAULAY, with an Introduction and Biographical Sketch of the Author, by E. P. WHIPPLE, and containing a new steel-plate Likeness of Macaulay, and a complete index. Six vols., crown octavo. Price, on tinted paper, extra cloth, $13.50; on tinted paper, half calf or morocco, $27.00.

Sherman's March through the South. With Sketches and Incidents of the Campaign. By Capt. DAVID P. CONYNGHAM. 12mo., cloth. Price, $1.75.

> "It is the only one that is entitled to credit for real ability, truth, and fairness."—*J. W. Geary, Maj.-Gen. U. S. A.*

Lieutenant-General Winfield Scott's Autobiography. Two vols., 12mo., illustrated with two steel-plate Likenesses of the General. Price, per set, in cloth, $4.00; half calf, $8.00. An elegant "large paper" edition of this valuable book, on tinted paper, price $10.00; half calf, or morocco, $12.50.

Milman's Latin Christianity. History of Latin Christianity, including that of the Popes to the pontificate of Nicolas V. By HENRY HART MILMAN, D.D., Dean of St. Paul's. Eight vols., crown octavo. Price, extra cloth, $20.00.

"In beauty and brilliancy of style he excels Hallam, approaches Gibbon, and is only surpassed by the unrivaled Macaulay."—*Mercersburg Review.*

Fleming's Vocabulary of Philosophy. With Additions by CHARLES P. KRAUTH, D.D. Small 8vo. Price, $2.50.

"To students of mental science this book is invaluable Dr. K. has done good service by the additions to the work of Dr. Fleming, and the whole volume is one which will be eagerly sought and cordially appreciated."—*Evangelical Quarterly.*

Long's Classical Atlas. Constructed by WM. HUGHES and edited by GEORGE LONG, with a Sketch of Classical Geography. With fifty-two Maps, and an Index of Places.

This Atlas will be an invaluable aid to the student of Ancient History, as well as the Bible student. One vol., quarto. Price, $4.50.

"Now that we are so well supplied with classical dictionaries, it is highly desirable that we should have an atlas worthy to accompany them. In the volume before us is to be found all that can be desired."—*London Athenæun.*